Behind the Teacher's Desk

The Rules Were Made for Everyone but Me

A novel about teaching from a teacher's point of view.

Dedicated to my mother, Miep, who taught grades 9 to 13
French for fifteen years,

and

to my mother-in-law, Marjorie, who for many years, was an
exemplary
grade eight teacher. She saved her class when the roof caved in.

1st Edition©cwilliams, 2013
2nd Edition©cwilliams, 2016
ISBN-13: 978-1540788528
ISBN-10: 1540788520

ebook by Bookbaby.com
Paperback by Createspace.com
Create space title ID: 6765835

Cover Art

by

Chris Kotyk

Acknowledgements

I would not have written this book without the encouragement of Irene Kauhanen, who inspired me to write it as a fiction novel and many friends who kept me going. Above all, I thank Madeline Holland, who read the raw, lengthy unedited manuscript several times, and made excellent suggestions. I thank Wendy Lukasiewicz, my evaluation editor and many colleagues and friends who gave advice and help. Finally I thank my in-depth editor Anne Bougie-Johnson who patiently nurtured a still rough manuscript chapter by chapter into a readable coherent book. Not least, I thank my agent, Johanna M. Bates for her good advice and friendly help. Finally I owe a debt of gratitude to the McCann School for Dogs, who so kindly allowed me to observe as many classes as necessary to write the chapter on the puppy obedience class.

Chris Williams

Reviews

Behind the Teacher's Desk is truth most of us don't know about. This behind the scenes novel about a young woman's personal and professional journey, opens a shuttered window to show what today's teachers are dealing with. It's a must read for us all.

Lynn Johnston

"Behind the Teacher's Desk: The Rules Were Made For Everyone But Me" is hands down one of the most riveting and well-crafted books I've read in a long time! I was completely drawn in from the opening pages, and absolutely loved the author's use of description of the different characters and attention to detail on all fronts. We feel transported not only into Claire's life, but her amazing life experiences inside and outside the classroom... and it was a wonderful and eye-opening view into another lifestyle that many of us either don't really think about or just take for granted. There is SO much more to teaching than just teaching! And Williams shows us many facets that we probably never considered before. This book covers so, so much it's impossible to sum up, but it felt like I was living through a wonderful woman's life, from her professional, romantic and social experiences, and it was interesting to see how it all tied together in the end, which I loved! An epic literary feat and very inspiring. I was really impressed and would recommend this book with the highest praise. (5 stars)

Indie Book Reviewer

Index

January

Chapter 1

<u>Finishing Up</u>

Wednesday, January 24

Paul Fraser was hunched over his filing cabinet drawer. He didn't know it, but his life was about to take a turn. A pile of out-dated files lay scattered on the floor of the small math office. He had already checked some of his colleagues' file drawers. "Where is the damn thing?" He flung another folder on the pile. He wanted to get his copy of George Gumbersahl's basic Math course organized into a fresh binder for start-up the next week.

It was snowing. His colleagues had all cheerfully abandoned ship two hours earlier when they heard the weather report. But Paul believed weathermen exaggerated their warnings for idiot drivers. Plus, if it did snow all night, school might be cancelled in the morning and he could work at home, if only he had that damned file. It was beginning to be a big *if*.

The file could be anywhere. Everybody in the Math department borrowed courses and lesson plans from each other.

Bandhura Abbasi, the Math head, was always helpfully lending stuff to new teachers. Some of them never returned materials to where they belonged. Paul got up and gave the dusty pile of discarded files a good front snap kick. Papers flew all over. It vented his frustration but he regretted it immediately. He sneezed. Now he had to gather papers from every corner in the room to put them in the recycling. More dust. He sneezed again. "Damn allergies." Wiping his face with his handkerchief, he glanced out the snow-splattered window. Checking his watch, he decided to go home. It was four p.m. and Deirdre and the kids would be expecting him. If only he hadn't promised to take them to a movie tonight. How could he have known that the weather would actually be as bad as the weatherman had predicted?

He put today's exams in his briefcase and locked the Math office as he left, deciding not to check his mailbox in the staff room. It was chock-full of junk anyway. He'd checked it at noon. With his furry boots and the faded grey car coat he'd worn for the last eight winters he'd taught at Amberton District High School, Paul Fraser ambled down the hall to the parking lot exit and stepped out.

As soon as he opened it, the wind tried to blow the door off its hinges. Sensing black ice under the thirty centimetres of fluffy snow, he stepped gingerly onto the sloped parking lot. He slipped and nearly fell twice. Paul made his way towards where his car should be. It was hard to tell. There were two mounds of snow parked up against the school. Blowing snow got into his eyes and mouth and neck in spite of his scarf and glasses. His hood threatened to bare his head with its thinning hair, so he held it tight in his free hand. So much snow was soon sticking to his glasses that he had to let go of his hood to wipe it off. The wind tried desperately to knock him down. He resisted and lowered his eyes to the ground watching where he put his feet. He was inching along when he heard the whoosh of a car behind him. Suddenly, he was jolted forward. His head hit something hard. He fell. He knew nothing more.

***

Jethro Mason, the school caretaker, was doing his final rounds, making sure all doors were locked. He stuck his head out the door to the parking lot, to tally the cars before leaving. He was anxious to get home, but he had to stay if there were any cars left out there in the snow other than his own. Damn. There were two cars, side by side. He looked again and saw something dark in the snow. He put on his coat and slipped and slid his way out to find Paul Fraser, his head bleeding, an arm visibly broken and his right foot crushed. As Jethro fumbled with his cellphone his hands shook with cold and fear. He dialled 911, then stayed, trying to help the unconscious Paul. Why was that ambulance taking so long?

***

At about the same time, a young man in a dark green parka and a green toque, his face almost totally covered with a blue and beige plaid scarf, was rushing up the steps at 684 River Road. He had a gift-wrapped box with a big red bow on it. Both looked big enough to fill an entire room in the little house.

Inside, Claire Hébert, a young biology teacher, had been in her den working on her computer, concentrating on report comments and trying not to be distracted by the aroma coming from the chilli con carne in the slow cooker in the kitchen. The doorbell distracted her instead. She grabbed her wrap, looked through the peephole and quickly opened the door. "Oh Matt, get in here!" She held in her tummy as her boyfriend with the box sidled past her through the narrow entrance. She had to push with both hands to shut the door against the wind and the snow. "I can't believe you're here already. You okay? It's only four o'clock."

He grinned and gave her a sideways kiss. "I couldn't be late today," he said as he slipped off his boots and headed towards the kitchen table.

Claire managed to clear her mail off the table just as Matt put down the already dripping box. She gave him a coy smile. "OK. You got me. What's in there?" Claire circled the table, studying the box. Her birthday was in February, but for some reason Matt always thought it was in January. She'd been hoping for a coffee brewer. The box was big enough. She was flushed with excitement.

"A present." Matt gave her a fond look. Now that his scarf wasn't covering his face, she saw the smile she loved.

She put her arms around his neck, kissed him and looked deep into his hazel eyes. "I guessed that and I'm very glad you came early." In the last two years she had fallen deeply in love with this guy again. Claire tried, but she couldn't play it cool. She quivered with excitement, her auburn curls bouncing. "Come on, Matt, what is it?"

"It's for you, Clarikins, for Valentine's Day."

She laughed. "Matt, Valentine's Day isn't for two weeks."

"Well, in two weeks you'll be too busy to see me and he'll have been euthanized." Matt nonchalantly took off his coat and flung it over the back of a kitchen chair.

"Euthanized? What's in there?"

Matt gently pushed the box to the centre of the table and nodded for her to open it. Claire slipped the ribbon off, removed the sopping wrapping paper and opened one flap of a big old carton. She heard ticking sounds. She gave Matt a suspicious grin. He liked playing practical jokes.

"What? You found a baby on the church steps?" she ventured.

"Shhh … he's asleep," Matt whispered.

Hooked, she lifted the other flaps, she saw a soft yellow blob of fur, snoring on a blue fleece blanket, an old wind-up alarm clock ticking in one corner. "Ah, he's so cute." Her expression darkened. "But I can't keep him, Matt." She looked sad. "I'm too busy reviewing F for that French *Sociologie* class next semester and working on grade eleven biology handouts to deal with a puppy right now, Matt." She paused, and then said sweetly, "Can you take him back?"

Matt walked to the other side of the kitchen and ran his fingers through his wavy brown hair. "But Claire, you love animals. You studied animal biology. You've told me a hundred times that you wanted a puppy."

"I meant in a few years, hon." She moved closer to him. "I don't feel confident in this job yet. I'm sorry." She took another look into the box. "He looks small to be away from his mother, Matt. Where did you get him?"

"From my friend with the kennel in Elgin Falls. Al and I thought he'd be perfect for you."

She stepped back and cocked her head. "Were you really thinking about me when you made this decision? A puppy? With a French immersion course added to my schedule? I should never have told them I could speak French, but... Good God, Matt. The time, the training... How did you ever think I could manage that on top of everything else? Please, Matt, take him back to Al."

"I can't, Claire. Al's gone ice fishing in North Bay. This was the last puppy. Nobody wanted him." Matt reached down and picked the puppy up, nuzzling it. He looked at her. "He's so cute. And I did consider you. You need a distraction from your job, Claire. Being a teacher consumes all of your time and energy. I'm not always here, so I want you to have someone to welcome you home at the end of a long day. Look at the little fellow, Claire. Are you sure you don't want him?"

"My job. That's always the issue, isn't it?" They'd had this discussion several times over the last eighteen months. Claire knew she was becoming a terrible workaholic and that Matt wanted her to be able to go out on weeknights when he was in town. But she wasn't ready. She turned around, her forehead scrunched with turmoil.

"Work fills the time available, Claire." Matt lectured. "This is a scheduling problem. Move some things around, take time for walks. This little guy will love you in return." The puppy lifted his head as though waiting for Claire's decision.

She sighed. "I'm afraid to keep him, Matt… at least not until I feel confident teaching the French *Sociologie* course and I have enough biology stuff on file that I don't have to prep at home every night. It takes four years to learn the job when you're a teacher."

"Aw … he wouldn't take much of your time, Claire. Come on. Please? Al was going to put him down! Could you put the death needle into him?"

She looked at the fuzzy little face, Matt's pleading eyes, the blizzard outside and weakened. "Let me sleep on it."

"Alright!" Matt slapped his thigh with delight, beamed at Claire and ruffled the pup's sleepy head.

"Don't get too excited...I may change my mind..." It was a teacher-like warning.

"Of course not. You're going to spend a cozy evening curled up with two handsome guys," he pointed to the struggling puppy and to his own shining grin, "and never look back." With a spring in his step, he lunged forward, popped a sloppy kiss on her cheek and cradled the puppy into her hands. "I'll just go get his things from the car," he said as he grabbed his coat.

Claire looked down at the wriggling puppy and sighed. She knew she would cave in. She'd had a retriever when she was a kid on the farm and had always wanted one of her own and she had to admit this one was adorable.

"How old did you say he was?" she asked as Matt stuffed his feet back into his boots. "Are you sure he's okay to leave his mommy?"

"He's three months old," he shouted as he opened the door and the wind blew a cold gust of snow into the entrance. He took a deep breath and barrelled headfirst into the storm again, closing the door behind him.

Claire's M.Sc. in Animal Biology took over. She took another look at the puppy. "Three months? You look much younger than that," she said to him as she put him on the kitchen floor and he began to wobble his way around chair legs.

The door opened and Matt reappeared, carrying a large dog crate full of stuff, his dark hair wet with snow. "What's in there?" she asked.

"Just a few things I scrounged, you know, in case you decided to keep him." They hauled the contents out of the crate and put them on the table: a baby bottle and some puppy formula, a food and water dish, a small bag of organic puppy food, a leash, a harness and more. Matt had thought of everything.

"You know, Matt," she said pensively. "He looks much younger than three months, Matt." She patted the pup's ribcage. "He's been starved."

"He was the runt of a large litter, Claire. So far he's had a rough life being shoved around and denied food by his siblings." A slow grin spread across Matt's face. "Being a soft-hearted smart guy, I took a chance on bringing him here. I knew you could save him. Al thinks he'll always be undersized, so he'll go well in your Lilliputian house." Matt was sounding like a car salesman who couldn't take *no* for an answer.

"I said *one* night..." she stuck out her chin in for emphasis. How could she take care of a brand new puppy? "Will you come over and help when you're in the country?"

"Of course."

It was all so sudden, but she'd see more of Matt and that was a plus. "Well, he's here for tonight anyway," she said.

"I want you to be happy, Claire." He looked hesitant.

"Come here, you sweet thing." Claire smiled and put her arms around him. "I know you do." As she pulled his head down to hers, the puppy nibbled lightly on her slipper. Their kisses morphed into smiles as they pulled apart.

Claire got an old pillow, covered it with the blue fleece to make a bed for the puppy and put it and the old clock in the crate and the whole thing into the warm nook under the stairs. The little guy was tottering around exploring, occasionally falling on his nose, but bravely picking himself up. He left a little puddle, then came to lick her foot.

"He's got spirit," she thought out loud, "and he's lovable." She cleaned up the puddle and prepared a bottle. Then she went into the living room and fed him on the sofa in front of the fire while Matt puttered around in the kitchen.

"It's dark already," he said, looking out the window over the sink. "It's really coming down now. I can't get home tonight, Claire."

He walked into the living room with a glass of wine for each of them. "Well, then I guess both of you will have to stay. And what will I do with you?" she teased as the puppy stretched on her lap.

"Feed me?" he asked coyly.

"Oh! Gosh, dinner!" She handed him the puppy. "The chili should be done." She took her glass of wine and rushed back into the kitchen. She put a French stick in the oven and minutes later they sat down to eat.

"How long will you be in Egypt this time?"

"A week, maybe two." He paused. "It's hardly worth going for less."

"I miss you already."

"Do you have any free time Thursday or Friday?" Matt sounded hopeful.

She took a sip of wine. "I have tomorrow off and I won't have any schoolwork Friday night, so we can spend the evenings and the whole weekend together. I have to be in school Friday, but I won't have marking until the second week in February. When do you have to leave?"

"Tuesday of next week. The thirtieth."

"What's Ecohydrelco got you doing this time?"

"Same old, same old." He shook his head, absentmindedly swirling the wine in his glass. "Checking out the purification systems we sold them. Testing the water. Seeing if it's all working as efficiently as possible—not leaking. Seeing how we can improve our product. Then I'll do my own bit of research." Matt took a bite of bread. "Boring."

But it wasn't boring to Claire. She was proud of him. He was brilliant. In the four years she'd been in California getting her Master's in education from U.C.L.A. and starting to teach,

18

he'd earned three Master's degrees in engineering at Queen's: geology, mechanical, and a combination of hydraulic and electrical. He had joined Ecohydrelco in Elgin Falls and now travelled the world for his work.

They finished dinner and went back to sit in front of the cozy fire in the living room. Outside, the storm raged. The puppy stood up on its hind legs against the sofa, wagging its tail and wanting to be placed on Claire's lap. She picked him up and couldn't resist nuzzling the fur on his head. "He's so soft." He raised his head and his baby teeth gently grabbed Claire's nose in a love bite, then he settled down on her lap for another nap.

"What are you going to call him?"

"What did they call him at Al's?"

"Stupid."

"Well, that's not going to be his name. I want to name him after a dog I loved. His name is Boomer."

"Okay. Boomer it is then." Matt's smile stretched from ear to ear.

"What?"

"I guess if you're naming him, he just might be sticking around…"

She was done for now. "Boomer," she said with a sigh.

"This was probably the first time in his life he— Boomer—didn't have to fight for his supper and a warm spot near his mother," Matt said as he watched her sit down again. His arm was around her as she let Boomer finish his bottle.

"He seems grateful," Claire said. "That's a good sign. Ya did good, Matt." She kissed him. "Sorry I'm such a witch about work."

A pleasant hour later, they were watching the nine o'clock news. There had been a car accident at a local high school. A teacher had been hurt. A hit and run.

Claire's face went white.

"It probably wasn't at Amberton, Clarikins." Matt sat up and tried to put her mind at rest. "They just said *a local high school*. There are three of them." He put his arm around her, hoping her fear would fade.

"A local high school could be my school. But…it can't be. A teacher? Who would run someone over and just leave?"

"Calm down, Clarikins. If there's anything to it, we'll hear it on the morning news. Try to think positive. It's just news because it happened at a school. It's probably nothing. You heard. There were a million fender benders tonight. I'm here. Boomer's here. Relax."

They put Boomer to bed on the pillow in the crate. He was already a good distraction. Claire spread some newspapers on the floor, in case nature called. Matt took Claire's hand and led her upstairs.

***

Matt woke with a start and turned his head to see the

20

clock. It was 2:13 am. He rolled over, expecting to find Claire next to him, but her side of the bed was empty. He listened for a minute but didn't hear any water running in the bathroom. Groggy but concerned, he threw back the thick covers and found one of Claire's pastel fleece robes.

As he stumbled into the dimly lit living room, he saw Claire sitting on the sofa.

"There you are," he said softly.

She looked up at him and smiled. In her hands was a framed photo of Tyler, her late fiancé. "Sorry," she said as she reached for the drawer in the side table.

That's progress, I guess, Matt thought to himself. That photo used to be on the table, not in it.

"Couldn't sleep?" he asked as he sat down beside her. Claire smiled at the sight of him in her soft pink robe. "What? Not my colour?" he joked.

"No, no, it's totally you," she said. Her face slid into a frown. "I had a dream about Tyler. It woke me up and I just had to see him."

"It must be hard, living with the memories," he offered. "I only know what it's like being divorced. I can't imagine having someone so close to me die."

"I don't know," Claire said as she rubbed her tired eyes. "Maybe it's easier than watching your relationship die slowly.

Maybe." She shrugged. "I don't think about him as much as I used to."

"Is that why you work so hard all the time…so you don't have time to think about Tyler?"

"Sometimes, but then at others, work makes me think of him more. When I'm preparing lessons. We used to do that together. That's probably why I'm so obsessed with organization and being prepared. Tyler was a perfectionist. He memorized all the dates and facts for his history lessons. I guess it rubbed off on me. Now my work always seems to fill the time he took to do his."

Matt looked at her and noted her slumped shoulders and hollow cheeks. "Seriously, Claire, I still think you should quit. Teaching has gotten so much more stressful in the last few years. It's burning out lots of teachers."

"I know. I will, but I'd be black-listed if I did it now."

"Could Tyler have been afraid of his classes if he wasn't prepared? Because if so, he could have transferred his fear to you."

"I never thought of that. Maybe. Sometimes. Kids these days can be so bold and can have an insensitive, aggressive attitude." She shrugged her shoulders, "I'm outnumbered about thirty to one in the classroom, and in high school lots of students are bigger than I am, and the public's respect for teachers has been in the basement for years. My friend Shirley told us she's been afraid in classes off and on for the last twenty years. Some days she didn't *drive* home from school, she *fled* home. Maybe Tyler was afraid, but we loved planning our lessons together and I never saw any fear in him. But that doesn't mean it wasn't there."

"Why did you and Tyler live together for so long without getting married?"

"Simple. We talked about it, but never took the time to plan a wedding. We were *prepaholics* and travelled or took courses during the summer. It just never happened."

They sat in silence for a minute. She leaned forward, resting an elbow on the arm of the sofa as she looked up at him.

"You can't replace Tyler in my heart, Matt. Tyler was Tyler, and you are you. I loved him, but I do want you to know that now I love you just as passionately, maybe even more."

"I know. I just wish we had more time for each other."

"Well, that's not something we can to solve tonight." She stood up and held out her hand. "Let's go back to bed."

***

Thursday, January 25

In the morning, the bells of her ringtone jolted Claire awake at a quarter past nine. She ran downstairs and fumbled around for her cellphone. She found it between the pillows on the sofa in the living room.

It was Dr. Chin Ho, her department head calling. The accident on the news had been at Amberton District High School and Claire's timetable would be affected. "Could you meet me in the science office at ten-thirty? We'll go over it then."

Claire was stunned at the news and started to hyperventilate. Matt had just come into the living room, where he sat her down and tried to calm her. "Breathe slowly, Claire... Slowly... Just concentrate on breathing, sweetie... Inhale... Exhale... There, there. It's better already. Good thing I'm here, eh?"

Claire was reliving the horror four years earlier when Tyler had died in a car crash caused by a teenaged driver. His parents were canoeing in the Yukon at the time and couldn't be reached. Claire had been alone to make arrangements for what was left of the man she loved. She had accepted his marriage proposal one week before.

Matt gently kissed her on the forehead then scooped Boomer into his arms. "Go do your business, buddy," Matt whispered. He pulled hard on the nearly frozen patio door and had to use a frying pan to clear a spot in the snow for Boomer. The puppy quickly piddled and stumbled back inside. Matt made some toast and cereal, which Claire didn't eat, then made some coffee. He fried himself an egg, had breakfast, then rolled Boomer's soiled newspapers.

Claire stared out the living room window at the magical world in her backyard, with its sparkling branches set against an azure sky. "As if nothing had happened," she thought. Boomer jumped at her legs, reminding her of his presence. "The timing might be wrong, but the dog was right," she told Matt as she picked Boomer up for a cuddle.

Matt finished his coffee and washed his mug. "I'll take care of Boomer and put him in the crate when I leave. You need to get to school."

"Thanks, hon."

"I'll clean off your car and shovel the driveway before I go."

Matt grinned. His smile made her want to stay home and hop back into the warm bed with him. But he went out to shovel snow and she went upstairs to do her hair and makeup.

Chapter 2

The Ripple Effect

At ten-thirty Chin Ho was waiting for her in the science office. "Good morning, Claire, how are you?" A sombre look clouded his friendly face. "Better sit down." Claire sat. Chin had taken his spectacles off and sat in front of her cradling his tired head in his hands. "It was Paul Fraser who was run down last night in the parking lot. He had worked late." He lifted his head. "We don't know what happened. Jethro Mason found him around four-thirty. It was damn lucky he saw him lying on the ground with all that snow coming down." Chin paused to gather his thoughts.

"He must have been walking to his car. Visibility was terrible and there was black ice underneath everything after that thaw the other day."

Claire was stunned. Paul was a Math colleague and good friend. "But how could somebody just leave him there?" Tears pooled in Claire's deep brown eyes.

"I don't know. Maybe it was a drunk, a student, or just anyone turning around in the parking lot and blinded by the storm. Who knows?"

Claire's face was ashen. Her knees felt weak. She wanted to escape.

Chin took a deep breath. The news was weighing heavily on him. "The police are investigating. Poor Deirdre was beside herself when she called Bertha Stack last night. They don't have any leads, but Paul's alive…struggling, but alive."

"Oh God." Claire liked Paul—she didn't want to think of him in the past tense. He is a kind colleague, husband and father, a creative, popular teacher who always has a joke on the tip of his tongue. She wondered how the staff could help his wife and family.

"He won't be back this semester," Chin said gently. He stood up and stepped to his desk, putting his spectacles back on. "I'll be brief. They've had to reshuffle the timetable. You're getting Paul's basic Math class." Chin took a sheet of paper off his desk. "Here's your new schedule."

Grade ten general science and grade eleven university-bound biology in the morning, grade nine basic math in the afternoon. She looked at Chin, shaking her head.

"I know what you're about to ask, Claire. Nobody else with any Math knowledge had a moveable slot at the right time for his schedule. Sorry. You're not the only one who hates last minute stuff. Here are your class lists and course outlines. I know you'll do your best for these kids."

"It won't be as good as Paul would have done. Who else got new classes? Who got my *Sociologie* class?" She'd asked before she realised it.

Chin looked through some memos on his desk and chose one. "Don Patterson and Gérard Coderre. They've hired a new French-speaking teacher to teach Gérard's French immersion *Littérature* class, and his Entrepreneurship." He frowned. "Your *Sociologie* class goes to her too. Sorry. I know how much you've been preparing for that. Principal Stack was really keen on her. Shirley had reservations but she had to concede that this girl's French is better than that of the only other candidate and sociology is one of her passions."

"So she's young, not ideal, but she's as close as they can get with the short notice," Claire muttered, rolling her eyes. "I'd trust Shirley's people skills over Bertha's any day of the week."

Chin cleared his throat. "Me too. But that's it. Gérard will take Don's science classes and Don will take Paul's senior Math classes."

Claire's mind was flipping from one issue to another. "But, who could have hit Paul?"

"I don't know. I've been thinking about it all morning. Everybody likes Paul, except maybe Chester. Paul has been ribbing him for years about the mess in his classroom. We've all had problems with students over the years, but nothing that would warrant…"

Angus Bertch, the physics teacher had just come in. "No way it could have been Chester, Chin." he interrupted. He always legs it out of school as fast as he can when the bell rings. With that storm he would never have been near this place as late as four o'clock yesterday, let alone four-thirty. He's worse than the kids…"

"But are they saying it could have been intentional? Did someone hit Paul on purpose?" Claire asked.

Chin shook his head. "I don't know. That was the impression Bertha gave this morning."

"But she does have a habit of blaming teachers and leaving us waiting for the other shoe to drop," quipped Angus.

Claire sat at her desk staring at the papers Chin had given her. "What do we say to the kids?"

"Bertha's orders: we're not to say anything to the students about the accident, just about Paul's condition." Chin responded quickly. "Keep the gossip to a minimum. The police want us to keep what happened confidential in case it was a student. And Bertha doesn't want to give them any ideas. Hopefully, by the time classes start next week the police will have it all figured out. Until then, we soldier on." Angus gave her a sympathetic look.

"Yes, sir." Claire gave them a weak smile and a mock salute.

"Let's talk about something else, Claire," said Chin. There was a pause. "Anything good happen in your life lately? I need some good news."

"Matt gave me a puppy last night. He should've asked first." She ran her fingers through her auburn curls, as if that would clear her head.

"Keep it." Chin snapped. Claire looked up in surprise. "People with pets are less stressed." He looked at her. "On a scale of one to ten, I'd classify you as a fifteen since September. It'll do you good to walk a dog for a bit every day after school. Not everything is solved by work."

"I'm keeping him, Chin."

"Good girl."

She scanned her class lists, recognizing some names for reputable, others for disreputable reasons. She didn't know the new basic Math group at all.

Chin rolled his chair back and looked at her. "Claire, you look like shit. Go home to your puppy."

"Thanks, Chin." She left for the privacy of her lab. Angus watched her go.

***

After collecting her thoughts, the enormity of a whole new course with virtually no prep time hit Claire. She would need a lot of help teaching a basic Math class. She knew the theory. Tyler had taught basic level students, but she had never done it herself. During the three years they had lived together, Tyler had stressed that basic students had poor work habits, lots of family and learning issues and poor attendance. She remembered him saying that basic kids needed a good course with simple explanations and plenty of practice exercises. Claire had zilch.

In the learning resource room, Brian McLean, the learning resource teacher or L.R.T., reminded her George Gumbersahl could be the answer to her problem. Nicknamed 'Gumless' by the kids, because he was the lone holdout on staff who wouldn't let them chew gum in class, George had taught basic Math for years. Claire sighed with relief. She rushed to the other end of the first floor. George was in his classroom in the Math wing, doing what Claire had been doing earlier that week: throwing things out and preparing for Monday's onslaught.

She tapped on the open door. "Hi, George," she said. She hesitated. George looked distraught. Paul was his friend, too. "How are you? I'd say *good morning*, but it isn't."

George, an independent, good-natured widower whose children were all grown, always wore a cheap but neat grey pinstriped suit. The grey helped to mitigate the chalk his jacket picked up as he demonstrated solutions on the blackboard. He was of the generation that stood up when a woman entered the room. "I suppose I'm as well as can be expected. How about you?"

"Same as you. Shocked, saddened, worried for Paul, having trouble taking it all in, and wanting to quit."

"Ah, yes, Bandhura Abbasi told me they gave you Paul's freshman basic Math class. Even though you look like you're about to keel over Claire, don't quit. You'll do a great job for the kids." There was a twinkle in his eye as he offered her a chair.

Claire sat down. "Brian told me you've taught the basic Math course and you might have some ideas for me."

"Well, he knows that I've written a self-directed course for it."

"Yeah. He told me that too." Claire blushed. "Twenty lessons." She knew about their friendly rivalry.

"He did, did he? Isn't that just like that old board toady, assuming I'll just give away twelve years of my work." George's face reddened and his eyes bulged. Claire thought that if he were a cartoon, his ears would have been spouting little clouds of steam. "I like to decide for myself who gets to use my course. I wrote it on my own time, on my own dime and tested it in my own classroom. I don't like it when colleagues consider it public property and leave it lying around in bits and pieces."

"Sorry, George." Claire blushed and looked at the floor. She knew how much she was asking. "I respect the effort you've put into it. I wouldn't ask if I weren't in a real bind. Any chance I can at least have a look at it, George? Please? Think of the kids. Think of *Paul*."

George's twinkle returned. "'Tell you what. I'll let you make a copy of it. It's what Paul would have used."

Claire leapt from her chair and gave George a big kiss on the cheek. "Oh, thank you, George! I know I can do it with a reliable course to follow." Then she became thoughtful. "Would you like feedback on how things go?"

George was still blushing. "That's not a bad idea. I may want to publish it for extra change during my retirement someday. Let's go get it now. I rammed it into Paul's mailbox yesterday afternoon."

On the short trip to the staff room, George talked. "I'm not teaching the basic Math this semester. They gave me an E.S.L. class instead—before Paul's accident. Can you believe it: a sixty-two-year-old Math teacher teaching English as a second language for the first time? Ye gads, it'll take all my free time to figure out what to do every day." He gave Claire a compassionate look. "We're in the same boat, kiddo."

"They know how hard you work and probably hope you'll write a course for it." Claire was kidding.

But George was serious. "I would, but I'm already past retirement age. If they could guarantee me another twelve years of good health and send me to summer school to learn what E.S.L. is and how to teach it, I'd be happy to do it," he said, with a smile followed by a downhearted sigh. "It feels more like they're trying to get rid of me."

In the staff room, George pulled a thick rolled manila envelope out from a solid mass of mail and memos in Paul's box and gave it to Claire.

"Don't you know any English teachers, George?"

"Never see any. They hide on the second floor. I never get up there. Heart condition. No stairs."

"Anne Uzbecki in the English department is a friend of mine. We started here together. She might know somebody, or somebody who knows somebody, who can give you some help. I'll ask her."

"Thanks, Claire. Any port in a storm."

"No. *Thank you*! You've saved my life." She meant her *love* life, and smiled.

***

Claire spent the next hour photocopying George's course. She relinquished the copier twice for panicked young teachers who had not yet photocopied exams that were to be written within the hour. She finished the afternoon looking over the well-planned Math lessons and organizing them in a three-ring binder. She returned the original to George. Then she relaxed and puttered around in her lab. At two p.m. she couldn't think of anything else to do and decided she would go home and check on Boomer and Matt. She was looking forward to seeing them. No homework tonight, she thought.

***

Boomer was jumping around in his crate where Claire saw him with a blue ball and a chew toy too. There was a note from Matt on top of the crate, explaining that he had gone home to shower and change and would be back that evening. He had really gone above and beyond for her and Boomer. She dropped her briefcase on the chair in her little den and quickly put the puppy out on the back patio, which Matt had cleared for him to do his business and run a bit. "There, you go, Boomer." She marvelled at what two good meals had already done for him. When he had finished, she wiped the snow from his paws and his soft little belly and let him scamper into the living room. Matt had even installed baby gates for when Boomer had to be limited to the kitchen. Claire spent a few minutes rolling his ball and watching him chase it. Once or twice he retrieved it, although he didn't quite know what he was doing yet.

That night, Claire and Matt spent a quiet evening sipping wine in front of the fire, ignoring a DVD, and playing with the puppy on the sofa.

"How's Paul doing?" Matt asked, tossing the ball.

"His wife Deirdre told Bertha Stack he'll be in Intensive Care for some time," Claire answered. "They're keeping him in an induced coma. God, I hope he comes out of it all right. That's all I care about."

***

Friday, January 26

Claire had set her first semester final exams with an eye to choice and fairness for the students and expediency for her. Considering that the zeros in her marks book told her that she could still expect between fifty and sixty late assignments from her 104 first semester students, she had used multiple-choice questions on the factual knowledge section of the exam. It would save time and help her meet the report deadline by letting the Scantron machine mark that part.

Before Christmas vacation, she had printed the mark records for each class, using student numbers instead of names and had daily urged her students to check the lists and hand in any missing assignments.

After Christmas vacation, a studious *mark-shark* who owed two assignments handed them in. At the other extreme was a kid who owed thirteen out of thirty assignments, none of which came in. By exam time Claire had twenty extra assignments to mark besides the 104 exams, all due within the week.

After marking it all, Claire had to align her semester results with board policy, which many students all knew too well. She was not allowed to give a zero. She had to replace all zeros with blank spaces. The official ministry marks program would then estimate marks for the blanks. Each student's result could then be based only on the assignments and tests he or she had handed in and the 'donated' marks. That could range from seventeen out of thirty to thirty out of thirty assignments and tests. Most kids passed, including the student who had handed in only seventeen out of thirty assignments. In fact, his mark looked good. He had obviously skipped any test he hadn't studied for. This injustice towards the responsible students who did all the required work and the phony high marks irresponsible kids got were two more reasons why Claire was considering looking for another career.

**

Friday, February first

The final day of semester one, at eight a.m., waves of students from all three classes came gushing in as if to a bargain basement sale. Claire frantically handed out papers, hoping she didn't place one in the wrong hand. Then it was quiet while the students scanned their exams for marking errors, compared notes with classmates and checked Claire's addition with calculators. Unless there was a problem the exam was quickly dumped back on Claire's desk and the owner dashed off to the next class. Most students just wanted to get the hell out. Claire was wondering if any of them even cared whether they'd learned anything. The way they scrambled in and out of classroom after classroom left no illusion that they wanted to listen to a teacher explain what the answers should have been.

Still, Claire was surprised at how many kids asked about Mr. Fraser. She thanked them for their concern and told them to hope for the best. The media had reported Paul's name and said his condition was serious. That's putting it mildly, she thought grimly. Many commented that he was their favourite math teacher.

Ignoring Bertha Stack's exam take-up day schedule had become a ritual at Amberton District High School. The teachers were scrambling, but if they could survive the mayhem of the whole herd in the first hour, the rest of the day would be theirs.

Claire had attempted to follow the timetable. By eight a.m. she had prepared transparencies with the answers for the multiple-choice questions for all three classes and had placed copies of exams with point form answers on lab desks for reference, *in case* any students wanted to do what Bertha's timetable had been set up to do: look over their exam carefully and ask questions about their mistakes. A few students took advantage of her effort.

An hour later, everything had settled down. All the same, Claire remained in the lab until ten to eleven, keeping busy with odd jobs in case anyone showed up late. Finally, she checked up and down the hall. Nobody there. She had done more than what was expected. She packed up, tying the exams in bundles and bagging them for storage. As she was groping in her purse for her keys, Mark Compren, an arrogant, university-bound senior and aptly named *mark-shark* from period three, barged in like a gust of arctic wind. "I need to see my exam," he snarled.

Masking her frustration Claire said, "Hello, Mark. You're late. I was just leaving."

Mark's father was a supervisor at the board. His son didn't ask, he ordered. "You're still here. I need to see my exam," he repeated coldly. Wishing she could tell him to get lost, Claire slowly fished the senior exam package back out of its bag, untied it and retrieved Mark's paper. She found her transparency, mechanically plugged the overhead projector back in, pulled down the screen, and refocused the image. "The multiple-choice answers are on the screen for you," she said, feigning cheerfulness. "Numbers 29 and 32 are the ones most of the students had issues with." She handed him a copy of the exam with the correct answers.

Claire watched as Mark turned his stocky football player frame away and sat in one of the back seats, studying his exam. He didn't look at the screen. Claire waited. She looked at her watch. Ten minutes... twenty minutes... half an hour... Who did this kid think he was?

When Mark finally stood up, Claire wasn't surprised by his rant.

"This exam doesn't follow curriculum guidelines! The multiple-choice is too specific and the other questions are too general." He jabbed page two with his finger. "You have to give me more marks for numbers 8 and 14 in part B, Miss Heeeburt, or I won't get my scholarship." He raised his voice to an authoritarian level, waved his exam paper around, and got into her personal space. "And in the multiple choice, questions 23 and 47 ask for details nobody'd remember."

"More than half the class got them right," Claire shot back, looking him straight in the eye.

"Give me three more marks each for numbers 23, and 47, one each for 8 and 14 and my mark will be 98 percent. I need that for the scholarship I want." Mark was glaring at her, pressing forward.

"What about the others?" Claire stepped up on the dais behind her lab demo table. She tried to look taller, to look down on him.

But her height didn't bother him. He was used to being short. "Screw them, Miss. Just change *my* paper."

Claire swallowed hard. "No. Those answers are wrong and incomplete."

Mark flung his paper on her desk and stormed to the doorway. At the door he turned and glared at her and Claire thought she heard him mutter: "Too bad you weren't the one in the parking lot." Then he left, slamming the door behind him. Claire paled and took a deep breath. Now she knew why he'd been so late: he'd been wringing marks out of his other teachers. She groaned. If only she had resigned in December. She knew this wouldn't be the end of it.

It wasn't. At the end of the day, Claire found his printed email to the principal in her mailbox. It had a handwritten bit on the back from Bertha Stack, telling Claire to come to her office, a.s.a.p. Her heart sank. After he had slammed her door, Mark Compren had emailed his father, Bertha Stack and Chin Ho.

Claire went up to the science office. The kid had covered all his bases. Chin, Don and Angus were there.

"Claire, I took another look at your exam. It couldn't be more reasonable," Chin said. "The students had lots of questions to choose from. But based on this," and Chin threw his copy of the email into the recycling box, "I hate to say it, but do yourself a favour and give the weasel the marks." Then seeing her expression and shaking his head, he added, "It's not worth the hassle if you fight it, Claire. Let's face it: integrity is out. The kid is smart and because his father is a supervisor,

Bertha will give it to him anyway. I don't want to lose you too. The good kids need a teacher who cares."

"He knows how to manipulate the system and he has probably bullied every teacher who stood in his way," she pleaded. Don and Angus nodded.

Chin smiled and shrugged his shoulders in abject agreement. "Yup. He's a bully. Go home and have a drink, Claire. Do you still have the dog?"

"Yup."

"Good girl. Go walk him."

***

Claire went down to Bertha's office in a *let's-get-it-the-hell-over-with* mood. She nodded to her friend Shirley Alquist who was just leaving as Claire went in. "I raised the mark, Bertha," she said nervously, knowing that was what Bertha wanted to hear.

The principal sighed with relief. "Thanks, Claire."

"Would you like me to call Mr. Compren?"

"He can wait for the report card to find out the result."

Claire sighed with relief. She didn't relish the idea of talking to the tree that had produced an apple like Mark Compren. Even Bertha didn't want to talk to her supervisor right now.

Back in the hall, Claire met Shirley. Her short but elegant French immersion colleague, whose real name was Siu Li, was dressed to leave.

In the eighteen months they'd been colleagues, the thirty-three year old Claire and sixty-four year old Shirley had developed mutual respect and a close friendship. Her husband, who had been a Math teacher, had died of cancer eight years before, leaving Shirley to finish raising their teen-aged son and daughter on her own. She and Claire supported each other and commiserated with each other when things went askew. This was one of those times. Claire told her about Mark.

"I refused him, too," Shirley said, smiling and nodding. "That's why I was with Bertha when you arrived."

"I'm glad I wasn't the only one," Claire said. "Mark quoted the curriculum document and claimed I couldn't ask specific questions in the multiple choice, or details in the paragraph-answer questions. Can you believe that? In biology?"

"Claire, the curriculum document he quoted to you was probably the one for grade twelve French immersion." Shirley put her arm around her friend. "I showed it to him as a last resort when I felt the power to prevent him prying grammar marks out of me slipping away. It's in French immersion that they only have to have *general* knowledge of the literature."

So the kid had gotten something else wrong. Claire could kick herself for having given in.

February

Chapter 3

<u>Moans and Groans</u>

Matt arrived after work and they had one of those leisurely weekends when they forgot they even had jobs. They topped it off at Claire's parents' for Sunday dinner. Aimée and Jacques Hébert loved their canine grandson immediately. In three days, Boomer had become a full-fledged family member.

***

Monday, February 5

New semesters always started with a staff meeting in the library. Claire's friends were already there, craning their necks looking for her.

"She's late. She hates to be late." Anne, always the practical one, was annoyed.

"The meeting started late, Anne," said Shirley, shaking her head and rolling her eyes. "Her coffee's cold."

Having introduced new staff members, Principal Bertha Stack had vaguely updated the staff about Paul Fraser's condition.

"Do they know who did it yet?" whispered Anne, who taught history and English and was the youngest and least experienced of the three friends. "It's creepy." She shuddered. "It could be anyone. You're a department head, Shirley. Did you hear at the cabinet meeting if they're questioning anyone at the school? Bertha isn't telling us anything we didn't learn from the news."

"After working here for a year and a half, Anne, you should know the administration don't trust the staff with any knowledge," Shirley said, nodding her head towards the principal.

Bertha was about to continue with her agenda when Vice Principal Kristen Jaworski stood up and whispered in her ear. Bertha was shaking her head vigorously and trying to stop her, but Kristen prevailed.

"Oh, oh" Shirley said, leaning forward in her chair. "This could be good."

"Listen," Kristen said loudly, stepping away from Bertha. "Enough gossip, everybody. Here's the skinny." A hush descended over the staff. "You've all heard that Paul is in an induced coma and Deidre is with him day and night. The children are staying with her parents. All we can do now is pray, but later, I'm sure Deirdre will appreciate some practical help, if anyone's looking to be useful. And there are no witnesses, no leads as to the driver yet, but please, let's keep that to ourselves. One of our own was hurt and we need to support the police. If anyone sees or hears anything relevant in the halls, they want to know. Now, back to our agenda…"

Bertha gave Kristen a contemptuous grunt as she got back behind the lectern.

Shirley and Anne sighed and slumped back in their chairs. There were mumblings from the staff as the meeting proceeded. Bertha was well into a list of housekeeping items when Claire finally snuck in. She'd been fighting with one of the photocopiers. Vice Principal Jack Penworth had left it all blocked up with pink paper.

"Hi, guys. Have they told us how Paul is?"

"Shhh! …Tell you later." Anne was eyeing Jack Penworth, Bertha's monitor for staff meetings. He had noted Claire's late arrival.

Jack then took forty minutes to tell the staff about how they were going to save two of his dubious initiatives. None of the teachers was impressed with Jack's put-on smile as he presented his new plans. They were always schemes to discourage teachers from sending anyone to him for discipline: the discipline procedure checklist, how to word parental warning emails, the paperwork to complete if they needed support from the office. Behind his back, the teachers groaned at his efforts and laughed at how often he didn't follow through on things he had offered to do. You could always find Jack in his office nursing his computer. The wrinkled backside of his suit testified to his indolent existence.

On the other hand Jack had once taken a correspondence psychology course. When he did see students he coddled them and believed almost every excuse and lie they offered. The smart ones saw through him. The attitude-laden kids took advantage. If a student was sent to Jack for discipline and had no excuse, Jack thought one up faster than the kid himself could. It seemed that to Jack, all teens had family problems and should be pardoned for anything they did, no matter how vile. But now the wind was blowing in another direction and Jack was sporting his best smile as he handed out his pink questionnaire about his initiatives.

Bertha finally adjourned the meeting at eleven-thirty. The teachers filled out the pink sheets, then rushed out to finish their final prep for second semester. To them, that was what counted. That was where they would thrive or dive.

After hearing what she had missed from Anne and Shirley, Claire was rushing to catch Brian McLean in the hall, when Bertha called her. "Claire! Claire! I want you to meet Eugene Putnam. He's joining the Science department," she said, puffing from the effort to catch Claire. "He'll be in your lab 324 in the afternoons. Eugene, this is Claire Hébert. She's one of our best. I'll leave you two to get to know each other." She smiled as she left.

Claire nearly choked with surprise at a compliment from Bertha. She had expected to be told off for being late. She reconfigured her face into a smile and turned her attention to the man now standing in front of her. "Nice to meet you, Mr. Putnam," she stuttered.

"Please, it's Gene."

Claire thought his wire-rimmed glasses gave him a vulnerable, academic look, but a sparkle in his eye hinted at spirit and possibly mischief. "Right," she said before taking a deep breath and nodding towards the stairs. "I'll show you the lab and where you can put your things. What brings you to Amberton?" "I want to work with Chin Ho. They say he's the best Science Head in the district. I'm aiming for a headship too—in a year or so."

She nodded. "He's a good one to emulate, alright." Soon they were on the third floor. Claire noticed Gene glancing into the windows of all the other labs as they walked by. "Here's our lab. I cleaned it up a bit during exam break."

She watched her striking new colleague as he looked around the room. He was a lithe five foot ten, close to her own age, in his early thirties, and showed an energy lacking in many of her colleagues. His wispy blond hair was neatly styled. He had an easy way about him and it was obvious that he knew what he was doing as he moved about the lab.

"Wow," he said, looking around. "You're to be congratulated, Claire. Everything's neat, clean and in working order." He counted the desks. "Hmmm… big room… eight lab desks for four… rare in a fifty year-old school… did they break a wall down?… each with a sink and a gas tap… even twelve tablet arm chairs… Main valves for water and gas?"

"Oh yes." Claire chuckled. "In this cupboard under the demo counter. Chin will give you a key."

"Good." He scanned the room. "I like this."

Back at the front of the room, Gene stepped on the dais behind the neat demo counter.

"Oh look, the computer isn't an antique."

Claire liked his easy smile. "We got it last year. Chin keeps us as up to date as the science budget allows."

Gene turned around and faced the blackboards. "And… here are the latest anachronisms."

"What? We can't use blackboards anymore?" Claire was astonished.

"Didn't you hear? The Ministry of Education wants us to use *Smart Boards* instead. It's one of their new policies."

"Couldn't we use both? I missed the first half of the meeting. Does Bertha have to buy *every* policy the ministry dreams up?"

"She doesn't, but she does. The way I remember Bertha, she'll insist we follow ministry decisions to the letter."

"You've met her before? And you still transferred here?"

"Oh, yes. She likes to look at lesson plans—to make sure we're following the ministry paradigm."

"Yep, you know her." Claire looked at Gene and felt a small flutter in her stomach. He had bang-on insight, she thought. "Bertha may have changed a bit from when you knew her last. At Amberton, she's wearing out her office chair."

"That could be an improvement. So where's your Smart Board?"

"Four of us—now five—share one. We don't use it much. It's in the storeroom. There's a sign-up sheet if you want to use it."

Gene looked disappointed.

"I'm still learning how to work the Smart Boards into my lessons. But look, Gene, it's lunchtime. Let's go to the cafeteria and grab a sandwich. We can eat and talk in the science office."

"You go ahead. I bring my own lunch. I'm saving for a wife," he said with a slight smirk. Claire felt heat rise in her cheeks and turned away. "Where's the science office from here?"

"Oh, ah…right, right around the corner. I'll let you in. Be back in a few minutes with my lunch."

Chin Ho had already assigned him a desk and introduced him to Don and Angus. Gene wasted no time diving into the drawers and making it his own. Meanwhile, Claire was in the cafeteria wondering what the heck this guy meant by "saving for a wife."

***

After lunch, Claire's first period grade ten general science class dribbled in. "Hi, guys, welcome to grade ten science." In the first weeks, a teacher establishes a routine. So do the kids. The two are not necessarily compatible.

"Hi, Miss Hébert."

"Good to see you again, Miss H."

"We'll let bygones be bygones, eh, Miss?"

Claire moved around the lab, asking each student his or her first and last name and checking it off on the attendance list.

As the bell went, one last boy arrived. Claire asked for his name. "Jimmy."

"Jimmy who?"

"Yup."

"This list goes by last names, Jimmy," she said semi-sarcastically.

"It's Jimmy *Hu*, Miss. H…u…" chimed three or four of the boys, laughing.

Claire found 'Hu' on the list and laughed, too. The class was a standard bunch of
yappy individuals ranging from studious self-starters to those she'd have to help a lot and a few she'd have to watch carefully.

Ricky Penworth, the son of the Vice Principal, was the only absentee. Leaving a spot for Ricky, she made a seating plan to help her learn the kids' names. Then she started to get the class oriented: safety rules, where things are in the lab, notebook guidelines. She identified the equipment in the cupboards under their desks and showed them the eyewash station and the first aid box. Second semester was on. Reality was sinking in reluctantly. There were no questions.

Claire handed out the course outlines. If they read them, the kids would know exactly what they'd be learning in grade ten and they would see how much time they would have to spend on each unit. Then, if they turned the paper over, they would see how their marks would be calculated. Claire, knowing no hormone-powered grade ten would do it on his own, read it to them. Then she asked if there were any questions.

The rogues made themselves known on cue. "What's the course about, Miss?" Dwayne Dufresne yawned.

"How will the marks be calculated, Miss?" Logan Stanley asked, grinning.

Pointing to the information sheet she had just read to them, Claire tried to go on...

"Do we have to do homework?" a new boy shouted from the back.

"Only if you want to pass, Maziyar."

The self-starters giggled. The bell signalled the end of the first half hour period and they stampeded out the door. Many course outlines were left behind. Claire collected them and filed them for when they would realize it was helpful.

***

Period two. "Hi, guys, welcome to grade eleven biology." Most of the grade eleven class was more mature. It had a number of students Claire knew to be good, reliable people, like Danielle Duncan, a future oncologist and her friend Tori Oliver, an amateur sleuth.

"Hi, Miss H. How was changeover?"

"Pretty good, how about you?" Claire was happy to have Tori in the class. She was brilliant, and she and her friends were fascinated by forensics. They had befriended Aisha Ames, who had been cyber-bullied last semester. "Hello, Aisha." Aisha, a bit fleshier than the almost anorexic figures so many of the girls had, slid into her desk and gave a brief nod. Claire liked her friendly smile.

Contrasting with these girls there were some overindulged sexily dressed minxes, whose parents had taught them that whenever they opened their lips gold flowed out. At home they only had to utter a whim with their prettily lip-sticked mouths, flutter their mascara-laden eyelashes and a subservient parent would give them whatever they wanted.

As for the boys, at the top was Sean Jacobson, computer geek and homework freak. Kariem Jazrawi, was smart but impatient with slower classmates. Artie Binton, a suffering son whose mother had drowned in a boating accident last summer, acted tough to cope with his now troubled family life. His friend Serge Leclerc had endured his parents' hostile divorce last year and was getting over it with a new girlfriend, Amy O'Leary, who was not in Claire's class. Jimmy Hu had a bad case of A.D.H.D. made worse by a serious hearing disability. He did try hard in class, but whenever things got noisy—as in the cafeteria—he took out his hearing aids.

The elevens had seen the lab, course outlines, semester schedules and evaluation sheets before, and took the introductory period in stride.

Chapter 4

<u>The Hickenman Room</u>

Monday, February 5

At Amberton afternoon classes flip-flopped according to the date. On every odd-numbered day, immediately after lunch, Claire was scheduled for her period three basic Math class. On even numbered days she had her period four spare after lunch and the grade nine basic Math kids at the end of the day. Mornings stayed as they were.

The room she was to use for the grade nine basic Math class was in a forty-year-old, cheaply built, drably painted east side addition that was used for overflow from any department. In the mornings Chester Hickenman, the resident geography teacher who was notoriously sloppy, taught in the room. In the afternoons, while Gene was in her immaculate lab, Claire would be stuck in the no-man's land that was Hickenman's room.

It was an eye-opener for Claire. She had not been able to get into room 241 during changeover. "Oh… my… God…" she stuttered as she opened the door. Only the floor was clean—in spots. The mismatched tables and chairs were scattered randomly. The fronts of the tables had been boarded shut to prevent students leaving rotting food in them. The tabletops had been scrubbed clean during changeover, but the graffiti would be there for generations.

On the right, in the far back corner, Claire could distinguish what might be part of a teacher's desk beside a bank of filing cabinets, which had piles of posters and student projects sliding off it. She walked over. The desk was covered with junk, including a disgusting half-full mug of cold coffee with an island of greyish green mould floating in it, assorted abused pens and pencils, a dirty remnant of an eraser, pencil shavings, stray change, loose papers, and mangled paperclips. Around her, all horizontal surfaces, except for the students' tables were covered with years' worth of dusty detritus: maps, projects, piles of faded construction paper, atlases, National Geographic magazines, a dented microwave, loose rolls of posters, and old student projects. There was one wobbly little table for Claire's stuff.

Chester Hickenman, or his predecessors, had taped posters, newspaper articles, maps, jokes and student projects all over the blackboards. They looked as if they had been there for decades. Except for the floor under the desks, the whole room was dusty and mouldy. There were no windows. The air was a melange of human exhaust and popcorn.

By the door, there was a one foot-width of leftover blackboard masking-taped into spaces for Chester's homework assignments. It was the only sign of organization in the whole room. Beside it were the only six feet of useable blackboard. Claire had hoped to use the blackboard for Math demonstrations, but that little space wouldn't allow for much, especially if she had to leave a solution on the board for kids who were behind in their work.

This was the type of classroom Claire hated. She dreaded the thought of being there for period three every day for five months. She wanted to escape. Every fibre in her body wanted to quit, but her stubbornness, conscience and professionalism wouldn't let her. She would see it through until June and then quit, she promised herself.

The bell rang. Claire was still organizing herself as two kids ambled in. She smiled at them and they looked her over. "Hello," she said. "Welcome to grade nine Math." There was no response. They were gawking at the room, which contrasted sharply with their neatly dressed teacher. Three more individuals dribbled in, found a chair they liked and moved it to the table of their choice. "Hello," Claire said. Again, not even looks were returned. Two boys arrived. Their t-shirts looked very thin for February. Three minutes after the bell there were only *seven out of fifteen* kids present. Two more minutes... nothing. That could be it for the day, Claire thought.

After introducing herself, Claire handed out the course outlines and started to give instructions. Two more sauntered in. *Nine out of fifteen*. The new arrivals greeted their friends and sat down, moving tables, scraping the floor with their chairs and noisily dropping their backpacks. Was anyone listening? The two latecomers chatted with their friends as if they were still on break. Claire took their names, fixed the attendance and gave a short review of her spiel. "Y'awready said that, Miss." Somebody had been listening! A glimmer of hope!

Not one of the students had paper or pencil. Some started to listen, but this room would distract anybody. They couldn't help fidgeting, staring, laughing and gossiping. Their attention spans were short and they seemed totally naïve about the purpose of school. Two more wandered in. *Eleven.* Claire took their names, marked them late, and tried to give them a quick repeat of what she'd already said. She skipped the evaluation side of the sheet. They would not understand the Math. These students would need a lot of help. She thought of George Gumbersahl and how grateful she was for his course.

On the class list some students had been identified as having learning or perception differences. Claire looked over the class: Britney Anderson wore hearing aids. Lindsay Landon, a puffy-eyed dyslexic girl with long stringy black hair reeked of French fries. Jimmy Church and Deepak Dhali had A.D.H.D. Only Joel Atkins' clothing reflected parental care and he had Asperger's. Timmy Vanderhout was fast asleep with his head on the desk. Narcolepsy? Drugs? Maxine Young had walked out when she wasn't looking.

Claire tried to encourage the kids to come up with five rules to make a good learning environment. She handed each student a notebook and asked them to copy the rules on the first page and to put the course outlines she had given them into a pocket inside the back cover. She printed the rules on the bit of blackboard. She didn't want to scare them. One or two wrote in their notebooks.

That filled the thirty minutes. At the end of the period, Chester Hickenman's fourth period class barged in. There was no Chester.

If she let her basic grade nines keep the notebooks and pencils, she would never see them again, so Claire ran around collecting them from table and floor before they got lost. Then she grabbed her things and fled the mayhem.

As she left the room, Claire leaned against the wall in the hall, taking a long, deep breath. She had survived day one.

"I know! Awesome, right?"

"Yeah! I got chips and a pop."

"I got a chocolate bar."

From a room across the hall, a gaggle of kids spilled out into the hallway. They were all chomping on snacks and there was a lot of happy jabbering. Curious, Claire walked over and peered into the classroom as nonchalantly as she could manage with her arms full of notebooks and pencils. Sitting behind the desk at the head of the room was a young, attractive woman. Her blonde streaked hair was neatly pinned and pulled back from her face and her perfectly pressed dark teal dress was styled to impress. That must be Naomi Harper, the new long-

term supply teacher in Shirley's department, Claire thought as she picked up her pace. She didn't want to catch her eye. Heading down the hall, the hyper teenagers continued to cavort as they jostled their way to their lockers. Claire cleared her throat loudly as she passed and they gawked at her
as if she had two heads.

Back in the science office, she thumbed through the notebooks. Most were blank: no names, no rules; the kids who had used their pencils had doodled.

***

Finished with classes for the day, Claire sought out Brian McLean, the learning resource teacher, who was helping a student at his desk. Four students were working with two educational assistants. She tiptoed in and waited for Brian to finish. "Excuse me, Brian, I got Paul Fraser's basic level Math class yesterday," she whispered. "Any chance I could get a peer tutor at this late date?"

Brian nodded as he reached behind him for the peer tutor binder. He flipped through some pages. "Paul signed up for peer tutors, so you get them along with the class," he said. "Jenny Harrington and Amir Singh will undergo training this week and next and after that they'll start to help you in class Mondays to Thursdays." Brian found more information on the application forms. "They're extremely patient seniors earning a credit for leadership and volunteer work. Amir wants to be a teacher, Jenny a nurse." Claire breathed a sigh of relief in anticipation of the help. She might just survive the semester.

Claire used the last half hour of her prep time to ask the bookstore secretary if last semester's students had returned enough science and biology texts for her to distribute them to her new classes.

Bernice Bradbury was referred to as *the Bookstore Barracuda*. Staff loved her. Students did not. She was the antithesis of Jack Penworth and never, ever bought any of the lame excuses kids gave for not returning a book on time. "I can check on the computer for you, but I can't go to the bookstore until I finish these calls," she replied, pointing to a pile of late book slips.

"Thanks, Bernie. Check the computer for me, would you?"

"Give me a sec," she said, as she dug the end of her pencil into her loosely styled hair and did a few clicks on her keyboard. "Hmmm… Hébert, you're in luck. There are enough for both your classes."

"Can I borrow your keys and an elevator key so I can take them to the third floor?" Claire gave her a cheesy grin.

"Oh. Sure. Just don't take off with the keys and don't leave the bookstore unlocked. If you promise, I'll let you take the cart so you can do it all in one trip."

"Thanks, Bernie. I'll bring the keys back right away."

Bernie waved her off and spoke into the phone perched on her shoulder. "No, ma'am, there's no fine for the inconvenience, but there should be." Claire grinned as she trotted off to the bookstore.

***

At the end of the day, Claire met Anne Uzbecki in the hall. Her classroom was not far from the Hickenman room.

"All set for tomorrow?"

"Almost." Claire exhaled. "I still need to print the first two Math units." She waved two folders of paper at Anne. "Let's go to the copier room. They should have fixed those damn machines by now." They walked down the hall. "Oh, that reminds me: Do you know anyone who could help George Gumbersahl with his E.S.L. course? He's never taught it before and I want to help him. He's letting me copy his whole Math course."

"Why does admin give teachers close to retirement courses they've never taught before? George is a mathematician. How's that poor man going to manage E.S.L.?" asked Anne as they entered the copier room. "Is it at least E.S.L. Math?

Claire shrugged her shoulders.

"I'll see what I can do."

"Thanks, Annie. Now I owe you one, too."

***

Just after three p.m., Claire, Shirley and Anne met in the third floor English office, their feet on the coffee table amidst a pile of books and a box of papers that was waiting to be shredded. They were there for some peace, an after-school chat, and a coffee fix while the parking lot cleared of impatient cars and inattentive students.

Anne, a practical-minded tall blonde with a B.A. in English and History, soon had the old coffeemaker dripping. She had worked as a computer programmer to pay her way through teachers' college and after one hectic *worst-case-scenario-to-thought-provoking* year of supply teaching, she got her first provisional contract. At twenty-seven, one year out of teachers' college, she had started teaching at Amberton District at the same time as Claire.

"I guess you can put that French dictionary away, eh Claire?" Anne said.

"Sadly, yes. I was looking forward to doing the *Sociologie* course. It would have been a challenge and I would have learned more than the kids."

"So what did you two do during exam break—other than marking and everything for the
January report? Shirley asked.

Claire told them of Matt's gift.

63

"Sounds like somebody's serious. Those dogs don't come cheap," Shirley said, a dog-lover herself.

"How long have you two been together now?" Anne asked.

Claire sighed. "We went steady in high school for two years, but that changed when he went to McGill in Montreal and I went to McMaster in Hamilton. We drifted apart until I met him again in a pub in the UK two years after Tyler's ... uh ... accident. I followed him back home and came here." Talking about her late fiancé brought back difficult memories for Claire and she took a deep breath.

"So, what's that? Almost two years, right?" Anne said, cheerfully filling in the blanks for the hesitant Claire. "Have you and Matt made any plans? Wink, wink, nudge, nudge?" Anne giggled.

Claire rubbed a hand over her face. "Don't you think I'd tell you guys? No, ... there's nothing to tell," she shrugged. Claire stood up to get herself another half mug of coffee. "Let's talk about something else." She was always more comfortable talking about work. "Can either of you tell me anything about Logan Stanley? His name raises a red flag but I can't remember why."

Anne and Shirley exchanged knowing smiles.

Shirley took a sip of her coffee. "I taught a Lauren Stanley in grade twelve French Immersion last year. She was brilliant. I'd bet Logan is her brother. And if he is, watch out."

Shirley sipped her coffee. "At the graduation dance last year, Lauren arrived reeling drunk, loud and violent." Shirley's eyes were intense. "Her parents weren't in either home. Bertha had to let the police take her away."

Now Anne laughed. "It must have been bad—Bertha doesn't do that sort of thing lightly."

"Ah! The cops insisted. They were there anyway. Except for socializing a lot, Lauren was okay in my class. She liked French," Shirley added. "Still, there were signs... She could get away with not doing any homework and still get a good mark." Shirley got up to finish her coffee and check to see if the parking lot had cleared a bit. "Lauren always had the latest technology with her. If her brother's like her, he'll be brilliant but trouble. Just pray that he likes science."

"No prayer allowed in the schools," Claire said with a sneer.

"The parents divorced a few years ago and both are remarried," Shirley said.

"I was wondering about the parents not being in *either* home," Claire said, spilling her coffee. Anne passed her some tissues from a nearby desk.

Claire threw the used tissues in the garbage and scanned the parking lot. "I'll be keeping an eye on Logan then," she said, looking at her watch. "Oh, my gosh. I've got to go." Claire quickly rinsed and dried her mug. "I forgot that I'm a Mommy now. Boomer needs to be let out and I have a lot to do before tomorrow."

***

Claire let Boomer out into the backyard and waited for him to come back. In her den, she went through her files to find the best support material to introduce the unit about human tissues and organs to the grade ten general science class. She had located some and was exploring further on the Internet when Matt arrived and lured her away. They walked to the park with Boomer and took turns holding the leash. Boomer jumped and cavorted and the crisp air was good for Claire, too. The snow-covered trees and shrubbery and the icicles on the eaves of the houses along the street took her mind off school for a while.

"How was the first day?"

"Good. Busy. You know: a hundred new kids, a new course and not enough time. I have a new colleague sharing my lab in the afternoon. I think we're going to get along."

"Oh, is she nice?"

"*He's* very nice. He knows a lot about the reluctant and basic level students like I have in the basic Math class. I'm looking forward to picking his brain. He teaches woodworking in the morning."

Boomer was pulling so hard that Claire lost hold of the leash. Matt grabbed it just in time. "He's pulling quite a bit, isn't he?" Matt was concerned. "Boomer's getting stronger fast. He's easy to handle now, but I think we should enrol him in obedience training."

"It is better if they go when they're puppies. I'll look into it." They went as far as the old log shelter in the park, Boomer's limit for walks if they didn't want to carry him home.

"Stay with me tonight?" Claire asked as she looped her arm through Matt's.

"And?" Matt was gazing lovingly into her deep brown eyes.

"Who knows? You don't fly out until late tomorrow."

Chapter 5

<u>An Inauspicious Start</u>

Tuesday, February 6

It was the first full day of semester two classes. As Claire scanned her first period grade ten list, one name jumped out: Ricky Penworth. He was Jack Penworth's son from his first marriage and she had heard that he could be impactful in class. Again, he was the only absentee. Not a good start, but perhaps he was sick—it was flu season. Part of her looked forward to the challenge of having him in her class: to see what he was like and if she could achieve something with him.

"Anybody know where Ricky is?" she asked after taking attendance.

There was a sea of shaking heads. She started her introductory remarks. "Just a few instructions on survival in this lab." Claire was walking around, giving each student a friendly smile as she spoke and tried to attach names to faces. Two were taking advantage of the electrical outlets on their lab desk to recharge their appliances: one a cellphone, the other a laptop. Claire didn't think it was right, but decided against making an issue of something that was in limbo until the tech committee examined it. "Listen people, always bring your science books. You might think we won't do anything because of some activity, but I can make use of even two minutes, so you'll need all your science stuff in class and your homework completed every day. And don't be late." She turned on a dime. "Could you three at the back please pay attention?"

Half the class was not actively listening. Logan Stanley had impressed Karla Kozak and Dwayne Dufresne with some comment and they were all guffawing.

"Second, if you have issues with me... er... Logan, can you and your friends please respect your classmates and not talk while I'm speaking?"

Logan and Karla stopped for about three seconds and stared at Claire. Then Logan grinned and put up his hand. "C'n I go to the washroom, Miss?"

Karla giggled.

"What I'm telling the class is important."

"I gotta go, Miss. Show me some *rispec*, Miss." He was hopping about holding his crotch and grinning.

"Hey, Loganboy, gitme a bag of chips while you're out, man." It was Maziyar Bizhani, the new boy, just transferred from Bellington High School. He had immediately identified and befriended Logan. He tossed a toonie at Logan, who caught it.

The class was watching.

"In a few minutes, Logan." Claire stayed calm.

"But, Miss," Logan whined, "I got a bladder problem. 'Sides, if ya don't rispec me, how can I rispec you?" Logan was obviously the leader in this class and he was raising the bar for the newcomer.

Logan was wasting time, the class needed to hear her instructions and Claire wanted to finish it this period. "Go ahead, then. But I'll need to see you after class." Logan sashayed out beaming a satisfied smirk to the class.

There was some snickering from his friends. Claire knew that Logan didn't have any medical problems, but she would double-check his file just in case.

"Second," Claire repeated, "if you have an issue with me, please do not try to discuss it with me in class. Wait until the end of the period. During class, I have the whole group on my mind. I'll be calmer and kinder after class when I can give you my full attention."

The grade ten class was in the biology lab for the first time. Heads were bobbing up and down as equipment was pulled out from under desks and examined. Every once in a while something fell, but Claire never left breakables on student shelves. She went on. "Third, the best way to learn science is to keep an organized notebook. Please pass these out." She counted out four handouts for each lab table to pass around.

"You need to identify the date you did the work and the page in the textbook to which it refers."

"Why d'we hafta put in a date?" Maziyar had stopped playing on his iPod to ask the question. "A date has nuthin' to do with science."

"Oh, yes it does," Karla giggled. "Human biology starts with a *date,* ya clod."

Claire ignored the remark. "Imagine how hard it would be to find a phone number if the phonebook wasn't alphabetized. Neat, dated notes make it easier to find work you missed in your own or in someone else's notes. It's part of learning to communicate."

"You don't need the alphabet, Miss. We can find phone numbers on 411 on the Internet, Miss." Justine Jones said. "Just type the name in the box. Besides, we don't have no textbooks yet, Miss." Heads nodded around the room.

In front of them, hunched over their work, Claire saw some kids taking notes and whispering together. Sylvia Woodhouse, Nathan Bergeron and Brendan Wong were working, a pleasant contrast to Maziyar, and Karla.

"You'll be getting them in a minute. Lets get back to notebooks now. Get into the habit of underlining titles and putting in page numbers."

"What fer, Miss?" Justine Jones shouted. She looked around expecting applause.

"It helps you find what you're looking for in the textbook or in your notebook." It was so obvious to Claire, but these grade tens had no idea how to keep a notebook and didn't understand. "Also, if you drop your binder and the pages fall out, you can easily put them back in order if they are numbered."

Logan returned with an authoritarian swagger, a bag of chips and a pop in each hand and hook-kicked the door so it slammed shut. His friends' faces lit up. He tossed a bag of chips to Maziyar. He had heard the bit about the notebooks.

"I don' ever look at it again anyhow so no, I don' care." Maziyar was tipping his chair back, acting cool and defiant to impress Logan, Karla and Dwayne. He was looking for allies.

"Put lines under titles in the textbook we don't have or in the notebook we don' have?" It was Logan, picking up from where he left off. The class laughed.

Others looked at each other and rolled their eyes in frustration at all the interruptions. They were bored with the jerks.

Claire ignored Logan. "Do your notes in ink, but answer the questions in pencil in case you make mistakes. The answers will stand out from the notes and, if there are mistakes, you can erase them and replace them." The good kids showed interest in this advice while the others ignored it like everything else. Then Claire handed out the textbooks. "Please take care of them. They cost a hundred and fifty dollars new," she warned. "We'll be starting with some general science review before we get to the unit on human tissues and organs. Any questions? Yes, Maziyar?" Claire tried not to show her annoyance. Two agendas were playing out in this classroom. She was going to have to do some serious thinking about this group.

"When d'we get to cut up dead animals?" Maziyar interrupted her thought.

"In grade eleven, during the anatomy lesson, unit five. You won't get to do that until you've passed this course," Claire answered pithily.

"Aw, damn! Science sucks."

"Watch your language, Maziyar."

"Say *please*, Miss."

At this Karla, his cousin, who sat beside Maziyar, whispered something in his ear. Maziyar turned around and laughed uproariously.

At the end of the class, Logan Stanley did not linger to speak with Claire. She made a note to catch him the next day. He skipped. Claire put a note in his *Gradecalc* file.

***

Wednesday, February 7

The staff room was abuzz with teachers. They had descended upon it like gulls to a chip stand. It was the annual teacher appreciation luncheon, sponsored by the Parents' Council. The parents had worked all morning preparing and displaying goodies around the room and a choice of beverages by the window. Two things were sure: it would be a tasty meal and there would be stimulating conversation.

"I hear Paul's doing better," Anne said as she and Claire filled their plates.

"Yes, I'm glad they finally brought him out of that coma. It's been ten days. They're hoping to operate on his foot tomorrow."

"Fingers crossed it all goes well," Anne said, holding up her free hand. "Do you know if the police have any leads yet?"

"Shhh! How would I know? We can't talk about it." Claire remembered Mark Compren's exam return day comment about it being too bad she hadn't been the one in the parking lot. Was that a lead? Mark? He was mad at *her*, not Paul and he probably heard about it on the news or from his father. Should she report it? Just a careless teenage comment. She shook the thought out of her head and stepped away from the bustle at the food table and bumped into Gene. "Oh, sorry!" she stammered as she regained her balance. Gene reached out and took hold of her arm. His hand was warm and strong. She looked at him and blushed.

"No problem," he said with a smile. "You alright?"

"Yeah, fine. Sorry. Thank you." Anne, standing beside Claire, cleared her throat not-so-daintily. Claire, thankful for the reminder, realized they hadn't been introduced. "Gene, this is Anne Uzbecki. She teaches English and history."

"Nice to meet you, Anne." Gene would have shaken her hand but Anne was balancing a full paper plate in one hand and a cup of coffee in the other, so he just smiled.

"Likewise," Anne replied. Claire couldn't help but notice the extra little flutter she gave her eyelashes. "So, Gene, is it? How do you…"

"Oh look." Claire stepped forward and nodded to the right. "There's George Gumbersahl, Anne."

"Huh?" Anne reluctantly swung her eyes from Gene's. "Right, George. Good old George."

"Have you had a chance to find any E.S.L. help for him yet?"

"As a matter of fact, I have. There's a teacher at Elgin Falls willing to help him get started. I told George all about it this morning."

"Did I hear someone mention my name?" George was grinning from ear to ear as he approached. "There she is—my port in a storm. Thanks, Anne. You saved my life."

"You're very welcome, George," Claire said.

Gene's eyebrows arched up as he looked to Claire. She winked as Anne said, "Hey, I did the helping, Claire."

"Sure, but who got you to help?" she teased. "George, have you met Gene?"

"Oh, yes. New to the science department, eh?" George was always eager to meet new people and talk. "This is a great luncheon. Professional development days used to be like this," he told the young teachers. "We'd have a motivational speaker from nine until noon, then after a long lunch we'd gather by subject group and exchange ideas that had worked with our classes. The next day everybody was eager to get back and try the new stuff."

"The good old days, huh?" Gene said with an easy smile.

"Hmph, you said it." George was having trouble balancing everything on his flimsy paper plate. Claire slipped a second one underneath the first. "Now the ministry uses professional development to try out theories spun by its officials. And when things go wrong, it's always our fault." Then his tone became jovial. "But this, my dear colleagues," he paused and took a bite of his B.L.T., "…this is motivational."

Shirley arrived from the far end of the room and introduced her new department member Naomi Harper to George, Anne, Gene and Claire. George was always enthusiastic to meet a pretty girl and shook her hand vigorously. Claire was less so. She hadn't met Naomi Harper officially yet, but had observed curious and distracting comings and goings at the new teacher's classroom door, which was diagonally across from the Hickenman room.

Shirley looked at Claire. "How did the girls' water polo team do last night?"

"We won three to two over Bellington. We're doing well," Claire said, without taking her eyes off her plate and getting ready for a forkful of salad.

"You coaching them again?"

"Just filling in. Karina Jackson's in charge of it this year. She played varsity in college. She's keen and knows much more about it than I do." Claire waved to Karina at the far end of the room. "I'm doing the Science Fair, the Eco Club and the Grad Committee."

"Does everyone have to coach a sport?" Naomi asked slowly in a Marilyn Monroe voice, her eyes wide. "I'm not good at sports." Claire thought she actually saw her shudder.

"Oh, that's the fun of teaching," Gene piped up. "Spending time with the kids, mentoring them."

"But, sports aren't mandatory," George explained in his friendly manner. "Some of us do other stuff like the Christmas Food Drive, the Drama Night, the June Park Day, the May Concert—to raise funds for the Music Department, clubs, the annual musical in November, and stuff like that." He took another large bite of potato salad and noticed the vacant look on Naomi's face. "Don't worry, it's voluntary." He swallowed.

"Oh." She sounded simultaneously bored and relieved.

"I run the Math Club," George continued eagerly. "It's for kids who aren't doing well in Math and need some extra help. It's every day after school." Naomi turned and left without so much as a backward glance as George finished.

"I guess she's the solitary type," Claire said. Everyone in the group shrugged their shoulders.

Not knowing what to say in front of Shirley who, she knew, had been against hiring Naomi, Claire turned to the dessert table and selected a decadent looking piece of chocolate cake.

"Enjoy it, Claire, you can work it off on hall duty," Anne whispered in her ear as she passed.

"Oh… man," Claire mumbled through her first bite. She had forgotten she was expected in the hall in ten minutes. Gene chuckled softly as he sauntered by and motioned to the corner of his mouth. Claire took a quick swipe at her own lips and felt the crumbs dislodge. She blushed again.

Before she could say anything to recover from the moment, she felt a hand on her arm. "Are you Miss Hébert?"

Turning around, Claire saw a neatly dressed woman with a sweet face and a shy smile, wavy black hair with the odd grey strand. Who could she be?

"Yes, I'm Claire Hébert," she said, as she swallowed her bite of cake.

"I'm Eric Thompson's mother, Elaine Bamford."

"I'm glad to see you. I've made a note to call you. Guidance told me Eric has Tourette's."

"How is my Eric doing? I hope he isn't giving you too much trouble." She had a British accent.

"Oh no, Mrs. Bamford, Eric has been quite good in class. He blurts his thoughts out once in a while and occasionally does some loud socializing, but nothing that I'd get upset about."

"You see, he sometimes asks shocking questions or makes shocking remarks."

"Yes, I've heard inappropriate language, but I'm used to it. The f-word rings loud and clear in the halls during breaks and dismissal," Claire chuckled. "We don't approve of it of course, but Miss Stack says if we sent every child who swears to the office, there'd be hardly any left in class."

Mrs. Bamford blushed. "It's called coprolalia. He also has echolalia, where he repeats something he has just heard."

"Yes, I've noticed that, too. I thought he was doing it to memorize things."

"He does, but they're also components of his Tourette's. Eric was often sent home from school before he was diagnosed. You may have noticed he occasionally has physical tics; making faces, grunting, all seemingly for no reason. Some teachers think he's being disrespectful. He isn't. This is his second high school, and he has been to five different elementary schools. He needs calm. Sudden changes or surprises... well, he just doesn't handle them well."

"Thanks for telling me, Mrs. Bamford. It's better to know."

Mrs. Bamford continued. "He's a good boy. But I worry about him, too. Eric is easily excited, angered, distracted. When he was younger, I could control him. Now that he's in high school and a lot bigger, it's not so easy. He can get violent. He has been talking about some girl... Sarah... Sandra... Samantha... I don't remember the name."

"He often talks to the girl who sits beside him— Samantha. She's kind and smart. She likes him, I think. He's a good-looking guy. In any case, he hasn't done anything I would call terrible in my class."

"Oh, good." The relief showed on her face. "He can have difficulty staying on task, if there are distractions. Once distracted he has trouble getting back to work. But perhaps you could let him stay near Samantha?"

"Oh, I think that can be arranged," Claire replied with a wink and a smile.

"Thank you!"

"Thank you for telling me, Mrs. Bamford. We'll talk again."

As Mrs. Bamford turned away, Claire looked lustfully at the cake on her plate. Just as she lifted the fork she heard another, "Oh! Are you Miss Hébert?"

Claire sighed and put down the utensil. The parents were nice enough to host this lunch, but it wasn't entirely free. Some wanted their five minutes of face-time.

"I'm Kariem's mother."

"Oh yes. Kariem, a very bright boy who…"

"Yes, but he has a tendency to interrupt in class." His mother would know, Claire thought to herself. "He loses his patience when things don't go fast enough and calls out answers for the others just to keep things moving."

"I've spoken to him about it a couple of times already…"

"Last semester," she interrupted again, "his teachers gave him extra responsibilities to keep him busy for when he thought the lessons slowed down."

"That's an idea. That would give other kids a chance to go through their thinking process," she said. But she also thought that then Kariem wouldn't have to learn to correct his bad habit.

"He could tutor somebody," his mother jumped in again. Claire wondered if she was at all aware of the irony. "You could ask him to make notes, which he could photocopy and pass on to help kids who can't keep up. Mr. Adams put him in charge of the attendance. We learn a lot from helping others."

"All good ideas, Mrs. Jazrawi. I'll see what I can do to keep him engaged."

"Thank you, Miss Hébert."

Claire looked at her watch. "Oh damn, it's time for hall duty." Her taste buds were screaming as she threw the leftover chocolate cake into the trashcan, checked her mailbox and hurried off. On her way out she bumped into Mrs. Atkins, who was just coming in.

"Oh ... are you Miss Hébert?"

"Yes, but I..."

"I'm so glad I didn't miss you! I'm Joel Atkins's Mom."

"Oh yes. Nice to meet you, but I have hall . . ."

"It's very important that I talk to you about Joel. He's a special case and needs some sensitive handling. Can I make an appointment with you for after school today or tomorrow?"

"Of course. How about tomorrow?"

"That would be good, thank you."

"I really have to scoot now! Sorry. Bye, Mrs. Atkins. See you tomorrow."

***

Claire hated hall duty. The hall was always crawling with students because the cafeteria was crowded and messy. Teachers were at a disadvantage—most of them knew less than a quarter of the student body and if they had to ask a rabble-rouser for his or her name, they usually gave a false one— especially if they didn't know the teacher. Claire just hoped no one had to be reported to the office as she walked along, watching kids eating, chatting, breakdancing, texting, snogging, or generally messing around.

One group was on the floor playing cards and eating. "Mr. Hickenman eats in the hall," they said pre-emptively as Claire walked up to them. Having seen his classroom and having observed Chester and several other colleagues— including Jack Penworth and Bertha herself—eating in the hall, she knew that the kids weren't lying. Instead of breaking up the group, she just reminded them, "Help to keep your school neat. Put all your garbage in the bin, okay, guys?" She knew the hall would still be littered with garbage after lunch. It always was.

The rule was: *No eating in the halls.* It was on laminated signs all around the halls. Still, with the cafeteria being too small for everybody, didn't putting garbage cans every thirty feet along the corridors imply permission to eat there? Or was the administration thinking they'd eat in the halls whether there was a sign or not, so let's just put garbage cans out and hope they'll use them?

On her second time around, Claire overheard voices in a shadowy alcove under the stairs. She stopped to listen. After a few seconds, she recognized Julie Pelegrino and her boyfriend Ethan Boyd. They had been in her grade eleven class last year. "Damian's been grounded 'til next September for going out in that blizzard." It was the 'grounded 'til next September' that caught Claire's ear, so she lingered, picking up bits of garbage and carefully putting one piece at a time in the bin so she could eavesdrop longer.

"Damian Stoker?"

"Uh huh. His Mom just got that silver Corolla last summer. It's gonna cost him to fix the damage," said Ethan. Claire's antennae rose.

"How d'ya know?" asked Julie, taking another bite of the slice of pepperoni pizza they were sharing.

"Damian called me last night," said Ethan, taking a sip of a family-sized cola. "We've been friends since grade eight. His parents musta gone out, or he wouldn't a' been able to use the phone. They took his cell off him and he has to flip burgers at their restaurant until he pays for the repairs."

"Mr. Stoker is loaded. You'd think he wouldn't even notice the money," Julie said, taking another bite of the pizza, "But my Mom worked for his mom. She's mega strict and Damian taking the Corolla in that snowstorm up Elgin Falls Road totally pissed her off. She was like fire-spitting furious at him for the damage. She's punishing him because he picked Cait up too."

"Don' worry. He'll get out of it, Julie. There were lots of fender benders that day. His Dad'll stick up for him."

"I hope so. Cait's in big shit, too," continued Julie. "Cait's mom says she shouldn't have gone out with Damian in that snowstorm. They could both have been hurt. Now Mrs. Somers is furious at Damian. She was already super pissed about having to drive Cait to Bellington for school every day since they kicked her out of Amberton when the football team ratted on her for conning them into to having some fun with Aisha Ames last semester."

"She isn't like grounded too, is she?" asked Ethan.

"Shit. Worse. Her Mom wants her to break up with Damian. That's like worse for Caitlin... she's totally hot for him."

"It isn't that bad, Julie. They live in the same neighbourhood don't they? They'll like see each other at the mall," Ethan said.

"Why do parents always do that to kids? Caitlin should, like, be able to go out with who'ever she damn well wants," Julie said, her voice rising an octave.

"Don' worry, I know Damian. They'll be together again. Cait sent him her full body picture the other day."

Claire nearly gagged as she heard that and put the last piece of garbage into the bin. She ambled on. Her pulse was racing. Had it been a silver Corolla that had almost killed Paul Fraser? Would the police know? If it was Damian who had hit Paul, he could have been scared and lied. She could hardly wait for her hall duty to be over so she could report the information to a vice principal. Claire was so preoccupied with what she had overheard that she didn't notice an urgent 'all call' for assistance in the cafeteria.

She made her final tour of the first floor hall. "Excuse me, gentlemen," she called to a couple of boys. One of them had picked the other one up and was twirling him horizontally over his head. "Please put your friend down!" The boy put him down and they looked back at her as they walked away, laughing. Claire smiled and walked on. You never knew what would happen on hall duty.

As she approached the cafeteria at the end of her last round, a wall of noise confronted her. Kids were talking excitedly, some were crying, their lunches forgotten. It was pandemonium.

"What happened?" she called to Lily Campbell over the din, surprised to see the Guidance Coordinator there.

"A fight. It was bad, Claire, really bad," she said as she let an emotional young girl pass. "Do you remember Spike Carruthers?"

"Not at the moment."

"Spike was Heidi Masterson's steady boyfriend last year. He dropped out last semester and Heidi dumped him. She's been going out with Dalton Peters since January. Well, Spike snuck into the school just now with a large, sharp rock in a stocking and started swinging it at Dalton."

"Did anyone get hurt?"

"Lots of people, Miss," a twelfth-grader said as he pushed past. The adrenaline in the hall was palpable.

"Didn't you hear the all call?" Lily asked.

"No, I was at the other end of the school, near the gym. I overheard…"

"Never mind. Some kids called the office when it started. Several kids have cuts on the head and neck. Dalton got the worst. He's in the nurse's office with Gene Putnam and the E.M.S. are on their way. He got hit at least three times."

"Where's Spike now?"

"Gérard, Martin and Bandhura got him. Bandhura heard about the slinging stocking and brought a meter stick to stop it. Smart, eh?"

"They must be in the office. My hall duty is over. I'm going to see if I can help. I missed all that?"

Lily shrugged before grabbing the hoody of a running boy. "Slow down, young man... What can I say? Never a dull moment..."

Claire rushed to the main office, where she saw Spike sitting on a chair. Martin and Gérard loomed over him, standing guard, their chests puffed out and their faces red. The secretaries watched the scene nervously. In the corner, Jack Penworth and Kristen Jaworski were speaking animatedly, which also drew the curiosity of Gérard and Martin.

Jack, the big man, was disagreeing with Kristen, the mere woman on duty. "Let me handle this," he said through his teeth, his voice deeper than normal.

"Just put him in your office, please, Jack," Kristen said, throwing her head back in frustration. "Until the police get here. They're on their way."

Just then, Gene came in with Dalton. In a flash Spike sprang up and kicked Dalton in the groin. Gene lunged forward, trying to break Dalton's fall, but he missed. Dalton hit the floor hard and Spike landed him a second solid kick square in the face, breaking his nose. Blood spurted everywhere as Spike shook his hair back off his forehead and smiled. It took Kristen, Martin, Gérard and Gene to subdue him again. This time they took Spike away. Jack remained frozen behind the counter. Claire tried to help Gene make Dalton more comfortable, but she started to hyperventilate and dropped to her knees. Gene noticed Claire's predicament but he was busy with Dalton, who was trying to breathe in between howls of pain.

The police arrived and slapped handcuffs on Spike while the paramedics took over with Dalton. Gene used a puffer the E.M.S. had given him to calm Claire's breathing. She sat down and wiped her blood-smeared hands on her slacks as she tried to control her anxiety. She watched as the E.M.S. loaded the groaning Dalton onto a gurney and wheeled him out of the office. Claire, Gene, Martin, Gérard and Kristen just stood there for a full minute, each of them sprayed in blood, unsure of what to do.

"Well," Jack finally said from behind the counter, his voice now thin. "Thank you for your help, guys. All in a day's work, eh?" Then he just stood there, bewildered.

They turned as a group, their arms limp at their sides, in shock. "Hey Jack?" Gérard said. "Look at us. We can't teach like this…"

"Oh?" Jack looked disoriented.

"Go home, all of you." Kristen said firmly. "We all need a shower and some clean clothes, Jack."

Claire turned to Gene and realized he looked as stunned as she felt. She had completely forgotten what she had come to report. Gene accompanied her to the parking lot.

***

Thursday, February 8

The next morning when Claire entered the science office, Angus was on his way out and Gene was already hard at work.

"That was quite the start to the term, wasn't it?" Claire said, as she dumped her briefcase in her chair and hung her coat on a hook in the corner.

"I never had one like it where I came from. Are you alright?"

"Sure. Another hall duty like that and nothing will faze me again, ever."

Gene looked at her and smiled. "You should have seen my wife when she saw my clothes. She wanted to take me right to the hospital until I could get it through to her that it wasn't my blood. Then she whisked everything off to the cleaners. She didn't want the girls to see it."

"I should have thought of that. I washed them myself. I missed walking the dog," Claire said.

"You have a dog?" Gene asked as he started loading his papers into his bag.

"Yes, a golden retriever. He's new. My boyfriend,"— that word always felt funny on her tongue—"gave Boomer to me as a gift."

"Boyfriend, huh?" His eyebrows rose with the question.

"Yeah, Matt. Boyfriend." Why did she always feel stupid saying that to people?

"Nice. My wife and I are huge dog lovers. So are the kids."

"How old are they? Your kids, I mean."

"Seven and ten. Both girls. They go to Amberton Heights Elementary."

"Okay, back to business, guys." It was Chin, who looked harried, his arms full of administrative paperwork. "How's that big general science class, Gene? Good impression or bad?"

"The general level grade nine is large. It might present difficulties. No reason to panic yet."

"It will depend on how or if the kids work." Chin knew how difficult it could be to get Bertha to split a class.

"So far they've listened pretty well, but this is only the third day. And that incident yesterday won't help."

"Don't remind me. They're bringing in the board psychologist to talk to anyone who feels traumatised," Chin said as he nervously flipped through papers.

"Great. Will they cover our classes?" Gene asked sarcastically.

"Dream on. Teachers just have to suck it up."

"I know. Don't we count? We had to be the police and the ambulance yesterday until the E.M.S. came and if Jack had had his druthers, they wouldn't have called them at all," said Gene.

"It was scary, Chin, really scary," added Claire.

"I heard," Chin said sympathetically.

"Especially when you started to hyperventilate…" Gene's voice lilted as he started imitating her heavy breathing.

"Okay, okay, enough," she said, her cheeks flushing. "I still have a job to do. I'm off to class. I'm sure half of my grade tens will take advantage of the psychologist to skip class."

***

With an actual lesson, Claire's general level grade ten science class behaved better. She assumed Ricky Penworth was still sick. He was absent again, as were four or five other 'traumatized' kids, including Maziyar, Logan, the mouthy Justine Jones and the rowdy Karla Kozak.

Their absence made Claire's day go extremely well. She was so pleased at the end of the day that she would have forgotten the appointment with Mrs. Atkins, if she hadn't been waiting in the hall. Joel was one of the quietest students in her Math class, usually staying at the outside of the group, never really joining in with the uncoordinated untaught. He worked and handed in his work to be marked. He ungrudgingly redid any questions he got wrong, listening to Claire's explanations for correcting mistakes. Once, when he had been provoked, he hurled a book at Jimmy Church. Claire hoped his mother would shed some light on this. With Boomer to walk every day now, she hadn't had time to read his entire identified file yet. It was thick.

Mrs. Atkins entered the room after the class had barrelled out. Only Joel left quietly, sweetly high-fiving his mother's hand as they passed each other at the doorway.

Mrs. Atkins dove right in as she took a seat beside the wobbly table. "Miss Hébert, my son Joel is a boy with a difference." She reached into her purse for some papers. "His best qualities are that he can be very quiet and is very intelligent and he likes to do his schoolwork. But he has Asperger's syndrome and has difficulty interacting with people."

"Yes. Guidance notified me. At first glance he seems to be a loner."

"It's more than that. When he's frustrated, he can become instantly violent and throw things. He hasn't learned to think before he acts. We're trying to help him understand that when something is bothering him there are solutions besides losing his temper." Claire got paper and pencil to take notes. "Last semester I talked to the learning resource teacher. Mr. McLean is happy to continue with what we set up. Joel knows he can go from any classroom to the learning resource room when he needs to, but you might need to remind him. Sometimes he'll act frenetically and you'll know he needs some quiet. If the sun is too bright, I hope you will allow him to lower the blind near his desk. Oh," she said, looking around, "you have no windows in this classroom. Well, that's actually better for Joel.

"He also has difficulty recognizing his own things amid similar items. So if you could put something he can recognize on his table; a sheet of paper or a book—no cutesy stickers, please, he's growing up."

"Mrs. Atkins," a blushing Claire said apologetically, indicating the mess around the room, which she assumed could be bothersome for Joel, "this isn't my room, but I'll think of something—I can put the notebooks out at the beginning of class. Their names are on them."

It was obvious that Mrs. Atkins had made this explanation many times before. "Joel takes everything literally. He doesn't understand body language, symbolism, sarcasm or other forms of humour or teasing. We're working on it, but we're not there yet. You've probably heard that he spent some time in youth detention last summer."

"No, I hadn't." Claire tried to hide her shock. "What happened?"

"One hot day last July, I was watering my garden and talking to a neighbour who likes to kid around. He was kidding me about drowning the flowers. She shook her head. "We didn't realize Joel was there. He attacked the neighbour and I couldn't stop it." She paused. "Another neighbour called the police. His father and I now have some professional help for us and for Joel, and we're dealing with his issues together. We joined a local Asperger's support group, too."

"That sounds helpful." Claire wasn't sure what to say. "You've had so much to cope with. Joel is lucky to have a mother like you."

Mrs. Atkins smiled, a bit sadly. "Thank you, Miss Hébert. I'm so grateful you understand and are willing to work with us."

Chapter 6

The Math Class and Bullying

Monday, February 12

Claire had her spare after lunch today. She didn't have to substitute for an absent colleague, so she could rush home, let Boomer out, grab a bite, send Matt a quick text, return to school and still have an hour to mark late assignments and enter results into her marks book and the *Gradecalc* program.

Some of the grade tens had found the terminology and diagrams of this morning's *Human Organ and Tissue* lesson overwhelming, so she decided to spend some extra time on it and make extra worksheets tonight. Why not? It was snowing again and Matt was in Egypt. If the handouts were good enough, she could keep them for next time she taught the course—if she stayed.

Determined to get the grade tens on track, she designed handouts that would help them learn the terminology. She made a crossword puzzle, then went on the Internet and searched for diagrams to label and charts to better explain the functions of the organs, their secretions and how it all worked. She hoped the class would be engaged in tomorrow's review.

***

The grade nine Math class could also be challenging, especially when period three came at the end of the day and everybody was tired. The morning had gone well and Claire was optimistic when it was time for the Math class.

She had to administer the short diagnostic quiz the administration had asked all staff to give. After taking attendance and sending the five students, who regularly worked with Brian McLean to the L.R.T. room, off with their tests, she passed the tests out to the others. Maxine Young and Chelsea Buck took one glance and walked out, leaving their tests on their tables. Six out of the eight remaining kids shouted that they had no pencil or pen. Claire handed each one a pencil she had marked with their names. Half the kids got up and asked the other half how they were going to answer the questions.

"You're supposed to do the quiz alone," Claire said, trying to usher the students back to their seats.

"But it's only the first week of school," Lindsay Landon complained.

"This quiz is for *me*, not for you," Claire pleaded. "You can't fail it. It's for me to find out what you need to learn." Blank faces stared back at her.

When the class was finally doing the test—in their sense of the word—Claire scanned the classroom and couldn't see

Leah Dewaard. Her test was gone too. She almost panicked. Was Leah another Maxine or Chelsea, someone who just walked out of classes? Was Leah out in the hall getting the answers from everybody she met? Claire caught herself. The basic kids didn't see the point of tests. Why did Bertha have to insist the basic kids do them?

She scanned the class. "Where's Leah?" she asked, trying to mask any alarm in her voice. Then she heard a great sloppy sneeze and Leah's head popped out from behind a filing cabinet covered with posters. "I's back here, Miss! I needs a tissue!" The pale, dark haired girl cheerfully waved her test paper above the pile of dusty old projects, wiping her nose with her sleeve. Claire breathed a sigh of relief and delivered a box of tissues. Perhaps Leah was used to nobody caring where she was.

Claire was reminded every day that these kids were challenged socially as well as intellectually. Gene had shared his ideas with her for helping the students meet their individual learning differences. Both of them were dedicated to helping them discipline themselves so they could achieve success at a level they could reach. The rewards—when they came—could be great.

Britney Anderson, who was partially deaf, was already an example. Claire couldn't watch every student in the class all the time, because Britney needed to have the instructions repeated at close range. But once she knew what to do, she put

97

in a lot of effort. When Britney had shown her the first lesson all completed and the second started in the first week, Claire had praised her: "Wow, Britney! Keep up the good work!" Now, as Britney was concentrating on the diagnostic quiz, Claire thought back to what she had learned from Tyler.

She never forgot that these kids' home lives could be terrible and that they were only exhibiting the behaviour they had learned in their families, where education and civility often didn't have a high priority.

***

After Tyler had tragically died Claire had been so traumatised that on impulse she had stuffed a suitcase and fled to the U.K. She wanted to get out of California and lose herself in the museums, the art galleries, the theatres, and the sights and sounds of London. When her money ran out, she found a job supply teaching and this gave her a chance to experience the British school system.

One day she had been relaxing before class with the other teachers at a seedy neighbourhood school when an unkempt, scraggly eleven-year-old named Kenny came in. "D ya see an'thin' differen' abou' me?" he asked the teachers, who were sipping their morning tea.

Nobody had noticed anything different, so Kenny pointed it out. "I's hit by a car this mornin', Miss, and I got throwed over a hedge and I landed on me knee." The Assistant Head Teacher then noticed that his trousers were torn and muddy and his knee had been badly scraped. She ran for the first aid kit, but Kenny's story wasn't finished. "Las' night me Da got out his blade an' started ta chase me Ma. Then me bruther tooked his knife out an' he was a chasin' me Da. So I grabbed mine and chased me Da and me bruther all 'round the house. Me Ma hid in a closet. After a while me Da was so drunk with the whiskey that he went a' rollin' down da stairs. He slep' there at the bottom, a pissin' an a snorin' all night. I hid in the attic. In the morning, me Ma an' me bruther had gone. I didn' know what ter do, so I snucked out an' comed here ta school."

What touched Claire most was that Kenny told the whole story as if it were just a regular day. What good were details of literature, math, history, and geography to a kid with a life like that? One of her supervisors in California had told Claire how much better these children's lives would be if only they would make an effort and learn the lifecycle of the Monarch butterfly. Yeah. Right.

After that, every day, she wondered who might have been raped or beaten or thrown out of the house, or cut himself or had not been fed anything the night before or even the day before, especially in general and basic level classes.

She had been in the U.K. for two years when she ran into Matt again in a pub one rainy weekend. She followed him back to Canada when the school term ended.

***

Claire's attention slipped back to her math class. The kids had settled down. They were working… in a sense. Three times, Claire checked behind the filing cabinet to see if Leah was still doing the test. Three times, she asked Leah to put away her cellphone. Three times, she watched Leah put it under her left elbow. Three times, she took it out again. "Okay, Leah," Claire said on her fourth trip to the back of the room. "Give me the cellphone, please. You can have it back at the end of class." She held out her hand and waited. Leah grumbled but gave up the phone. Claire put it on a corner of her wobbly little table. Leah didn't know better, but that didn't mean she shouldn't learn.

A lot of the behaviour of the basic level math kids was unacceptable, and Claire had to guide them gently ever closer to mainstream behaviour patterns, tirelessly explaining the math or life skills at whatever level they needed. The peer tutors Jenny and Amir would help a lot when they joined the class next Monday. Claire couldn't wait for them to start.

After forty-five minutes, the ten-minute diagnostic test was over. Three of the kids returned to their regular work. The others socialized or found excuses to slip out into the hall, saying they were off to the washroom or the L.R.T. room. One reorganized her backpack. Another drew cartoons on the bit of available blackboard. Most listened and tapped along to their music players or played videogames. Only Britney Anderson and Joel Atkins worked at the assigned math lessons. Maxine Young returned, put her head on her table and promptly fell asleep. Where had she been? Where was Chelsea Buck?

At ten minutes before dismissal the alarm clanged. Lockdown. Claire covered her ears for a moment, then quickly looked into the hall. "Inside! Inside everybody!" she called to nearby hall wanderers. They rushed into the room, as she bolted the door from the inside, put the 'okay' sign in the window and got everybody sitting out of sight, on the floor. Claire could only hope that another teacher had taken in Chelsea. After twenty minutes of shushing and fidgeting, the *all clear* was called.

"Was that a fire drill?" Leah asked when she came to retrieve her cellphone.

"No, sweetie, it was a lockdown."

"Jeez, Miss, loud noises scare me. Why do we have to have stupid alarms? Why couldn't we just go home right after school? Now I gots a headache."

"I don't know what it was, Leah, but there must have been a reason," Claire took a deep breath. "Alarms are there so the Principals can keep us safe."

On her way to the science office, Claire bumped into Gene. "Nothing to worry about, Claire," he told her. A detective working on Paul's case had a quick question for Jethro. He forgot about his taser. A student saw it and reported it. All's well that ends well and all that, eh?"

"Seriously?" Claire's tired eyes widened. "The kids get the wits scared out of them because a cop forgot to take his taser off before entering a school?"

***

When Claire got home that day, she was worn out. Matt was still in Egypt and she might have called him, but he had texted her. They'd be going to India from there for another five days. Claire was too tired to figure out what time it was there. He must be busy. It was the only text she had received from him. She let Boomer out of his crate. Until now she had had no idea how glad she would be for Boomer's company.

***

Monday, February 19

The next Monday Claire was excited when she got home from school. The peer tutors had started to help her in the math class and that took a huge load off her shoulders. Matt was back from India and wanted to go for a walk with Boomer and then have dinner out. She checked her face in the small hallway mirror. He might be flying out again soon, and Claire wanted as much time with him as possible.

When she had reunited with Matt Granger, her high school sweetheart, in London almost two years before, he had become a bit of a nomad and seldom stayed at his sparsely furnished flat. He had cancelled his landline and now texted all the time. Recently divorced then, he escaped his loneliness by travelling for work and it worked well for him—until Claire came back into his life. It was serendipity, a happy complication. After a pint in the neighbourhood pub, they had fallen back into each other's arms. Matt had locked his eyes into her deep brown eyes, had tipped her chin back and kissed her passionately.

Claire could hardly wait to see him after his two weeks away. Invited for four-thirty, Matt arrived promptly at five, giving Claire more time for her schoolwork. He knelt down to give Boomer a good rub. "You're feeding him right, Claire. He's starting to look like a teenaged dog." He gave her a quick kiss.

"That's all I need! Another teenybopper in my life!"

By now Boomer had been to the park so often, he knew how to get there. He was pulling hard on the leash. "He's getting strong," Matt said. "You're doing a good job with him, Clarikins."

"You sure love dogs."

"I love you." He tugged lightly on her hand and swung her around to face him. She giggled and leaned into his kiss.

"I know," she said with a smile.

"Do you?" he asked. "Being so far apart much of the time, I worry."

"It's not always easy but we manage, don't we?"

Matt nodded.

"It's like Gene said the other day…"

"Jean?"

"EUgene. The new teacher I'm sharing my lab with. I told you about him…"

"Oh yeah, right, of course."

"Well, we were in the science office and I was telling him about Boomer and he said how cute it was that you'd given me a stand-in for company while you were away." Claire chuckled lightly and looked over at Matt.

"Really, a 'stand-in?, 'cute'?" He dropped her hand and turned away.

"I thought it was funny, that's all." She gave the pup's head a tousle. "Gene likes to joke around and talk in riddles."

"If you say so," Matt said a bit tersely. "Sounds pretty smart, this Gene."

"Oh, he is. Great teacher, too. I want you to meet him sometime."

"I can hardly wait," Matt said through his teeth as he picked up a stick from the ground and tossed it for Boomer.

Claire stood back and watched them play, feeling content. She had been looking forward to Matt's return for two weeks and wasn't about to let the moment pass too quickly. They walked home arm in arm and had dinner together. Then they sat in each other's arms listening to their favourite music until passion took over and Matt led her up the stairs. At ten-thirty, Matt slipped away. He had to get ready for his trip to Mexico on the twenty-third. Claire was fast asleep. She had forgotten to finish her prep work for the grade tens.

***

Tuesday, February 20

It was lunchtime and Gene was startled when Claire gushed in and slammed the office door. He turned around and his smile faded. Claire's eyes were teary and her hands were shaking.

"I didn't get my prep finished last night." Claire sniffed, as she plopped into a chair. "And a kid in my grade ten class is becoming impossible."

Gene was surprised to see Claire in such a state. "Just one?" he said, trying to lighten the mood. "Spill it, Claire. What happened?"

"Matt came over and I didn't get my grade ten handouts done last night and I had to use the textbook. These kids won't read even one page without a handout for help.

"Since start-up, four kids in that class have been giving me a hard time. The worst one, Maziyar Bizhani, does no classwork, ignores everything I say and is always talking to his friends or texting when he's not playing with techie toys. He treats my class like a rec room."

"I've heard about him." Gene nodded. "Shirley's been talking about him as well. From what I hear, he's a piece of work."

They sat, Gene on his desk, Claire in the old upholstered chair. She lifted her head from her hands. "Really? Shirley?"

She sighed as her own situation refocused. "I've rearranged the seating plan three times in two weeks." Gene handed her a box of tissue. "Thanks… I let the kids be part of the development of the classroom rules on the first day. Maziyar participated the most, actually." She blew her nose.

"He's the boy they got from Bellington, right? He's new and wants to show off," Gene said compassionately.

"Is he?" Claire said. "He always has to be the centre of attention."

"He was traded to Amberton in January for disciplinary reasons."

"So, Bertha and the Bellington Principal swapped losers who had burned all their bridges and I got the booby prize," Claire said with a tinge of bitterness. "As far as I can tell, he's far from stupid. He's as creative as he is disruptive."

"And that's saying something." Gene raised his eyes to the ceiling with a sarcastic smirk. "Thanks, Bertha."

Claire let out a deep sigh of overpowering fatigue. "Every time I remind Maziyar's group of how they should be behaving, they stop for a couple of seconds, give me the 'duh' glare, and continue whatever the hell they're doing. With the rest of the class unwilling to read the textbook and without handouts to guide them through the reading, these jerks had a receptive audience for their shenanigans and today it spread to the whole class.

"For two weeks, I've tried to change their behaviour— especially Maziyar's. He's the leader now. I've been direct. I've cajoled. I've moved them around. I even called his father. That was an experience! He speaks *profanish*. In the lab Maziyar and his friends' disobedience is dangerous. He won't stay where I put him. He walks around and touches everything. He twists everything I try so it works against me." She looked at Gene helplessly. "I should be able to do more than just ask them politely to stop their shenanigans and work." She got up and paced. "I'm sick of always having to be so bloody polite."

"I agree." Chin had just come in and heard the conversation.

"I've tried everything—threatened to take his cellphone away, talked to him, sent him to the office. His notebook cover is now decorated with 'MISS HEEEBURT'S SCIENCE CLASS SUCKS SHIT' in big letters."

"You know that's a load of horse manure, don't you, Claire?" said Chin.

Claire looked at Chin. "Well, today I couldn't ignore it and I grabbed his phone as he was texting. I surprised myself at how fast I did it. Maziyar freaked out. 'You can't do that!' he yelled. 'That's my property!' He got up and tried to pull it out of my pocket. I had to dodge him. Then I 'invited' him into the hall."

"Did he go?" asked Gene.

"He stomped out. He almost hit me with the door. I was seething and dreading the conversation at the same time. I don't function well on anger and I can't fathom a kid thinking it's okay to be that disrespectful to anybody."

"It's not disrespect, Claire. It's abuse. It's absolute bullying," said Chin.

"I told him if we couldn't settle the issue, I would have to involve Miss Jaworski. Maziyar's reply was vicious. 'Go ahead, Miss, I've already talked to the bloody Vice Principal and complained about your stupid fucking class and your lousy teaching. Damn it, I hate your puking class.'"

Chin and Gene looked at each other and kept listening.

"It hurt, but I stood my ground. I was not going to allow myself to be thrown by this kid. My options for handling him rushed through my head."

"They're pathetic," Chin said.

"Yes," Claire went on, using her fingers to count the

'options.' "I can only speak to Maziyar politely. I shouldn't raise my voice. I can't touch him, I can't return his rude, cruel words in kind, I can't give him an effective detention, and I certainly can't overpower him. Maziyar knows all of that."

"But he, on the other hand, is not legally shackled," Chin said. "He's protected because he's a minor. He's bigger than you. All you can do is send him to the office, and he can decide not to go, or worse, to push you around. So what did you say?" asked Chin calmly.

"I was still hoping to defuse the situation, so I suggested that if he didn't like my class, he could transfer to another. Don Patterson teaches the same class I do, at the same time."

"What did he say?"

"Oh, that set him off again," Claire said, dabbing her nose with the tissue. "He started by calling Don a queer, then he got into my face and said, 'I want to drive *you* fucking crazy, bitch. Then when you're on stress leave, maybe we'll get a real teacher. Go fuck yourself, ya fat-headed, stupid piece of trash,' and he stomped down the hall. He's a smoker. That's how close he got."

"Claire, you need to tell Kristen," said Chin.

"Let's make an appointment for after school. I'll come with you," offered Gene, and he emailed Kristen to make an appointment.

***

"You need to hear this, Kristen" Gene said as they knocked on her open door after classes. Kristen looked concerned as soon as she saw Claire's face. Gene shut her door.

"What's wrong?" Kristen was worried and got up to put a comforting hand on Claire's shoulder. Unlike Jack Penworth, Kristen Jaworski considered both sides of student-teacher confrontations and assumed the teacher was telling the truth. After all what was in it for the teacher not to tell her exactly what happened? While Claire was collecting her thoughts, Gene gave Kristen an outline of the story, adding snippets of things Maziyar had done in Shirley's class.

Kristen listened attentively. She knew the story wouldn't be over yet. "How did the rest of the class go?"

"At first I just stood in the hall, stupefied and shaking," Claire said. "But I managed to get through it. The others knew something had happened. You could hear a pin drop. Except for Maziyar's friends, everyone worked. The good kids gave me the strength to go on."

"Have you tried to contact Maziyar's parents?" Kristen knew the likelihood of that accomplishing anything was slim, but what other options were there?

"I called Mr. Bizhani at work last week. He has never had any respect for the school system, even before his son was transferred here. Maziyar used to live in Bellington with his mom. Dad hates it that Maziyar now has to live with him in

Amberton. He told me his son could do what the f--- he wanted and hung up."

"The apple doesn't fall far from the tree," Gene mumbled.

"Obviously not," Kristen murmured. "What about Maziyar's mother?"

"I called her, too. She's a better bet. She's remarried. She has a haughty Middle Eastern accent and she requested Maziyar's exact words. I told her what I could remember, and she promised to speak to Maziyar when he comes for his next visit."

Claire turned to Kristen. "I don't know what else to do. Did he talk to you about my classes?"

"No, Maziyar hasn't come to see me," Kristen assured her. "But he may have talked to Jack."

Claire was only partly relieved to hear that.

Then Kristen took charge. "O.K. Email me a résumé of the incidents. Point form is good. Just hit the high spots. I don't expect every little detail since day one."

"Okay," Claire said as she wiped her eyes again.

"You've done all you can, Claire. Let me take it from here. You go home and forget it ever happened. Maziyar's my problem now."

***

Maziyar did not come to class the Wednesday. Thursday, Claire was amazed that he settled in submissively. He talked a bit to a reluctant girl one desk over, but stopped whenever Claire looked at him. Still, he hadn't been suspended. Claire thought his parents must finally have taken action, but Kristen had emailed her. He had skipped his appointment with her and might be lying low to avoid suspension. Claire was torn between letting him dig his way to more trouble and reporting his presence to Kristen. She didn't have to decide.

Claire had just started showing a PowerPoint presentation when there was a knock on the door. Kristen stepped into the room. "Miss Hébert," she said, "Sorry to interrupt."

"That's okay. What can I do for you?"

Kristen immediately made eye contact with Maziyar, who was closest to the door and said, "I need to see you. Now."

"You're in for it now, Mazzi," a few of his friends chimed sarcastically.

Claire held up her hand to signal to the class to settle down. "Maziyar." She shook her head indicating the door.

With a barely audible grunt, Maziyar stood up and grabbed his backpack. "You're in
trouble now," Logan said snidely.

"Are you sccaaared?" Dwayne Dufresne taunted for effect.

Inwardly, Claire smiled. To the class, she said, "Okay. Show's over. Back to work." Kristen waited for Maziyar to slouch past, and then winked to Claire as she shut the door.

"Carry on," she said.

Chapter 7

After the Technology Meeting

Thursday, February 22

The promised meeting regarding a policy for electronic gadgets in the classroom started at four o'clock in the library. Parents were invited, but many couldn't come. They worked until five. Four o'clock was a compromise for the teachers, who finished in the classroom at two-forty. Still, there was a reasonable showing of parents and teachers to defend or attack how technology was affecting the classroom.

Anne attended out of curiosity. Claire and Shirley stayed because their incidents with
Maziyar Bizhani had been about technology. Those who attended got an earful of
everyone's opinion on cellphones and handhelds and the array of the good and the bad that technology presented in the classroom. There were so many opinions that Claire was convinced that they would all be dead and buried before the committee made a decision—if ever.

***

When it was over Shirley, Anne and Claire met at Jake's Pub for their own meeting. They were beyond famished. A busboy brought them water, warm buns and butter. Soon, they were devouring the carbs.

"Have your peer math tutors started yet, Claire?" Anne asked.

"Yes, they're a godsend," Claire nodded, buttering a bun. "Patient and helpful. Paul picked a couple of good ones. They reach the kids student to student, in a way I can't." Claire bit into the bun as if she hadn't seen white bread for years. "By the way, have either of you heard how Paul is doing?"

"I heard from Bandhura Abbasi at the heads meeting yesterday that he's out of intensive care and they're starting to do physio with him in bed. Now that they've operated, the foot has a lot of healing to do before he'll be able to do much with it, but they're strengthening the rest of him," Shirley said.

"We should visit him in the hospital some time."

"Good idea. It will be a while before he can come home."

"I don't suppose they know who was driving the car yet?" Anne asked.

"Oh my God!" Claire went white and covered her face with her hands.

"What's the matter?"

"On my hall duty, the day of the Teacher Appreciation Lunch, I overheard a conversation between Julie Pelegrino and Ethan Boyd. Apparently, Damian Stoker was driving his mother's new Corolla the afternoon Paul was hit and he told his parents he hit a tree."

"That's interesting!" Shirley and Anne said, looking at each other. "Have you reported it to the office?"

"Right after I heard it we had that incident with Spike Carruthers and Dalton Peters over Heidi Masterson. I ran into that and it blew Ethan and Julie's conversation right out of my mind. I feel terrible. Remind me to report it tomorrow. The Corolla was silver and had a dent and Jethro's car had a dent with a paint mark on it but I don't know what colour the mark was."

"Way to go, Detective Hébert!"

Claire shook off the compliment. "Speaking of detective work, can either one of you tell me what's up with Maxine Young?" she asked, taking another bite of her bun.

"She's a troubled soul," Shirley said, "but, lucky for me, she loves French and she's very good at it. She's in Naomi Harper's grade eleven Immersion class."

"What's a grade eleven immersion student doing in a grade nine basic math class?" asked Anne with a bewildered look.

"Good question. Maxine hates math with a passion and she won't do anything she doesn't want to do, which is why she has failed it twice—with under twenty percent. Guidance has put her in basic math, hoping she'll succeed there. If she doesn't, she can't graduate," Shirley explained.

"When do you have her, Claire?" Anne asked, buttering another bun.

"Third Period."

"Hmmm," Anne said. "That's when I always lose Brad Hillman."

"What grade?" Claire asked, eyeing another bun.

"Eleven."

"So, they're sneaking out for a little alone time, huh?" Shirley said. They all chuckled. "Maxine's boy crazy."

"They don't sneak. They just walk out and give you a big mouth and run if you challenge them," Anne said. "They know we can't leave our classes."

Then came the inevitable interruption. "Hi. My name is Alanna. I'll be your server today. Can I bring you something to drink?" Alanna McPherson was an attractive, athletic Amberton student.

Claire immediately recognized the voice and looked up, astonished. "Alanna? I didn't know you worked here."

Alanna blushed. "Oh hi, Miss Hébert, Madame Alquist, Miss Uzbecki. Nice to see you." She looked at the three teachers, a bit hesitantly, looked back at the kitchen, then back at her customers. "I got the job last week. Just trying to earn some money for university. This is my first real day on the job since training."

"Well, that's a great thing for a grade eleven student. Your parents must be proud that you're planning ahead."

"Well, not really. I haven't told them."

"Why on earth not, Alanna?"

"I'm hoping that if I can pay for some of my post-secondary, they'll have to let me have a say in what courses I take."

"Oh, I see."

"Dad's in business so they want me to go into accounting or business and I want to go into computer arts or animation, or both."

Alanna eyed Claire and Anne. When she saw the compassion on their faces she said, "My parents have been telling me who I am my whole life, but I want to choose my own career." Then she switched back to her responsibilities. "Can I bring anyone a drink?"

"Sure. You won't tell, will you, Alanna?"

"Are you over nineteen?" Alanna asked, straight-faced.

The three of them looked at each other and laughed.

"Go ahead, it's after school time anyway," Alanna blushed at her own joke.

They ordered two Screwdrivers and a Singapore Sling.

"I'll be back in a few minutes to take your order." Then she was gone.

"Well, I'd never have guessed that anyone could tell Alanna McPherson what to do," Shirley said. The three thought about it for a minute.

Alanna returned with their drinks, took their orders, and left.

After a few sips, Anne shook her head. "Who owns the child?" she asked.

"What do you mean?" Claire asked.

"Who... owns... the... child?" Anne repeated. "Take Alanna. Her parents gave her life and pay to shelter her, feed her, clothe her. They think she—her life—is theirs to mould. Alanna's parents are in business, so she has to go into business. Her parents are Presbyterian, so she has to be a Presbyterian. Even until after W.W. II, the son was expected to become whatever the father was. The state pays for health care, education and protection for her and her family." Anne was slowly stirring her drink with her straw. "Alanna lives in these media saturated times and she wants to make her own decision about a career. She's rebelling intelligently and I admire her for it."

"I do too. Parents don't always know what's best, and if kids aren't allowed to make some decisions, they'll never be good at it as adults," Shirley said. "And who defends the kid when the parents are wrong? Alanna's great at art. She also does a lot of the photos for the yearbook."

"She's coming back," Claire warned, nodding in the direction of the kitchen.

"That's exactly my point, Shirley," Anne whispered. "Often a teacher, a guidance counsellor or a friend can see things a parent doesn't. They should have some clout."

Alanna arrived with three chicken salads. She placed their orders in front of them. "Is there anything else I can get for you?"

"No, nothing else, thanks, dear." When Alanna left, Shirley said, "Boy am I hungry! Staff meetings usually make me lose my appetite…"

Claire had finally guessed. "It reminds me of Nadeena Hami too, Anne."

"We've all noticed the change in her clothing and deportment," Shirley said.

"I'm positive it's the parents insisting that she wear the hijab."

"And I'm equally sure she hates it," Claire said with a sigh. "Last semester she was so garrulous, so fun-loving, so bubbly in my class. Now, I see her in the halls and she's solemn, silent and sedate. Her friends think she's depressed. I've seen the concern on their faces."

The three of them ate in silence for a few minutes. "It's a religious thing, obviously, but some Muslim girls have real problems in North America. I hope you told Guidance," Shirley said as she prepared a forkful of salad.

Claire nodded. "God, I wouldn't want to run a school these days." She was testing for her friends' opinions. "In fact, more and more I'm thinking I won't last as a teacher, either. I'm young enough. I have my Master's in animal biology."

"Oh, Claire, you're just tired today," Shirley said, grabbing the dessert menu from the middle of the table. "You're a natural. You love the little ankle biters. Schools need people like you. It's been a hectic few weeks since changeover. Anyone for dessert?"

"Nah, not today, guys. I have to walk the dog," Claire said as she reached for her coat. She left a generous tip for Alanna. "Boomer needs exercise and I like to throw the ball for him at the dog park. It's good for me, too. I usually have to go get it myself!"

"Sounds like some of my classes," Shirley said as she and Anne put their tips on the table and headed for the cash register. "Ask a question and if you want an answer, you have to give it yourself!"

"Yeah, but Boomer will eventually learn to fetch the ball."

***

"Hey Boo! Wanna go to the park?" Claire rushed into the house, slammed her briefcase onto the chair in the den and let a bouncing Boomer out of the crate. After the meeting and the pub, she was in the mood for a good walk and some fresh air, no matter how cold it was.

Boomer knew the words *walk* and *park* and licked all over her face as she attached his

leash. She put on her old coat with the blue tennis ball in the pocket, grabbed her hat and gloves and locked the house.

In the well-lit dog park she let him off the leash and was watching him cavort when a familiar figure was coming her way. "Hello, Gene."

"Oh hi, Claire. How are you holding up after Maziyar?"

"Surviving. What are you doing here?"

"I'm exercising Prince Charles." When he noticed Claire's bemused look, he pointed to a black retriever with a reflective collar streaking after a yellow tennis ball. "Sorry, he's my dog. He goes by P.C. for short." Gene said with a grin. "He likes to chase the ball."

"I was just imagining the real Prince Charles chasing a ball," Claire giggled. "That's my puppy Boomer over there. I just got him in January. He was the runt of his litter. He's still small for his age, but he's growing fast."

"He's got good conformation. Does he fetch a ball yet?" P.C. returned with his tennis ball as Boomer cavorted behind him.

"We're working on it."

"Hold on to him for a bit, Claire." Gene tossed the ball a few times and P.C. retrieved it. Claire saw Boomer's head swivel from the ball to the black dog and back. He saw the attention P.C. was getting. Then Claire threw the ball for him while Gene held P.C. back. "Fetch, Boomer!" she yelled, as Gene had done. Boomer sprang into action, chasing the ball down to a round of applause from Claire and Gene. He looked thrilled the third time when he finally brought back the ball and got lots of praise. "Good boy, Boomer! Good boy!"

"Your puppy's smart, Claire," Gene said, patting P.C. on the head.

They threw the balls for a few more minutes. Then Claire lobbed hers far up a nearby hill and Boomer didn't come back. Claire and Gene wandered to the tree line to look for him and found him, jumping up on Matt, his whole back end wagging.

"Hi, Matt!" Claire exclaimed. "What are you doing here?"

"You weren't home, so I figured you'd be here," Matt said as he got Boomer to sit and brushed the wet snow off his pant legs.

"Matt, this is my new colleague Gene Putnam and his dog P.C. Gene, this is my friend Matt Granger."

Matt's eyebrow raised. "That's *boyfriend* Matt Granger," he stressed with a slick smile as he reached a gloved hand toward Gene. "Nice dog, Gene. How old is he?" Matt asked.

"Two."

"Do you come here often?"

"I will be. I just moved in down the road. P.C. and I like our exercise." He patted P.C. on the head. He had sensed something. "But I'd better get home. I've still got work to do tonight. See you in the morning, Claire."

"Nice to meet you, Gene," Matt lied.

"Bye, Gene. Boomer thanks you for the fetching lesson," Claire said as she watched him and P.C. leave.

"Seems like a nice guy," Matt said, as he searched Claire's face for any signs of what she might be thinking.

"Yes, he is. I like him. He's a team player. He helped me out this afternoon when I had a
nasty situation with a student. Good sense of humour too. Er... where's Boomer?" Claire looked around, unaware of Matt's concern.

"Obviously," he said through tight lips.

"Oh, here he is," she said. She grabbed Boomer's collar and clipped the leash on as she
turned and fell into Matt's arms. "Take us home, my strong sweet *boyfriend*."

"Hey, you...how's my girl?" asked Matt, eager to hold her. She looked tired.

"Exhausted. It's been a hell of a day." She blinked up at him. "How are you? I didn't expect you today! You're off to Mexico tomorrow, aren't you?"

"I know, that's why I came to the park. Your car's in the driveway, so I figured you'd be walking Boomer." He put his arm around her and tried to keep the edge out of his voice. "We finished today's work early. So...this Gene..."

"Oh, Matt, lighten up!" Claire exclaimed, suddenly catching on. She reached down, picked up a handful of snow, and threw it at him.

"What happened to being so tired?" Matt sputtered as he wiped the snow from his face and neck.

"I'm never too tired for a snowball fight," she said through a giggle.

Matt smirked and quickly formed his own snowball. Boomer jumped and barked as they laughed and pelted each other with snow.

As they started making their way out of the park, Claire said, "I never did ask the other night, how did it go in Egypt and India?"

"It was okay. I got a lot of useful information on that trip. They're beautiful countries. But right now I'm too distracted."

"How's that?"

"You're too much of a distraction! Spend the evening with me?"

"Oh, Matt. We had that stupid tech meeting. There's some work I have to do for tomorrow on a unit I haven't taught before. I wasn't expecting you."

"Aw, I was hoping… come on… not even a couple of hours? I leave for Mexico tomorrow and I'll be gone for ten days." He put on his best puppy dog eyes. He was exaggerating the length of his trip in the hope of persuading her.

Claire scrunched her face and looked at her watch. "Well, okay. I have an idea," she said. "It's seven-thirty. I got some stuff done before the meeting. I have to finish the grade tens'

handouts, and if I can juggle the other stuff a little, it should be okay. Can you come back in say, forty-five minutes? I may have a surprise for you too, Mr. Granger."

"Now you're talking!" He patted her behind. Her body responded with a tingly rush from her toes to the hair on her head. "You have an hour, Miss H."

***

A short hour later, Matt was at the front door. Claire had changed into a negligée and was in the kitchen, lacing a couple of hot chocolates with peppermint schnapps and mini marshmallows.

"Well, hello," he mumbled as his arms slipped around her from behind and he began nibbling her neck.

"Hello," she said leaning back and letting her head fall onto his shoulder.

"I take it you got your work done…" His lips found her earlobe and his hand meandered up and down her trim torso. The rose-coloured satin slid like water through his fingers.

"Uh-huh," she muttered, losing herself in his touch. "Only one hitch—a kid named Logan left his whole test paper blank."

"Really?" Matt couldn't have been less interested.

She straightened up and tried to focus on the drinks again. "Yeah, I can't figure it out."

"Maybe somebody dared him to do it." Suddenly he spun her around, bringing them face to face. With deliberation, he kissed her slowly, thoroughly, and her mind went blank…almost.

Shaking her head, she pulled away and took a deep breath. "He gets ping-ponged from one parent's mansion to the other every other day."

"Huh, still with the work? Well, I guess I'll have to try harder," he said light-heartedly as his hands began to roam. She looked at him, smiled and he knew she needed to finish the conversation. "Alright, that's not my idea of a stable home base for a fourteen-year-old." Matt himself had led a nomadic life for four years since Jennifer had left him and now that he was back with Claire, and had met Gene, the travelling was rapidly losing its appeal. He just didn't know how to make the transition—or if Claire would want him to.

"I know. Where does the kid belong?" Claire pushed away, her finger tracing a slow, circuitous path down his chest, then turned to put sprinkles on their whipped cream and handed Matt one of the drinks. "Every child needs a home where he can feel safe with people who love him and care for him."

"And discipline him," Matt thought.

Boomer was playfully nipping at their feet. "That's why Logan is a jerk in class. He wants his parents' attention, not mine."

Matt laughed. "Now you sound like a liberal-hearted administrator, Claire. You're making excuses for the kid's behaviour."

"I guess so." She smiled weakly. "The bad behaviour needs to change, no matter what the reason."

"Isn't there a counsellor who can help this kid?"

"There is, actually. I'll talk to Lily Campbell in the Guidance Office tomorrow and get the ball rolling. If she doesn't know what to do she'll know someone who does."

Matt sipped his hot chocolate and grinned. "Clarikins, this is good stuff!" he exclaimed after a second sip. "Now, it's getting late. Let's leave work behind for the rest of the evening." He took her free hand and led her into the living room where he turned on the fireplace and put on a slow playlist on Claire's docked iPod. They melted into the sofa together, their legs intertwined as they sipped their drinks. As they snuggled and kissed, both were reminded of their own high school days when they were so in love and in lust. It never took them long to get back to that point.

At ten-thirty, Matt knew he had to go home. He longed to spend the night, but knew better than to ask. Claire never wanted him to stay over on a school night, but tonight had given him an idea. They kissed and parted at the door, and Claire went to finish her schoolwork.

***

Friday, February 23

After lunch, Claire went to see Kristen Jaworski in the office. She knocked on the door. "Kristen, I apologize for being so late with this, but it happened the day of the Spike Carruthers affair."

"Oh? You look serious. What's up?"

"During my hall duty I overheard a conversation between Ethan Boyd and Julie Pelegrino. It was about Damian Stoker and an accident he had with his mother's car on the same afternoon as Paul Fraser's accident."

Kristen's eyebrows shot up and she picked up a pen. "Hmmm... I see. What did they say?"

"They talked about Damian Stoker and his mother's new silver Corolla. Apparently Damian told his parents that he had hit a tree on Elgin Falls Road when he went to pick up Caitlin Somers." Claire blushed and looked at her hands folded in her lap. She should have told Kristen this days ago.

"Wow, really? That just may be the clue the police need. They're having a hard time because there were no witnesses." Kristen wrote the information on the scribbler on her desk. "I'm sure they'll be very interested in this information. They have taken pictures of the tire tracks in the snow and taken samples of the paint that was left on Jethro's car. They know the make, the model and the year of the car, but they can't find the exact car. If this matches, Damian isn't only in trouble with his parents. I'll call Lieutenant Wajowski right away."

Claire took a deep, shuddering breath. "Keep me posted, will you?"

"I will," Kristen said as she started to dial the number. "You did the right thing here, Claire."

Claire smiled weakly. "Better late than never, right?"

***

Claire met Anne in the hall outside the Guidance Office. "Did you see Guidance about Nadeena today?"

"Yes, Lily Campbell is on the alert," Anne replied. "What are you up to?"

"I just told Kristen about the silver Corolla."

"And?"

"She said the police would be interested. How did your talk about Nadeena Hami go?"

"It's amazing what the Guidance counsellors can do," Anne continued. "Lily has seen grade nines arrive, looking adorable in fashionable clothing. Then they become Goths, all black and white and spooky with chains, spider web stockings, spikes and tattoos. They get even moodier in grades ten and eleven with black nail polish and black lipstick and spiked collars and rings in more body parts than we want to see and then, sometime between grades eleven and twelve, most re-join the human race."

Claire grabbed her hand. "But most Goths are doing it of their own free will. Is Nadeena?"

"That's the point and Lily knows it. She won't drop the ball."

Chapter 8

<u>A Birthday Celebration Turns</u>

Tuesday, February 27

It was the end of the day. Claire, Chin, Gene, Angus and Don were in the Science office updating February's paperwork.

"I've had a lot of absentees this week, Claire," Angus said. He was doing his attendance for the month. "Is there a flu bug going around?"

Claire turned towards him. "Maybe. But I have a kid who has only been here four days since February fifth."

"You win. Who's the kid?" Gene swivelled his chair around.

"You'll be surprised. It's Ricky Penworth, the V.P.'s son."

"No surprise there at all," Don said. "I had him last year."

"I've heard a lot of talk about him in the staff room." said Chin. "He *is* a flu bug. Rumour has it that he was socially promoted every year since grade three and then pushed out of Amberton Heights Elementary into here just to get rid of him."

"They're exaggerating... aren't they?" Gene asked.

"No, they're not," said Don. "He's a piece of work."

"What reason do his parents give for his absences?" Chin asked.

"His mother always says he's sick or claims she needs him to do things around the house. She and Jack are divorced, you know," Don said.

"Yeah, I know. No surprise there." said Claire.

"How is he in your class?" asked Chin.

"He refuses to sit in the seat I assigned and he doesn't participate, period. He plays on his cellphone or on his computer at the back of the lab. Since start-up, Ricky has missed most of the first two science units and the first five quizzes."

"Have you talked to Jack?" Chin asked.

"He doesn't see a problem."

"What about talking to Kristen?" Angus asked.

"Ricky's not in her end of the alphabet—she gets the kids with last names A through L and Jack gets the rest,"

"There's no way Ricky should be on Jack's list for discipline. He's his son, for God's sake. That's a conflict of interests," Chin said.

"I know that and so does Kristen," Don said. "But she told me neither Bertha nor Jack saw any conflict in having a 'professional' father in charge of his son. They refused to assign Ricky to her. She left it at that—smart girl, actually."

"Parents and kids shouldn't even be at the same school, in my book. How are you coping?" Gene rubbed a hand down his face.

"I do the same with him as with anybody else. I can't make up for what he didn't learn in previous grades," said Claire.

"How is he on tests?"

"I give frequent small quizzes. So far, he has skipped them all. The other kids—even Maziyar and Logan—are learning to appreciate my system."

"It's a good strategy. I use it myself. They're not afraid of the little quizzes and they get higher marks. It also helps for the larger tests," Angus said, "They review more often."

"Well, it isn't working with Ricky. I can forgive the quizzes he missed while on the cruise, but he has missed both quizzes in the four days he's been here since he returned. It's unfair to the others. I usually don't return the marked quizzes until everybody has done them," Claire said.

"No, Claire, hand them back. Make a 'B' version for him. And I'd talk to Lily Campbell in guidance if I were you." Chin advised.

"Been there. Done that. Lily is as frustrated as anyone with this boy."

"It's strange," said Don, "Jack and Muriel block any effort to help their son. They spoil him rotten and facilitate him doing whatever he wants. I pity the kid."

"Me, too. But he's still a spoiled jerk and he needs to learn. The second day he was here his father was out of the school at a meeting. I confiscated Ricky's cellphone and made him get it back from Kristen. Ricky promised her he'd never play on it again and that he would work in class."

"Did he keep his word?" asked Don, with a sarcastic smirk.

"Are you kidding? The next day Jack called me into his office. On the drive home with his father, Ricky had told him that I was unreasonable, boring and couldn't teach. Jack asked to see my lesson plans for a week."

Chin Ho was shaking his head, his eyes closed. "I'm afraid you're going to have a tough semester, Claire. Maziyar, Dwayne, Karla and Logan are in that class too, aren't they? Let me know if there's any way I can help."

"Yeah, me too," Gene said.

"I've read his guidance file. Ricky's I.Q. indicates he could do a lot better. So I'm hoping to motivate him with easy successes that can't be attributed to cheating. But so far even when I ask him the simplest of questions, he cannot or will not answer. Could he be doing it on purpose? I can't figure it out. Moreover, the Penworths insist on extra time on assignments and quizzes, overlooking his spelling errors and letting him do all tests in the learning resource room," Claire said as Don took a bite of his apple.

"Brian McLean won't allow that because the Penworths refuse to let him be tested for learning differences. Ricky doesn't qualify," Don said. "I don't know if that's helping or hindering the situation."

"Nothing can help a kid with those parents," Chin said.

"Every time I talk to Muriel she implies he has exam phobia, dyslexia, or some such thing. It changes every time. She demands that Ricky be allowed to use his laptop in class, because he can't write and she insists his homework be emailed to her daily. They spoil him with videogames and are totally blind to his behaviour."

Don turned his chair, looked at Claire and pointed at her with his half-eaten apple. "I think she does his homework for him. She insists he be allowed to answer essay questions in point form because he can't write. I think the real reason he can't write or print is because he doesn't get any practice. He doesn't get to do anything."

Claire's eyebrows raised and she gave Don a look that said: message received.

"Does he have a science notebook?" Chin asked.

"He doesn't. Or he didn't," Claire said. "The one thing he did in my class while I was standing over him was some garbage-dump standard stuff on a bit of torn paper. I told him he needed to get a proper notebook or open a file on his computer and take notes in class and show them to me every day. The next day he showed me a complete set of notes he had bought from Artie Binton."

"Who's he?" Gene asked.

"He was in my grade ten Science class last year and took great notes," Don said. "He photocopies them and sells copies to the new kids. Ricky must be a good customer."

"When I challenged him about the photocopied notes, Ricky just said his Mom thought they were terrific, gave me a 'whatever' roll of the eyes and marched to his seat at the back of the lab, giving high-fives to several boys on his way and then laughing. 'Dumb assholes! I just sneezed all over my hand,' he said. No wonder the kid has no friends. I had to let five boys go wash their hands."

"Has he done any of the quizzes he missed after school?" Chin asked.

"No, he won't do anything after school. He has to catch a ride with his father and just doesn't show up. I think it's the only time Jack spends with him."

"So when can you get him to do quizzes?"

"He will only do them in class while I'm teaching and I can't monitor him properly,"

"So he can cheat," said Don.

"It's not fair to the others—but he still fails," Claire finished.

"Sorry, guys, I have to go to the office," Gene said. "I just got an email.

Chin was looking at the attendance screen on Claire's computer. "This month, Ricky missed fourteen out of eighteen days!"

"The first two weeks he was on a Caribbean cruise with his grandmother. Don, what was his final mark last year?"

"I gave him thirty-three, but Bertha gave him fifty percent."

"Can I fail him for chronic absenteeism?" Claire asked.

"I'm afraid not," said Chin.

***

Wednesday, February 28

At lunch the next day in the science office, Claire was redoing the seating plans that had changed daily because of additions and deletions to her classes and trying to set up the weightings for marks for the courses she was teaching. "Shoot!" Claire said a bit later. Matt was in Mexico and again she was hoping to get stuff done so she could spend more time with him when he returned.

As she speed-flipped through the manual, Angus came in. Claire looked at him and blushed. "Do you know how to get the mark weightings set up on this thing, Angus?" she asked. "I need to do this more than twice a year to remember it."

"Let me have a look. I did mine yesterday. They've changed it again." He checked her latest moves on the screen. "Oh, yeah. I think you're putting the class numbers in the wrong place. They've moved them to here, you see … and they've added the parents' email addresses in the third column, so you have to bring that over too. Just click and drag the icons."

"Thanks," Claire said. She did the required moves for grade ten biology and followed the results onscreen. "Did they change the learning skills?"

"They'll be changed for September."

"Oh goody. I can hardly wait," Claire snarled. She set up the marks program for her other two classes.

Don got up from his desk, an energy bar in hand. "By the way, what's with the drop-in centre on the second floor?"

"The what? Where?" Angus, Chin and Claire looked at him.

"That Naomi Harper woman. Her room's a kid magnet. They go in and out at will, all day. They drink pop, make popcorn, and sell snacks. I bought this energy bar there just now. The cafeteria staff's mad as hell."

"Huh, I have noticed a lot of unusual activity there when I'm in the Hickenman room," Claire said.

"Oh God, you're in the Hickenman room?" Angus said, an exaggerated shiver wobbling down his thick shoulders. "He can be totally obnoxious. He hates sharing it."

"I've noticed. Oh, it's the best of times…" Claire started and gave the men a smile. "Well, somebody should look into the Harper room. But it won't be me, I can tell you that."

***

Wednesday, afternoon, February 28

"Jenny, Amir, can you come here for a minute?" Claire was putting her books on the wobbly table. "I have some leftover Valentine's chocolates today for the kids."

"Wow! That's a lot, Miss H.," said Jenny, looking in the bag. "Can we give them as rewards for work done?"

"That's a great idea, isn't it, Miss?" Amir said as he placed the kids' notebooks and pencils on the tables.

"Let's try. Everybody likes chocolate," Claire said.

"We do too," said Jenny, unwrapping the red foil from one and popping it in her mouth.

Claire smiled. "Today's the last day we're allowed to give candy. The government's 'healthy food policy for schools' kicks in tomorrow, so we have to give them all away this period."

"Understood," Amir chewed, his cheeks bulging.

"We have rewards for work done today," Jenny said to Lindsay Landon, the French fry girl. "Do you like chocolate?"

"Sure do! Hey, Deepak! We're getting chocolates today for math!"

"I don't care. I don't like chocolate. It's bad for my A.D.H.D.," Deepak responded. He dumped his books on a table and ran back into the hall.

"Well, thank God I don' have A.D.H.D then," Maxine said, dropping her bag on her table. She had arrived on time for a change.

"Let's try to do some work then, Maxine," Claire said, jumping on the chance to motivate the girl.

"I only wanna work with Amir, Miss." she pouted, then plopped herself onto her chair and sat, refusing to take out a pencil until the bell went.

"I'm a bit busy at the moment," Amir said, reaching a hand upward. Jimmy Church and Deepak Dhali were taunting Joel by playing 'try to get your cellphone back' around the tables. With a swift turn and a quick grab, Amir nabbed the phone. "Ha, got it! Now, sit."

Before the boys had a chance to go after it, the bell went and Claire ushered all the hall stragglers into the room. She sent those who were to go to the L.R.T room off with their workbooks and started everyone else working on their lessons.

The chocolaty bribe didn't impress the entire class, but they all agreed it beat the usual grind. Claire, Jenny and Amir worked the room, helping and handing out red foil-wrapped rewards for completed math pages.

Forty-five minutes in, the first balled foil missile flew across the room. Jimmy chuckled and Deepak returned fire. An all-out war erupted as Claire sat slumped at the wobbly table, marking as fast as she could. Maxine Young had stayed for the treat, but got hit on the cheek by one of the little missiles and left.

"Isn't this getting a bit wild, Miss H.?" asked Jenny, ducking red missiles.

"Back to work, please, Jimmy!" Claire said. Jenny tried to herd him back to his seat as
he flicked little red balls in all directions.

"Gotcha, Jimmy!" laughed Deepak.

Claire put on her stern face, but she was pleased. Thanks to the chocolate everyone, including Maxine, had already done more work than usual. Best yet, Jenny and Amir had seen how well the kids could work when they were motivated.

***

Wednesday evening, February 28

Claire was still pleased with her day when the doorbell rang. "Matt? What the hell?" Claire said, as she saw her man standing on the front step, dressed in a tux and tie, a black limo in front of her house. "What are you doing here? You're supposed to be in Mexico. You didn't get fired, did you?"

"I came back to surprise you because I missed your birthday." He smiled mischievously as he pulled a bouquet of roses from behind his back.

"Well, you succeeded!" she gasped as she sniffed the roses and gave him a hug. "It's cold. Get in here." She was flustered, her cheeks burning brightly.

"I missed you so much," he said, as she arranged the flowers in a vase. His toes tapped in his shiny dress shoes as he embraced her from behind.

"You didn't have to do all this, hon, you already gave me Boomer."

"I've booked us a limo ride and a candlelit dinner.

"What?" Claire turned on a dime. That car is for us? Suddenly, she forgot all about school and ran upstairs to change into something dressy. In love and forgetting all her usual instincts, Claire was in another world.

Matt smelled success. He did a little jig while she was upstairs. He had concocted a plan to prove to Claire that the sky would not fall and that the world would go on even if she went out on a weeknight. He had no idea what Maziyar had done to her last week when she hadn't had her handouts ready. Claire had forgotten it too. Five minutes later, she was ready and gorgeous in a little black shift, her chestnut curls bouncing around her shoulders. "Wow," Matt said as he helped her into her coat. "You're amazing."

"That makes two of us, then." She smiled and turned into his arms for a squeeze.

They laughed and sipped muscat de rivesalte and ate olives in the limo as it drove them around and dropped them off at the *Bonaparte,* where the maître d' escorted them to a secluded table. Time stood still during a leisurely, elegant, romantic dinner. Back in the limo, "I hope you'll forgive me for fibbing, Claire."

"Fibbing?"

About the length of my trip to Mexico," Matt said. "I wanted to surprise you." He surprised her again by gently putting a succulent chocolate covered strawberry into her mouth. She crushed it between her tongue and her palate and savoured the juice and the chocolate as they melded together.

"Of course you're forgiven." She closed her eyes and savoured another strawberry. "This is heaven, Matt. The whole evening has been magical."

"Good." Matt exhaled and sat back with a satisfied look on his face. He told her about his next trip, a two-day jaunt to Nevada. Then, after another strawberry, "Isn't this a lovely way to spend a Wednesday evening?

Claire sat up with a jerk and stared at him. "Holy crap, Matt! I have to teach tomorrow. The grade ten class from hell will roast me alive if I don't keep them busy. I haven't made their worksheets. Without them they run amok. They won't read a word without a worksheet to follow." She tapped on the glass separating them from the chauffeur and asked him to take them straight home. "Thank you for all this, Matt, but I still have a lot to do tonight."

At 684 Riverside Road, Matt gallantly helped her out of the limo. "Come on, Clarikins, be a sport. It's only one night. You can just get a worksheet from the Internet in the morning." He tried to grab her on the way to the door. She dodged him. He followed. "A change is like a vacation, isn't it?" he begged, rapidly losing his dramatic touch to desperation as he hoped to postpone the inevitable.

"Yes, it was all that and more," Claire stepped past him on her way to her door. "But it's past ten-thirty, Matt. The evening's over." She turned to face him for a moment. "Thank you for a lovely dinner, but tomorrow is another day."

"What do you mean?" He didn't expect an answer. He wanted her to feel just a bit guilty for sending him home. He followed her into the house.

"Oh dammit, Matt, you know you've got to go." She spun around. Her eyes were like lasers. "Didn't you tell me you had a plane to catch for Nevada tomorrow morning? Knowing you, you haven't packed yet and there's school tomorrow for me and I have grade elevens to tutor *before* class."

"Yeah, if they show up." Matt's mood was clouding over.

"That's a risk, but teachers have to set the example."

Matt had hoped the evening would lead to something more, but his desires had gone out the window.

"I'm sorry, Matt. I have to make those worksheets. You have no idea what happens if the kids don't get them."

She was showing him the door after the lovely evening he had planned. Suddenly, he lost it. He turned to face her. "Oh, dammit, Claire, other people go out on weeknights and teach." That lit another fuse.

"There are also teachers who care more for their social life than for their students," she shot back.

"For God's sake, Claire, two weeks ago you were thinking of quitting!" he shouted. "In fact, you should quit. Why in hell do you care so much about your damn classes? Don't I mean anything to you?"

Claire took a deep breath. "I know I've been talking about quitting, but for this semester I'm still a teacher. Every student is someone's son or daughter, and I cannot live with myself if I don't do my best. I want to be more than an automatic lesson dispenser with a text. And yes, you do mean something to me." But she wasn't going to answer that question with specifics right now.

Matt looked at the floor. "You have time for everything but me: the students, your girlfriends, extra-curriculars, the dog, Gene, Paul..."

Her answer came like lightning. "Didn't I see you after school on a Monday two weeks ago... and today?" She let that sink in. "My extra-curricular responsibilities increase in March. We'll see each other on weekends and at the Ecology Club when you get back from Nevada."

"Always work, work and more work. Do I have to join your damned profession if I want to see you?" Matt turned away. "Do I have to volunteer? Is that all we'll ever have together?" He enunciated each word as he looked at her.

The question hit Claire in the heart. She straightened up to her full height. For a moment she turned and looked at the ceiling. Then she faced him, her thoughts swirling. "N-no," she pouted.

"So? What do you want then?" It was as if Matt expected a contract signed on the spot with no thought for what was important to her.

"I want a relationship—a loving, trusting, mutually respectful relationship," she sputtered. She softened her voice. "I do love you, Matt, really I do. I love you with all my heart and soul, but you arrived here unexpectedly before I even had a chance to start the stuff I needed to get done for tomorrow. I know you meant for this to be a surprise and really, it was magical, but I made plans that would keep me very busy *because you told me you'd be in Mexico until Monday* and I thought I'd be alone." Boomer was barking, trying to divert their attention.

Claire felt tears welling in her eyes. She didn't want to blubber. "You can't expect me to drop everything because you

<section>147

suddenly show up." She sniffed and grabbed a tissue from the box on the counter. There was a moment. Matt looked at her. Boomer looked from one to the other. He hoped it was over.

It wasn't. Claire turned to him again. "You have a job that takes you away from me all the time and I'm coping with that. I have a job that keeps me busy late into the evening. Both are good jobs, Matt. Learn to live with it, dammit."

Now Matt was hurt. "Didn't you have a good time?"

"Of course I did. Didn't I just say so?"

"So, isn't that the most important thing?" He took her hand in his.

"Yes, but tomorrow is also important and I want to get through that too. For that, I have to finish my handouts. You said you had a plane to catch and your trip will be better if you're well rested—and if you have luggage." She emphasized the last four words.

He didn't answer. He pulled back his hand, glared at her and left, slamming the door. She watched him drive away, missing their usual lingering kiss at the door, the connecting wave as he turned out of the driveway. Her heart sank. She deflated. What had just happened?

For a moment her determination came back. She would shut the issue out of her mind and go into her study to finish the work for tomorrow. She could analyse this to death later, she told herself. Still, it kept pushing itself back into her mind. She couldn't remember what she needed to do. Miss Practicality,

Miss Workaholic, she thought. A tear rolled down her left cheek and fell on her keyboard. She wiped it off. She got more tissues and cried. Boomer hopped on her lap and licked the tears. The handouts didn't get done.

In bed the sleep Claire needed didn't come. She was analysing her relationship with Matt and kicking herself for ruining the magical evening he had planned for her. She was sorry. Was it too late? Had she messed it up for good?

March

Chapter 9

<u>Five Months with the Same Bunch</u>

Saturday, March 3

Three days dragged by without a word from Matt. Claire, tired and depressed, tried to focus on anything other than last Wednesday's falling-out. She thought about poor Maxine, who had walked out for most of ten days in February. She was in class a bit more now, but still insisted she couldn't do the work and freaked out whenever she thought it was hard. Claire had been documenting her behaviour since mid-February.

The peer tutors were helping, but Maxine always wanted Amir and if he was busy elsewhere she would tour around the classroom, pulling notebooks out from under kids' pencils or rummaging through backpacks. She excelled in obstreperousness. If it were a marketable life skill, Maxine would be rich.

Claire tried to be friendly and help her with the math, but she would just rant. "Why d'I hafta do this crap anyways? I told you, I'm stupid an' I hate math," then she would fold her arms and pout. Claire had learned to stop before she walked out.

150

Claire called Mrs. Young, but the woman sounded spaced out. When Maxine found out about the phone call, she told her, "Don' bother callin' my mom, Miss. She don't do nothin' nohow. My parents don' care. I could spend the night in a garbage bin an' nobody'd come lookin' for me. I done it."

Claire felt sad for Maxine. She had read her file. The girl had not been identified with learning differences. It only labelled her as rebellious and stubborn and having a vile family situation. Her I.Q. was better than normal. She should be able to do the work, even though she had failed both academic and general level math. Everyone needed two math credits to graduate. If only her home life were better…

***

Later at the dog park, Claire finally allowed herself to think about Matt. How could she nudge the situation back to where they had been? Where was the damned reset button when you needed it? They had known each other since they were little kids in Elgin Falls. What if he thought the ball was in her court? They had both made mistakes last Wednesday. But if this was all it took for him to drop her, then maybe he didn't love her as much as she thought. Her mother would say she'd be well rid of him. But she didn't want to be rid of him.

She threw the ball for Boomer. Claire and Gene now met regularly at the dog park. She enjoyed his company but couldn't help wishing he were Matt. She saw them coming and threw Boomer's ball towards Gene and P.C. The dogs came romping back together "How was your day, Gene?"

"Not bad."

Gene put out his hand to let Boomer sniff and knelt down to do some serious rubbing. He looked at her. "He's going to be a beaut, Claire, a real beaut." P.C. came back and wanted his share of the rubbing. "I love retrievers. Too bad he's a male. Natalie and I want to breed P.C. and I'm looking for a nice little bitch for him. But they're expensive. We want to breed retrievers and train them for service."

"So that's the *wife* you said you were saving up for that first day." Claire shook her head and couldn't resist laughing.

"Sure is," he winked, "Besides, what would you have thought if I'd told you I was saving for a bitch? Besides, the wife I have at home is already paid for."

"Oh, Gene!" Claire poked his arm.

"Well, she is. The wedding wasn't cheap, not to mention the ring and the dinners I have to buy to make up for all the trouble this mouth gets me into."

Claire laughed for the first time in days and was truly thankful for his friendship. "I can only imagine," she said sadly.

"I can see how you might have taken that comment the wrong way."

"You think? I mentioned it to Anne and Shirley and they're still curious."

"Do me a favour and don't explain it to them. I like being an enigma," Gene said with a laugh.

When it started to get dark, Claire, buoyed by Gene's light-heartedness, headed home with Boomer. Enough was enough, she decided. She would bite the bullet. She wanted her Matt back. What could get them together again? What could he not refuse? Suddenly it hit her. He had always wanted to see Algonquin Park. As teacher advisor for the Eco Club, she could plan an overnight field trip for club members in May! That was it. Now she was really excited. She found her phone and her fingers flew.

Hi, she started out and waited. He didn't have to know she was coming home from the dog park where she had met Gene.

Hello, Matt responded. *Been meaning to call U.*

Me 2. Plz, can we forget about the other night?

The minutes passed. Claire was starting to worry.

Maybe, he finally replied.

You always wanted to see Algonquin Pk.

Yes.

I could plan an Eco Club fieldtrip to Algonquin for May.

?

We could reconnoitre it tog, Mrch Break.

Her phone rang and Matt's smiling face appeared on the screen.

"I'm in," he said.

***

Monday, March 5

Claire was monitoring her grade tens as they wrote a test on Unit three. They had found it particularly difficult. She hoped they would do well. Suddenly, Dwayne Dufresne stood up. He had a drinking box in his hand and came to the front of the classroom.

"Thank you, Dwayne. I'll put that in the recycling for you. You just sit down and write your test."

"It ain't empty, Miss. I gotta meet my mother."

"I'm sorry, but students can't leave class during a test."

"I gotta meet my mother, Miss."

"Do you have a note?"

"Didn' know I had ta have one."

"Finish your test. It isn't long. Then you can go." Claire always left her cell in the science office, or she would have called the mother.

Dwayne persisted. "I hafta meet my mother, Miss. I promised her." His voice raised and his eyes darted to the door.

"Why didn't you tell me at the beginning of class, Dwayne? I could have given the test before you left or after you came back."

"I forgot."

"Return to your seat, Dwayne. The sooner you finish the test, the sooner you can go."

Heads were starting to pop up all over the room now. Maziyar and Logan had stopped writing and were gawking and chuckling to each other. Claire asked them to settle down and get back to the test. They did not.

Dwayne stood his ground. "I gotta meet her NOW!"

"I'm sorry, but you can't go until you finish the test, Dwayne."

"But I HAFTA meet her." He was glued to the spot.

Claire called the office. There were no parents in the office.

"I tole you," Dwayne shouted. "I wasn't meetin' er in the office!"

Had he? The rest of the class was laughing out loud now. Claire felt her control slipping away. She looked at Ricky's empty seat and felt as powerless as she was.

Justine Jones, an obnoxious girl, ventured into the fray. "Didn'cha hear him, Miss? He *hasta* meet his mother!"

Claire, fighting to look serene, explained again that she could not let him go because he had a test to write and suggested again that he write it quickly, then leave. He protested again. By this time so many in the class were engaged in the issue, that Claire had to raise her voice to be heard. It didn't help.

"But his mom's here, an' she has ta see him, an' she ain't in the office," shouted Karla Kozak from the back.

"Wha' part of that don'cha understand, Miss?" Maziyar and Logan threw in. The class was a sea of wide eyes and dropped chins, all glaring at Claire. For a moment, time stood still. She couldn't remember seeing a class with everyone—including Maziyar and Logan—paying attention to the same thing at once.

Reality returned. I'm on my own, Claire thought. I'm outnumbered thirty-three to one and I have to work with these kids for four more months. This is no TV show. There is no script. Think, Claire, think!

Claire checked the corridor to see if the mother was in the hall. Nobody there. She felt stupid doing this for a grade ten kid, who hadn't bothered to learn even basic school rules. For all she knew, he could be meeting a pusher or a bookie. There was more snickering. More kids were shouting in defence of Dwayne. Inside, Claire was crumbling. Dwayne was thick, unscrupulous, muscular and big enough to push her aside or worse, and he had similar friends in the class.

Suddenly Marcie Jameson, a shy, quiet girl, clamped her palms over her ears. "Please stop," she cried as she began rocking back and forth in her seat. "Please be quiet. I'm getting a migraine." Claire saw the tears in her eyes from the pain. "Please, Miss. Can I leave? I need to take a pill."

Claire agreed, defeated and wanting her class to write the test. She salvaged what she could by letting Dwayne leave, too. He came back a while later grinning victoriously and finished his test with the others.

***

Just before the end of the class, Marcie, who had met Lily Campbell in the hall, returned to finish her test. Lily had invited Marcie to lie down in the Guidance Office while her medication took effect. Claire asked Dwayne to stay after class and tried to explain to him that not getting a note and not telling her he had to meet his mother before class had caused a lot of trouble. She added that these rules were in place for a reason. All students needed to follow them, so things could run smoothly in everyone's best interest.

"Yeah, whatever," he muttered and turned away.

A few minutes later, Marcie handed in her test.

"I'm so sorry for the noise, Marcie. How are you feeling now?"

"Well enough to finish the day," she said weakly. "But, you know, Miss, this wasn't your fault. These kids are so immature and they don't realize what a good teacher you are. They're wrecking it for those of us who want to learn."

"Thank you, Marcie." Claire smiled. She had been wrong. She was outnumbered thirty-two to *two*, maybe better.

Marcie gave her a hug, which along with her encouraging words, was exactly what Claire needed. Claire walked her to the door and through the throng of grade elevens, watched as Marcie went to her locker to get her books for period two. This had been one of those moments that made teaching worthwhile. Ironically, she realized, it was the Dwaynes who made such moments stand out.

That night, Claire noticed that neither Dwayne nor his friend Darryl had submitted their tests.

***

Tuesday, March 6

The next morning Kristen, who was responsible Dwayne Dufresne and Darryl Howard, was at a workshop. Claire found Jack Penworth at his computer, cleared her throat and asked, "Is it acceptable that two students don't hand in their test papers? And what's the policy when a kid gets up during a test to go and meet his mother, with no note or prior warning?" She looked at him expectantly.

"Er... I don't know if that... er... if that has ever come up before... I'll have to think about it..."

"What about the missing test papers?" she pressed.

"Are you sure the papers are missing? Have you looked everywhere?"

"Yes, I'm sure. I checked my briefcase last night and their desks this morning: no tests to be found. I've double-checked each test to see if another test might be hooked to it at the staple. Nothing. Dwayne and Darryl's papers are not there. But the boys were in class and I saw them write the test."

Jack stared at her blankly.

Claire stifled the urge to roll her eyes. "Dwayne Dufresne and Darryl Howard were both present. Based on the rules I remember, they should get an automatic zero. But you won't let me do that." Claire hesitated; she had no idea what a V.P. like Jack would support. "What should I do, Jack?"

It took a long time for him to answer. "You can't give zeros."

Claire was so irritated that these buffoons were making extra work for her that she wanted to give them zeros or worse. She wasn't good at thinking according to the current liberal philosophy and, having recently returned from teaching abroad for five years, she needed some advice to keep out of trouble with the Amberton administration herself...

Jack finished what he was doing on the computer and swivelled his chair around to face her. "You'll have to give them a chance to explain," he said.

Claire's jaw dropped. This indulgent thinking went so counter to her philosophy about educating youth. "It wouldn't be fair to the others to have them write the same test again."

"No, of course not. You'll have to make up a different but equally demanding test."

"But what about all the kids who did their work and in spite of the test, came in, wrote it, and handed it in?"

Jack was pensive. Claire said, "None of the other kids had the advantage of seeing another test on the same topic before writing theirs."

Jack still looked pensive. "Dwayne and Darryl wouldn't lie, would they?"

Claire responded in a flash. "Oh yes, they would. I haven't got their papers. I saw them write the tests in class. I don't have them."

"We don't give zeros. If they lied, they'll be suspended."

"Would the parents believe us or them?"

"You'll have to prove the boys are lying. We need concrete proof."

"Isn't my word good enough?" Claire asked. "Don't you believe me?"

No answer. Jack just shrugged.

"Thanks, Jack" Claire said, turned, and left.

***

At the end of the day Claire bumped into Shirley in the staff room. Frustrated, she explained the situation. "Why doesn't he believe me? What's in it for me to *pretend* they didn't hand in their tests?" Claire asked.

"If it makes you feel any better, my word isn't good enough either, and I've been here a lot longer than Jack. If Jack does anything, he'll have to face the kids' parents, and they will probably defend the kids. The kids lied to us. They'll tell their parents the same story or worse. The parents will believe them."

"That's what happens with Ricky every time. He's in that class, too, when he shows up," Claire said. "Too bad Kristen wasn't there."

"The only person who cannot make the administration uncomfortable is the teacher. Right now that's where you're at, my dear."

"So what would you do, Shirley?"

"You can't win. This is a classic he-said-she-said. Bite your lip and follow Jack's advice—whether you like it or not."

Claire was clearly piqued. "Drat!"

"Claire, my dear, you need something to look forward to. I was planning to visit Paul Fraser in the hospital for a bit after school. Want to come?"

"Sure. That's a great idea, Shirl. How's he doing?"

"He's on the rehab floor now, and he's slowly starting to put weight on his foot."

"Wow. And to think he could have died." Claire said, shaking her head. "How are his spirits?"

161

"He's optimistic and determined to be back to school in the fall. The kids want him back. They love him—the good ones do anyway. They visit him in the hospital."

"Do you know if the police are anywhere near finding the hit-and-run driver?"

"I think they're looking into the lead you gave because it's the only one they have. As Bertha told us again at the last heads meeting, there were no witnesses. We still can't tell the students anything. Police orders."

"But how can they be sure?"

"They've sent paint samples from both cars to the police lab. They have their forensic ways, but it'll take a while. They can tell the make and the year of the car by analysing the paint, but not who owns it or who was driving it. That's where the conversations we overhear can be helpful."

"I wonder what the hit-and-run driver, whoever he may be, has been thinking all this time."

"If it's Damian Stoker, not much. He's a juvenile and wouldn't get much of a sentence. The weather would have been a factor in the accident."

"Yes, but Julie Pelegrino said his mother will be furious and she'll be harder on him than any judge could be. So if it is him, ..."

" ...So he'll get what's coming to him from his family if not the court.'"

***

After school Claire and Shirley headed for the hospital. Paul was learning to walk between two beams with the help of a physiotherapist. When he saw them he almost fell over with excitement.

"Hi Claire! Hi Shirley! It's good to see you!" The physiotherapist helped him to a wheelchair where he could put his leg up. They gave him the fruit-basket they had picked up on the way, and Claire pushed him to a visiting area while Shirley brought him up to date on school gossip.

"And how are you doing, Paul?"

"I'm getting there. The arm's almost good as new, the ribs have become weather predictors, the head can be achy and the memory is sometimes fuzzy. The foot's the biggest challenge. I've lost some muscle tone all over but Nicole, my physio here, is a great help. She'll have me ship shape in no time. So how's my math class doing, Claire?" he asked when all three were settled.

"I absolutely hate the room but I love the class. I got George Gumbersahl's course and I don't know what I'd do without the peer tutors you chose."

"Chester can be quite persnickety about his room. I used to rib him about it. Maybe too much. Glad you're enjoying the class, though."

163

"Are they keeping you up to date on the police investigation?"

"I don't really want to know. I figure when they've solved it I'll hear about it. I have other things on my mind." He smiled and tried to wiggle his toes. "So I hear you're retiring, Shirley…" They stayed until Paul had to be wheeled back to his room for dinner.

Chapter 10

Techno Geek, Algonquin Plans, the Naomi Effect

Thursday, March 8

The first time Claire saw Sean Jacobson was one night after school first semester. She was walking back to the science office. He was on a stepladder with his head amongst the myriad of coloured wires in the hall ceiling. Claire didn't know him, so to her this looked like significant mischief. She told him to get down and get out of there. He obeyed placidly—which is why she remembered the incident. There was no attitude, no backtalk. He just walked away, head bowed, leaving the ladder in place as if for later. He didn't look like someone who had just been caught doing something he shouldn't.

Now that he was in her junior class, Claire knew what Sean had been doing: passing a wire from a computer lab into a teacher's classroom. In the last two and a half years, he had helped many teachers set up computer systems at Amberton District High. He was able to make any PowerPoint projector or a Smart Board or even the old video players work from the school computers, most of which had developed the eccentricities of old age. Sean was the unofficial computer expert for the staff.

Sean often missed classes and a blind eye was turned. He earned a lot of leeway with his tech-support of the staff because he had an eidetic memory. His marks were beyond excellent. Claire soon saw that he was always ahead of everyone else in his reading and his homework, in spite of missing classes almost as often as Ricky Penworth.

Sean did what the Board of Education should have paid a large team of technicians to do. Requests to the board for repairs to equipment took weeks to be processed. When one of their two and a half technicians finally did arrive, the guy would fix the one and only issue on his work order and rush off to the next school. Sean was available and flexible and many teachers took advantage of his enthusiasm, knowledge, and skill. Sean loved it. Had he been born in the fifties, he might have been another Bill Gates.

Today Sean helped Claire set up her video equipment for a pig dissection video. When they had seen it Claire asked them to answer some questions that followed the information in the video on one of her handouts. She wanted them to review it while the information was fresh in their minds. The result would be a useful note. After March break, the class would be dissecting foetal pigs, and today's work would prepare them for that experience.

Hannah Jessica May and Farah Marie Zahar were in a *grown-up-Barbie* phase. Instead of doing their work, they were admiring hairdos in fashion magazines.

"Put away the magazines, girls, and please answer the questions on the handout." They both looked up at Claire as she sauntered by their table and got to work. "Thanks, girls."

Claire walked on. Elisa Rollins was bouncing to the beat of the music blasting in her ear-buds and doing no work. Claire tapped on her desk and mimed taking the ear-buds out of her ears.

Elisa reluctantly removed one bud. "Could you turn off the music and do the assignment, please, Elisa?" Claire asked.

Slowly and deliberately, Elisa turned a disparaging shoulder to Claire. "I'll do it at home," she muttered, replacing the ear-bud.

"Sorry, Elisa, that's not how it works. It's your job to work here and now, so I can help if you have a problem." Claire felt stupid restating the obvious to a seventeen-year-old.

"Why don'tcha go help somebody else?" she muttered under her breath.

Claire heard it. "You need to be working, too."

Elisa glared at Claire, her jaw hanging slack. She slowly reached into her backpack, took out some wrinkled sheets of paper from something that had once been a notebook and painstakingly leafed through them to find one with some blank space. She tore off a wedge. Then this seventeen year-old eleventh grader—a product supposedly just over a year away from university readiness—needed to borrow a pen and a science text. Having ignored the video, she took her time, hoping that Claire would go on to somebody else. She did, but Claire's peripheral vision brought her right back. "Elisa, put away that cellphone and answer the questions."

Elisa shot back, "For God's sake, Miss, there's only five minutes left."

Claire checked her watch. "And you're supposed to be working for those five minutes. Turn off that cellphone or I'll confiscate it and you'll have to reclaim it from Mr. Penworth." She hoped Elisa would obey.

Elisa turned away again, then muttered, "Ye gads, woman, why can't you be cool like Miss Harper?" and began texting.

Two minutes later Claire snatched the cellphone. She told Elisa she would get it back from Mr. Penworth at the end of the day. "Fuck it! There's only one minute left before the bell, fer Chrisesake!" Elisa screamed. Teacher and student glared at each other for a moment. Elisa's hatred was palpable. "Gimme back my fucking phone!" she yelled. Claire's speechlessness was deafening. The bell rang. Half the class bolted out the door. Claire turned towards her desk, held the warm cellphone in her pocket and refused to return it. "I hafta leave right after school an' I ain't gonna spend the whole afternoon without my fucking kit, bitch!" Elisa shouted as she left the lab, kicking a filing cabinet and knocking over the recycling box on her way out. She slammed the door open and stormed into the hallway.

Her classmates waiting at the door looked bored. They were used to this sort of thing.

In the hall, Elisa was creating more havoc by trying to persuade two classmates with well-known unreliable reputations to be witnesses to prove that Miss Hébert had been ignorant and unreasonable. Claire went to the P.A. system, and called for Mr. Penworth. After what seemed like too long, she saw Kristen Jaworski, who was there on another errand. Claire called her and gave a brief account of the situation. The noise level in the hall dropped and the witnesses vanished.

"I'll take the phone," Kristen said. "Elisa, come with me."

"Thanks, Miss Jaworski," Claire said.

Elisa shot daggers with her eyes. The hallway had started to clear when Jack arrived. Huffing from walking down the hall, he came to a stop beside Claire and watched Kristen retreating.

"More trouble in class eh, Miss Hébert? Usually I expect the students to come to me, not the other way around, Miss Hébert." He smiled thinly as he made to follow his colleague back to his office.

"I don't think this one would have gone to the office, Jack," Claire replied, then went to the science office to type a report in Elisa's file.

***

At home, Claire dumped her books on the chair in her little den, grabbed the leash and jogged to the park with Boomer.

"Hey, I heard the noise in the hall with your grade elevens," Gene said as the dogs greeted each other.

"Who didn't?"

"How did it turn out with what's her name?" Gene asked, throwing the ball for P.C.

"Elisa Rollins." Claire was admiring P.C. "Kristen took care of it. She's great." Gene threw the ball for Boomer.

"With a dog, if they don't do what they're asked, they just don't get a treat," Gene said, as he threw the ball again.

"I doubt if refusing Elisa a dried pig's ear would have motivated her to do the work, Gene. But the basic math kids perked me up after lunch."

"I like those so-called *challenged* kids," Gene replied. "Many of them are so happy to be out of the quagmire they call home that they like coming to school."

"Especially when it's cold outside." Claire rubbed her hands together. The sun was setting fast. Boomer had just returned with the ball. She threw it again.

"Most have substandard people skills, but you can blame it on their upbringing. It's never personal. Many of them love us in their way. But you look cold. We'll walk you home. P.C., Boomer, come!"

***

At the house, Gene was waving goodbye to Claire and Boomer as Matt's car pulled into her driveway. Claire turned towards him. Boomer was already clawing at the door.

"Hey, hey!" Matt called to Boomer as he got out. "Don't scratch the paint, buddy." He picked him up. "Hi, Claire. How are you?" He gave her a kiss hello. "Wow, he must have had a growth spurt. I won't be able to pick him up much longer. Have you enrolled him in the puppy obedience class yet?"

"We start the week after March Break."

"I see you and your dog park cum lab partner are doing well." Matt looked towards Gene's receding figure as he put the dog down. "At least you're not alone, I guess."

"He walks by here because he lives down the street, Matt. Besides, Boomer and P.C. are buddies." Claire knew he was suspicious of Gene, but… Could Matt really be jealous? "How was Nevada?" she asked, changing the subject as they entered the little house.

"Boring. It was only a day." Inside, they took off their coats and followed Boomer to the sofa in the living room. "I've been there so many times now, it's just work to me. I don't get to see much."

"That's too bad. I'd love to be able to sightsee offseason." Claire moved closer to him and took his hand. "Let's talk about

171

March Break and Algonquin for a minute. It's the sixteenth to the twenty-forth. Can you do that?"

"I'll text the boss." Within minutes, he had an answer. "Absolutely." He rubbed her fingers with his thumb. "Are we tenting or staying in a lodge? And what do we have to plan with the rangers for the school trip? How fast can we get that out of the way and enjoy ourselves?" His hand was progressing up her side…

Claire playfully eluded him. "We'll be camping. Dad is letting us borrow his old R.V."

"That's great…" Matt's voice trailed off. He got close again. Her warmth was distracting him.

"My list's in the den…" She went to get up but he stopped her from leaving the sofa. "From what I remember, we need to look at permits, campsites and find out where we can cook and sleep and investigate the cost and activities available on the Victoria Day weekend."

"How long do you think that'll take?"

"Not long. A couple of hours at most," she said leaning into him. She indicated a variety of pamphlets on the coffee table. "Once I have everything confirmed by the rangers I can make handouts for the kids."

He ignored the pamphlets, smiled, and began nibbling on her fingertips. "Then we can walk the trails and spend nights looking at each other."

"Or not..." she laughed. Matt raised a quizzical eyebrow. "There's a great trail with a lookout over Rock Lake and Whitefish Lake. I'd love to hike it with you," she said. "Just the two of us..."

"Just the two of us? Deal! And bring the camera." He kissed her playfully.

"Yes." She pushed back a couple inches.

"Now that's a word I like to hear," he said as his lips found hers again.

She gave in to him and they had a long deep, meaningful hug. Then she added, "But we'll camp at Mew Lake in March. The Rock Lake campground doesn't open until just before May twenty-fourth weekend."

"That's okay. Any trail will be new to me." He stole another kiss. "Hey, Clarikins?" He hadn't called her Clarikins since last week. He was getting his confidence back... testing the waters again. "Know what I'm thinking now?"

"Oh, I think I have a pretty good idea," Claire said before she got up and sashayed up the stairs. Matt was hot on her heels.

***

Friday, March 9

Claire had invited Shirley and Anne to her house for an afterschool gabfest. Anne arrived first. She had been at a History workshop.

"Where's Shirley?" Claire asked waving her guest into the kitchen.

"She was with another delegation of students when I left," Anne said as she hung up her coat and grabbed a chair.

"Do you know what's up?"

"A bunch of Naomi Harper's students have been complaining to Shirley. It's probably about Naomi. I see the goings on from my door during breaks and during class I hear it. There's a real problem."

"Well, Shirley didn't want Naomi in the first place. Bertha forced it."

Anne nodded.

Boomer, just released from his crate, jumped at Anne's knees. Claire grabbed his collar and put him in the backyard. She popped a k-cup into the coffee brewer for Anne and set out the cookies she had brought.

Claire's cellphone rang. She read the text and her smile faded. "It's Matt. Something's come up and he can't see me this weekend," she explained.

"That sucks—after everything you did to have the weekend free."

"Yes..." she pondered for a second, then dropped the thought. "What about Shirley?" Claire deflected. "Will she have to talk to Bertha?"

"That's my guess. I've heard mutterings. The academic classes are angry and I can only assume it's because of Naomi's classroom management—or lack of it." Anne stopped to take a sip of the coffee Claire had handed her. "Yum! Caramel vanilla. What are you having?"

"I like Belgian mocha. Let's go sit in the living room."

No sooner were they comfortable than Boomer began scratching at the door. Claire let him in and as soon as she sat down, the doorbell rang. Shirley came in, bursting with news.

"Let's get you set with a coffee first, Shirl. Then you can relax and tell us all about it."

When she was in the soft chair, her feet on a floor pillow, she started. "It's been a nightmare. For over two weeks groups of grade eleven French immersion kids have been coming in complaining about Naomi Harper. They say she sends them into the hall to figure out the grammar sentences and correct each other's exercises. During their *Littérature,* she tells them to read while she sells snacks in the classroom. They're reading a book many find challenging. They need help and they're not getting any. She hasn't handed them any of the support materials I gave her."

"You're joking!"

"I wish. Hall wanderers come and help themselves to snacks and Naomi puts their money in a box. The French class complains that it's distracting and they're right. She also makes and sells popcorn. The room reeks of it."

"Totally unacceptable!"

"Bertha loves it, but that's not all. Naomi is using the English text for the French *Sociologie* course."

"That was to be *my* course!" exclaimed Claire. "I worked hard at that, brushing up on my French. How can she do that?"

"She's not doing it with my approval, I can tell you that."

"Wait, wait," Anne waved a hand as though to rewind the conversation. "Why does Bertha like what she's doing? It doesn't make sense."

"Well, Naomi's basically running a drop-in centre and Bertha likes that she has increased the attendance for a lot of borderline students."

"Misfits. Back asswards logic, that is," Claire said, astonished.

"Today's delegation—Tasha, Mike and Natalie, three of the best students I had last year—were astounded when I told them I had given Miss Harper materials to help them. They begged and pleaded with me to talk to Miss Harper. I went to see her after school today."

"You don't need coffee, Shirley. You need a stiff drink," Anne said.

Shirley grinned but continued. "I went to her classroom after her 'Breakfast Club' kids had left. I needed a minute to think. I wanted to keep an open mind—you know, what works for me might not work for her."

"You're being extremely generous," Anne said. "I'd have torn her head off. She may be improving attendance for some kids, but she's causing lots of others to skip to buy snacks, which they eat as they wander the halls."

"My mind was whirling," Shirley continued. "She was counting the day's take at her desk when I walked in.

"I looked around the room. What a mess! There was garbage everywhere. The chairs hadn't been put on the tables for the cleaning staff. There was chalk-dust everywhere—including all three microwave ovens, which were perched on precarious piles of paper and magazines. The walls, blackboards and bulletin boards were covered with posters, magazine cuttings, jokes, and pictures of llamas, all stuck on with masking tape. In fact, there was all kinds of llama stuff: mugs, a stuffed toy, a costumed model, some children's books, postcards, cartoons, one fashioned from duct tape... And there sat Naomi, like a rose in a garbage heap. She shook her head. God, why llamas? They spit!"

"What did you tell her?" Anne asked.

"At first I was speechless." Shirley took a sip of her coffee. "I just had to take it all in. But Naomi was cheerful and asked me what I wanted.

"I asked her how things were going. She said things were going well. They made sixty dollars and fifty-five cents today. When I went to sit down, I had to wipe crumbs, a crushed pop can and a candy wrapper off a chair."

"Ick," Claire muttered.

"I told her that her French immersion students had been complaining that she hadn't been teaching them anything."

"And?"

"She called them complainers because they had to read *La Sablière* in French. She said they probably couldn't find an English version in the library. I asked her if she had read *La Sablière*."

"What did she say?" Anne looked suspicious.

"She said she was going to read it tonight."

"I knew it!" Anne said, shaking her head.

"It would take more than one night," Shirley said, "but I decided not to react. I asked her about the room and when it was last cleaned."

"I bet she blamed the caretakers," Claire said. "We've all heard Jethro complaining about her room."

"Apparently some of her Breakfast Club kids do it once in a while," Shirley said. "She promised to ask them to sweep it again Monday morning.

"And what about all the garbage? pop cans? dirty mugs? Does she have any recycling boxes? garbage bags? cleansers? Where did she get all this stuff?" Anne asked.

"She brought it from her last school. Chester helped her get it in. She asked me if I didn't think it was cosy and a great idea? Naomi did not catch on that this was not a casual visit. I replied that it was certainly kid-friendly."

"Yes, but she's overdoing it," Claire said.

"I told her that the food sales during class and the kids visiting any time were not accepted practices in our board."

"How did she react to that?" Anne asked.

"She just said that Bertha knew and was okay with it."

"Yes, *Miss Imaginary Excellence*, would like this. It fits. Bertha wants all the square-pegs-in-round-holes to feel comfy at Amberton," Claire said.

"I asked her if Miss Stack had actually seen the room. I was seeing red flags everywhere."

"Has Bertha seen it?"

"No, and she said Miss Jaworski likes it too because she runs the breakfast program and they get the cash every day. I asked her if Miss Jaworski had seen the room. She hasn't."

"Of course not. If she had it would have been closed down."

"But—get this—she says there hasn't been any reason for Kristen to see her room because she doesn't have any discipline problems."

"Well, you can't have a problem with something you don't have," Anne said, laughing.

"At the end," I said, " 'Naomi, you and Miss Stack and I are going to have to talk about this some more. Some of what you are doing is really good, but from the point of view of my department, there are some things here that need to be addressed. But let's leave it until Monday.' She was okay with that and wished me a nice weekend. It took me ten minutes to type a report and now I'm here."

"You look worn out, Shirl," Claire said, putting another k-cup in the brewer.

"I have to do something about Naomi," she sighed.

"I thought that her French was excellent," Claire said, with attitude.

"I thought she came so highly recommended," Anne said, mocking Bertha.

"Yes, but that can also mean her last principal was trying to scrape her off." Shirley ignored their teasing. "About half of the Immersion classes have come to see me. I can't ignore this any longer. It won't go away by itself."

"If she encourages kids to read the English version instead of the French, she doesn't do directed French conversation with them," Claire said, thinking out loud. The situation was coming into focus.

"How long has she been teaching?" Anne asked.

"Too long, I'd say," Shirley said. "I feel a headache coming on."

"Will she be transferred out, do you think?" Anne was hopeful, sitting on the floor with Boomer.

"This won't be enough to get her moved. She'll be here at least two years if Paul doesn't come back," Shirley said. "Oh God, I miss you and Gérard, Claire."

"Now I know that's where Maxine goes when she leaves my class," said Claire. "She sneaks out less than before, but still..."

"She's in Naomi's French Lit class, so she knows about the junk food," Shirley said, between sips of her coffee.

"If Maxine likes French and Naomi isn't teaching it, sooner or later there'll be an explosion," said Claire. "Just wait."

"Naomi has worked hard to set up her so-called classroom, but she does very little with the kids." Shirley took a deep breath. "She really shouldn't have that timetable, but we were in a tight spot." Then she moaned. "Oh misère... I have to talk to Bertha on Monday."

"Let's hope Naomi isn't related to Bertha," Anne quipped. "Then she'd be here forever!"

"But there's worse news," insisted Shirley. "We're losing two good students because of Naomi and Chester. Fey Yen Tang and Huang Tang."

"Naomi's lowering school standards to those of the misfits who are attracted to her room like gulls to a garbage dump," Claire said.

181

"Don't you have to report this, Shirl?" asked Anne.

"I did. You'd think Bertha'd be upset about losing academic students," Shirley said. "Ascension snatched Fey Yen and Huang up on the spot, mid-term." Shirley took a sip of her coffee and sank further into the chair. "The problem is that Bertha actually likes what Naomi is doing and unless Bertha takes my position seriously on Monday, Naomi has no problems."

Chapter 11

Jack Blunders and Frustration with Techies

Monday, March 12

Claire looked around the cozy office and wondered how on Earth Lily Campbell managed to keep track of the huge pile of files on her desk.

"How's your math class doing, Claire?" Lily adjusted her wire-framed glasses and smoothed a hand over her skirt.

"They're settling in well." Claire leaned back into her chair and resisted the urge to slip off her well-worn leather pumps. "Jenny and Amir are a godsend. I give the kids a brief lesson and they help the kids while I mark. When I've marked someone's lesson I go and explain where they went wrong and how to get it right. It's going better than I expected."

"Except for the ones carrying on like Maxine, right?"

"Well, thanks to Miss Harper's 'do-it-yourself' classroom management style, she is spending more time in my class. She still sometimes disturbs her classmates though and doesn't do much math."

"That doesn't surprise me. She absolutely abhors math. But if she's in class, that's a step in the right direction," Lily said.

"She looks tough with her faded, torn jean jacket," Claire said, "but if you look in her eyes, you see sadness, sensitivity, and pain. Have you noticed that she never smiles?"

"No, I hadn't, but now that you mention it…" Lily said. "All her teachers—except French—complain that she has attitude."

"I've read her file and, like Ricky Penworth, she has normal to good intelligence. She was such a little cutie in her grade one photo!"

"Yes, I've seen it too. She becomes more and more morose from grades six to eight…"

"…Until her grade ten photo, which shows her as sullen and angry," Claire concluded.

"Her family isn't anything to brag about. I've asked social services to keep an eye on her case. Her mother is often stoned and I suspect her father beats her—or worse. But she does need two math credits to graduate and after failing general level math twice, we're hoping the third time will be lucky and she'll succeed in basic. Have you called the home?" Lily pushed back from her desk and leaned back in her chair.

"Yes, once. After a great hassle getting through, I got an earful from Maxine's mother about her stupid, lazy, good-for-nothing daughter and abusive drunk of a husband."

"It's no wonder the poor kid acts tough, Claire."

"Before she hung up, Mrs. Young gave me an unedited diatribe of what she thought of teachers and school. Maxine was right: her parents do not care."

Lily was thinking. What was there to say? Sadly lots of parents are too busy or too ignorant to care about their kids—nothing new there.

"But I care." Claire asserted. "There's something about Maxine. She's a fighter. There's spirit in there—other than being a pain in the class—and I want to coax it out for the better. I want to do more than document her activities for Jack. All he does is email me that I should be patient, give individual help, call the mother, get you involved, and offer rewards, all of which I've been doing and none of which involves any effort from him.

"Recently I've been noticing that she does work for Amir. She's on the hunt for a
boyfriend and Amir's not interested, but if he'd be willing to make her a special project… with certain parameters, of course…" She let the sentence hang in the air for a moment.

"Oh, I see," Lily said thoughtfully. "That might work, Claire. Just do make very sure that Amir's okay with it and that Maxine doesn't get out of hand."

"How is she in French?" Claire asked.

"Oh… she's furious at Naomi. They all are."

"I know. Shirley's going to have to do something or there'll be hell to pay. That might be why Maxine stays in my class now."

"Quite possibly. Well, you are making progress," Lily said as she stood up and smiled. "Keep up the good work, Claire. You're making a wonderful difference there.

Tuesday, March 13

Claire asked Amir to make Maxine his special project the next day.

"But Miss, she doesn't want help. She hates math and leaves all the time. She's interested in guys, not math." He blushed deeply and looked over his shoulder as though someone might overhear. With a couple of minutes until the bell, the room was still empty. He lowered his voice and whispered through his teeth, "I don't want her coming on to me!"

Claire felt bad as she watched him fidget. "Please, Amir, she won't work for me or for Jenny. You said it yourself, she likes guys."

"Oh, Miss," he groaned and blushed even more.

"Can we figure out a way that you can be comfortable working with her? For example, start with short intervals, keep her at arm's length, and do not go back until she has some work done..." She smiled, hoping Amir's charitable nature would overcome his fear of becoming Maxine's plaything.

186

He shuffled his feet and took a deep breath. "I guess I can try. She never does any work anyway. I do want to be a teacher."

"Great!" Claire thumped her fist in her hand. "I promise you, I'll keep a sharp eye on her and I'll intervene if she starts to bother you, Amir. Jenny can help me keep watch."

"Okay, Miss, I'll do it."

"I really appreciate that, Amir."

Amir started the 'experiment' as soon as the bell rang. He spent enough time at Maxine's desk to explain the exercise to her, but kept her at a physical distance. He treated her with respect and kindness as he did with all the students. Maxine couldn't remember her parents ever being patient, kind or encouraging to her. Claire smiled as she observed from her wobbly table, noting Maxine's pencil moving and her focus on the page, just to get Amir to come back.

As the class came to an end, Claire waved Maxine over to her desk. For once, the girl looked almost relaxed. "How did it go today?" she asked as she accepted Maxine's notebook.

"Pretty good, I guess," she said, looking around. The last two students had dashed out of the room.

"I'm glad," Claire said, leaning against her wobbly table. "How are your other classes are doing? I heard you're very good in French." Claire wanted to let her know she was interested in her.

Maxine hitched her messenger bag higher on her shoulder and mimicked Claire's posture. Claire knew that teenagers often find it easier to talk when they're not making direct eye contact. "They're okay," she said grudgingly.

"Okay?"

"Yeah. 'Cept maybe French."

Claire nodded. She had figured Maxine would be having problems in Naomi's class. She wasn't a self-directed learner.

"It's shit, ya know." Claire remained silent, leaving Maxine all the room she needed to talk. "That teacher's a useless bitch. She don' do nothing."

"Have you tried asking her for help?" Even as she said it, Claire knew how feeble the suggestion was.

"Ha!" Maxine scoffed. "Like she would help. She only hears the sound of coins hitting her cashbox. Screw it. Screw her. I'm never gonna learn anything in that class."

"Does it help to know that you're not the only one who feels that way?"

"Oh, I know." She straightened her shoulders. "The other kids sit back and watch. They're hoping I'll blow up and chase the bitch away."

Claire's gaze went to her toes and then to the ceiling. "Don't," she finally said, shaking her head. "I know it's hard to hold it together when you're mad. I really do. But, take a breath, Maxine. Count to ten. Blowing a fuse won't help."

Maxine gave a wry smile and turned towards the door. "What will?" she sneered and walked out the door.

***

Later Tuesday, March 13

At the end of the day, Claire stood at the photocopier across the hall from Bertha's office. She needed thirty-four copies of a worksheet for the grade tens, then she was going to meet Anne for a coffee.

"Don't worry so much," Claire heard Bertha say through the door, just as it opened. The principal stood, holding the door open as she tried discreetly to tuck her blouse into the waistband of her wrinkled beige midi. "Have a nice day," she said as Shirley appeared in the doorway and stepped into the hall.

Shirley turned before Bertha could shut the door. "I hope you heard me, Bertha," she stated firmly. Claire stared at the copier as she listened to the forceful tone of her friend's voice. "I need somebody who can actually teach the grade eleven Immersion *Littérature* class. And Naomi needs to teach—and I mean really teach—the *Sociologie* in French. Would you please consider that?"

"Yes, yes, I'll think about it."

"Marthe Moreaux did a fine job in my grade ten *Littérature* class last year," Shirley insisted. The door was beginning to close. "Those kids know her and like her."

"I'll think about it Shirley, and I'll talk to Naomi. Have a nice evening."

The door clicked shut. "You too," Shirley nodded to it.

Claire cleared her throat delicately as the copier finally stopped. "Good meeting?" she asked as Shirley turned and spotted her.

"Ugh," Shirley said with a fake smile. "Great."

Claire quickly grabbed her copies and hooked an arm through Shirley's. "You need a coffee and a chance to unload," she said as she moved them out of the office and down the hall. "I was just on my way to have both with Anne."

"You're right," Shirley said. "That was so nerve wracking!"

"I got that impression."

"I just want this damn Naomi situation dealt with— properly."

"I know. She's becoming a menace to the whole school."

They walked into the English office to find Anne slumped in a chair with her feet propped up on a stool. "I'm as tired as this coffee," she said, motioning to the pot. "Help yourselves."

"What a day!" Claire said. "I need a laugh."

"Hear, hear," Shirley agreed as she dropped herself into a chair.

Anne sat up, suddenly smiling and looking much more like her perky self. "There was a new supply teacher in my class last Friday afternoon. A Miss Sharon Prady. Young, first time here," she said as Shirley and Claire both leaned in. "It was day one. But Jack Penworth must have hit the wrong button on his computer and set her worksheet for day two."

"I love this already," Claire said, smiling. "He's always on my back because he somehow thinks I can't do my job... Go on... "

"The morning went well. But period three is grade twelve literature and period four I have grade ten drama. I left work for both classes. The twelves were to work on their essay about *The Handmaid's Tale*, but because Jack's supply info sheet gave the wrong day, Miss Prady gave the grade ten drama exercises to the grade twelves and the grade twelve essay to the grade tens."

Claire and Shirley exchanged smiles. "Uh oh ..."

"The twelves didn't mind a bit."

"I can believe that," Claire laughed. "Miss Prady probably isn't familiar with the course codes."

"They assumed I was giving them a break from the drudgery of essay writing."

Claire nodded. "It's plausible. And the tens?"

"They hadn't read *The Handmaid's Tale*. They told her, but Miss Prady didn't believe them. You know how 'tactful' and 'polite' they can be with supply teachers," she said, rolling her blue eyes. "How often do kids use not having the book as an excuse? How often do they lie? You can't blame Miss Prady." She shrugged and decided not to finish the sludge in the bottom of her cup.

"But for once they weren't lying. They really couldn't do it because it was grade twelve work."

"I'm sure they refused boisterously," Shirley offered.

"Sure did, and the louder they got, the more Miss Prady insisted they do it."

"Oh dear!" Claire giggled.

"Then they insisted that she call the office, and get someone she would believe to explain that there'd been a mistake."

"But she wouldn't call the office, I bet."

"Nope, Miss Prady stood her ground," Anne said, pulling a face and wagging her finger.

"Which *can* be the right thing to do," Shirley replied. They all knew students considered it was open season on supply teachers.

"Totally," Anne agreed. "She told them to start reading the book, but they didn't have it. She found some old copies, distributed them and told them again to start reading and use the dictionaries if they didn't understand.

The kids told me it was Ricky Penworth who threw the first book out the window. The others followed suit and they didn't stop with the *Handmaid's Tale*. Brian McLean downstairs looked out his window and it was raining books!"

"You're kidding …"

"Nope! He said at first he couldn't believe his eyes. Then he heard the stomping of feet and the laughter and swearing upstairs and knew the kids were running amok in my room.

"Brian hailed Martin Parker and together they bounded up the stairs and got there just as Dwayne Dufresne was mooning Miss Prady from the top of my desk. The kids were throwing books and shooting spit balls and get this, Martin said that Ricky Penworth was sitting right in the middle of it all, his arms crossed and smiling like an angel."

"On him that's proof of guilt, Anne," Claire said, laughing heartily.

"Ricky? An angel?" Shirley shook her head and began to laugh so hard tears started dribbling down her cheeks.

"Martin yanked Dwayne off the desk and dragged him to the office. By the time they got there, he had spilled the beans. Ricky had started the whole thing and egged them on. He named some others, too. Most of the class got into it—even the kids who are usually well-behaved."

"What happened to the teacher… what was her name?"

"Miss Prady. Brian stayed with her until Lily Campbell could come up to console her. Kristen was meeting with the police canine unit in her office. Miss Prady was shaking. It wasn't her fault. Jack got the day wrong. Brian finished the classes. The poor girl was a wreck."

"The good stuff always happens when you're away, doesn't it?" Claire said, wiping her own eyes. "Oh, I needed that."

"Me, too," Shirley said, her face relaxing into a contented smile.

"Too bad there won't be any repercussions for Jack. He caused it."

"Well," Anne said, sighing. "March break is three days away. Where are you off to, Claire?"

"Algonquin Park for the week."

"Sounds nice. Camping?" Shirley asked.

"Yep, Matt and I want to check out the facilities for an Ecology Club fieldtrip in May. After that, we'll hike and enjoy ourselves with Boomer."

"Matt doesn't mind?"

"Heck no, he loves it. He got himself a police check so he could volunteer. He enjoys teaching kids about the environment. He inspired Sylvia Woodhouse and Brendan Wong to study water birds and wetlands last semester."

"Sylvia's a wonderful student. Is she going? When do you leave?" Anne asked as she got up to wash her cup in the sink.

"I'm sure she and Brendan will go—on the fieldtrip, I mean—not with us for March Break."

"I'm glad you cleared that up, Claire," Anne snickered, drying her cup.

"Anytime, Anne…" Claire said sarcastically and the two of them playfully crinkled their noses at each other. "We're leaving right after school on Friday. We're mostly packed already. It'll be a long drive but we're going north instead of south so I hope there won't be as much traffic." She was counting down the hours. As the term was progressing, her workload had increased significantly and her time with Matt had been severely limited. She'd had to put him off for days, hoping he'd survive on a text message or a phone call here and there.

"That sounds nice," Shirley said. "We all need the break."

Claire looked at her watch and jumped up. "Oh gosh Boomer… gotta go… the parking lot must be sane by now."

"How about you, Anne?" Shirley asked as they walked down the hall. "Plans for the break?"

"Florida, my friend, sunny Florida."

***

Wednesday, March 14

It was report card day. At Amberton High the preliminary reports were still printed on paper and the teachers distributed them in class. Next year, the staff hoped, the *Parents' Portal* would be up and running. On it, parents would be able to see report information—up to the minute class marks, assignments due and attendance—on a day to day basis on the school website if they had a computer.

But the Amberton Board wasn't there yet. As soon as the kids had their reports, they would be up yakking to their friends, comparing marks, analysing teacher comments and nosing for loopholes. It was a cacophony difficult to teach over so Claire waited until the last five minutes of each period to distribute the reports.

She spent her spare marking seventeen assorted late items from her science classes and entering the marks both in her book and in *Gradecalc*. "This one's two weeks late," she muttered, as she searched for the right spot on the spreadsheet. "Why didn't she hand it in on time for the report?" She picked up a sloppy, scrawled lab write-up. "This kid is considered normal. He has no individual learning plan; he hasn't been identified as anything, so he should be able to hand his work in on time. Still, here are two late assignments from him… hmmm… I suppose I should be grateful they're finally here. *Note to self: kiss his butt*." Chin smiled as he heard her from his desk across the room.

Claire didn't remember assigning the next kid's effort. She checked the columns in her marks book. No match. The girl was missing four out of seven pieces of work and had just handed something—anything—in. She checked the identified students list. *Out-to-lunch* didn't qualify as a learning difficulty. The girl's name wasn't there. Claire tried to find a compatible marks column where she could park the mark and entered it. At least it would raise the girl's pathetic percentage a little.

"How did they get this way? Is this the way they want to get through school?" she grumbled out loud. "Why do we go to all this trouble when they themselves are so blasé about their education?"

"Hang in there, Claire. March break's almost here." Chin Ho took a stack of reports off his own desk and started for the door. "Thank God."

"I heard that," she said as she entered the last mark, then grabbed her stuff for the math class and headed for the Hickenman room. She'd be glad to get away from that dump for a week.

As she came around the corner, Jenny and Amir were standing at the door. They were beaming. "Hello, guys," she said as they stepped aside so she could open the door. "What's up?"

"Miss, can we set up a notebook with a page for each student?" Jenny blurted.

"We want to stick stars in it to encourage the kids to compete with themselves, you know, not with each other, 'cause that wouldn't be fair." Amir smiled brightly. Proud of his success with Maxine, he wanted to do more.

"What do you think, Miss H.?" Jenny bounced a little on her toes.

"Sounds like a good idea." Claire was pleased that they were thinking about their leadership assignment outside of class.

"We thought Thursdays—because that's our last day of the week with them. The winners could have a special treat."

"That depends on what the treat is," Claire cautioned. "No junk food, remember."

Amir and Jenny looked at each other and shrugged their shoulders. "How about permission to listen to music the following week?" Jenny asked.

"They already do that *without* permission," Claire replied.

Jenny and Amir smirked at each other and shrugged. "Get out of class early on Thursday?"

"How early?

"Five minutes?"

"Hmmm. That might be workable. And they'd sure like that." In fact, Claire thought she'd probably like it herself.

"Can we do that then?" Their eyes were lighting up again.

"I have to ask Miss Stack, so don't get your hopes up, but it's a great idea. I like it. We'll figure something out. Let's go in."

"How about a ten-minute break in the cafeteria?"

"Mid-period or at the end? It's another good one, but keep thinking. Make a list of possibilities without sex, sugar, drugs, or other stimulants and get back to me tomorrow."

"Ah, do you have to ask Miss Stack?" their eyes were pleading. "Couldn't you talk to Mr. Abbasi? He's head of the Math department and easier to find." They meant 'more predictable' but didn't say it.

"Sorry guys, Miss Stack is responsible for the school. She has to know—especially if we do it *every* Thursday."

Claire put the workbooks on top of a pile of stuff on the wobbly little table and they all slid to the floor in a cloud of dust. The disgusting mug with the mouldy coffee was still on Chester's desk. It had grown so much bigger she was considering taking it to the biology lab for analysis. How could Chester keep his room so messy? So filthy? No wonder Fey

Yen Tang left Amberton. Fey Yen was allergic to mould and in this rubbish heap of a classroom Chester was cultivating the stuff. Jenny and Amir picked up the notebooks and put them on the desks. Students were dribbling in.

Joel Atkins came in. He found his workbook and pencil and got to work.

"How's it going, Joel?" Claire asked.

"Doin' okay, Miss." He wasn't a talker, but he was polite.

"Good. Ask me if you need anything, okay?"

"Yes, Miss."

One by one Paula, Whitney, Cory, and Jason got their workbooks, Claire marked them present and they left for the learning resource room. Timmy was asleep at his desk. Cory woke him up and he shuffled after them.

Amir was helping Deepak Dhali whose hyperactivity was getting the better of him again. Deepak, after several attempts, agreed to get ready for math and Amir promised to return to help, when even the hearing impaired Britney Anderson had jumped as Jimmy Church arrived.

Jimmy liked to enter with flair and in his mind, flair meant noise. He did whatever it took to be noticed. He jumped into the room with both feet and the vibration in the floor knocked a pile of books off a precarious shelf by the door. "Ta daah!" Jimmy didn't even notice. Jenny restacked them. Claire looked at Joel, who was startled, but had learned to expect loud noises during the first few minutes of class.

Jimmy got Deepak back out of his chair and they were now sparring by the filing cabinets. Claire didn't like the rowdiness because others did want to learn and some, like Joel, Leah, Jewell and Britney, were prevailing over difficult physical and learning problems to do so. But Deepak and Jimmy were not prevailing over their A.D.H.D. and they had moved right in Joel's face. Joel began packing up his books to leave. Claire nodded to him to let him know she understood. It infuriated her that Joel, the hard worker, had to go elsewhere while the disrupting kids got to stay.

As for Maxine, Amir's tutoring was working out well. Amir had been spending five-minute intervals with her and she found that after a few days, having focussed on it, she was starting to understand the math. Once Maxine was working, Amir passed by her desk to encourage her. She thrived on the attention, the kindness, the encouragement, the praise, the improved marks—and Amir. Claire stopped emailing Jack Penworth with daily reports. Jack didn't notice.

*** *

After school at the dog park Gene was telling Claire that he was getting worn out with the technology use in his grade ten Science class.

"I want to do something about it. There must be a provisional policy from the ministry or something." Gene said as he flung the ball for P.C.

"I saw something, somewhere: first offence, the cellphone or game can be confiscated by the teacher, to be returned at the end of the period. Second offence, the student takes the item to the office vault, returns to class and retrieves it at the end of the day. Third offence, the parents have to come and get the cellphone from the V.P. Unfortunately, nobody except Kristen Jaworski and about two and a half teachers would follow it," Claire said. "And Jack won't support it."

"You can always tell when kids are looking at their cellphones." He turned to look at Claire. "Today, I counted six kids absorbed by tech games or giggling at nudes on their knees." He chuckled. "I put Tariq Tareem on the spot. As soon as I walked in his direction, I could tell that he was pocketing his cellphone. It was a no win for me. I had to teach the lesson, so I kept taking up the homework questions."

"And Tariq resumed his game or admiring whatever Internet porn he may have been looking at as soon as your back was turned, right?" Claire said, as she threw the ball for Boomer for the umpteenth time.

"Of course, but I didn't think he should get away with it either. So when I got back to the front of the room, I asked him to answer question five.

"Tariq looked stunned, trying to see what page was open in his neighbour's textbook. 'Sure, sir, just a minute, sir… What page are we on, sir?' I told him the page. Tariq clumsily flipped through his book. 'What question, sir?'

"Number five, Tariq. He read the question, thought for a few seconds, then said, 'Dunno, sir,' closed his text and his eyes went back to his lap."

"It happens all the time, Gene."

"I know, but it shouldn't. They are using the technology for all the wrong reasons. I turned to another student and she answered immediately."

"I bet she wasn't playing games," Claire said.

"I didn't want to waste the class' time again by asking another techie, Claire. There were at least six others huddled together giggling, probably looking at someone's girlfriend's nude body shot. At the end, I had just finished handing out the reports, when I managed to nab Tariq on his way out. I asked him how many times I had told him not to play videogames while I'm teaching.

"'I wasn't playing a videogame. I was looking for my pencil." Gene mimicked the boy's slack jawed intonation and Claire chuckled. "'Tariq?' I said."

"'I wasn't doing anything, sir.'

"'Were you texting? Let me see your cellphone.'

"'No, sir, you can't have my cellphone.' He squirmed away from me. And, not wanting to quarrel with a lying teenager, I asked to see his answers for the questions I had assigned yesterday.

"He replied, 'No, sir. I wasn't doing anything, sir. Besides lots of other kids were playing games. It's multitasking. It's a good thing. Gerry, Phil, Jessie, and Simon were all playing. Why didn't you center them out?'

"Because," I said "they would have wasted precious time just like you did, and we have a course to cover, Tariq, and there have been studies proving that multi-tasking befuddles the mind."

"There's not much point in making a fuss over Tariq Tareem playing games on his cellphone. He's in Jack's half of the alphabet," Claire said. "You'll never prove anything to Jack's satisfaction. Ricky constantly plays with a handheld. Jack will repeat his mantra that the policy is under review and that if your classes were more interesting, perhaps the kids would listen to you, yadda, yadda, yadda."

Gene flung P.C.'s ball with a vengeance. "In a class of thirty, would everyone always be interested in the lesson?" Gene asked through his teeth. "And how can anybody interest a kid in fundamental science knowledge when he can push a button and make his own imaginary world in *World of War Craft* on a tablet? How can any teacher compete with a Steven Spielberg or a James Cameron film? Even constant use of a Smart Board will eventually bore them as everything, from stone tablets to Internet PowerPoint presentations, has done over the ages."

Claire understood only too well what he was saying. She had a question of her own: Why were teachers and admin not working as a team?

***

Friday, March 16

As soon as school was out, Claire cleared off her lab tables and her science office desk for the cleaning staff. She was anxious to get home, but the cleaning staff had to clean up after 879 teenagers and get rid of the rodents in the walls behind the lockers during break. Claire checked the contents of the student cupboards and threw out the garbage. She shook her head at the stupid, tactless, soap operatic notes the kids left behind and threw them out. Finally, she reorganized her briefcase and jotted down a brief lesson plan for each class for the first day back. In the basic math section she added a star to a reminder to tell Jenny and Amir that their idea of letting kids out five minutes early on Thursdays for excellent work had been approved by Bertha. They would be pleased.

The inadequate parking lot of the old 1930's school was a chaotic confusion for the first fifteen to twenty minutes at the

205

end of any school day. On the day before a holiday, the kids were so adrenalized that they paid even less attention to traffic. Claire was taking no chances. As she watched the traffic from her lab window, she noticed how many silver cars there were. She thought of Paul Fraser and of Tyler. The police still hadn't made an arrest in Paul's case. Even the kids were talking about it. They wanted their teacher back and the culprit punished.

As Claire looked forward to Algonquin, she made a mental note to visit Paul again when they got home.

Chapter 12

In and After Algonquin Park

March 16-25

Claire couldn't wait to hit the road. It didn't matter that the sky was grey and it was blustery and the temperature was minus three degrees Celsius and dropping as they drove first east, then north. They left after work on the Friday, overnighted in a trailer park and arrived at Algonquin Park the next day.

Their hook-up at the Mew Lake campground was within easy walking distance from Rock Lake, where they would camp with the students in May. Matt agreed that it was a great location.

They spent evenings barbecuing, then sitting outside the R.V. wrapped in blankets on their chaise lounges and looking for wildlife. Seeing none they stared at the stars and hoped for a display of the aurora borealis. It was too early for bugs. Claire was mesmerized. "The stars are amazing."

"There's no light pollution in the park, that's why we can see so many," Matt said. "How many shooting stars have you seen?"

"One, I think."

"I've seen three and look, there's another. See it, Claire?"

"Oh, I missed it. But isn't it breathtaking? The Eco Club kids are going to love this," sighed Claire as she snuggled up as close as Boomer, the blanket, and the camp chair would allow.

They wasted no time making the arrangements for the fieldtrip. Claire got enough information and a contact person for the handouts she wanted to make.

That out of the way, they spent a sunny, exhilarating yet restful week around Mew Lake and Rock Lake, as Mother Nature got ready for a new spring. They wanted to hike Booth's Rock Trail to a lookout over Rock and White lakes, but it was steep and closed until May, so they promised themselves they would do it in May. They hiked or snow-shoed every day.

With the chaos of their daily lives replaced by northern silence, Claire and Matt relaxed and enjoyed each other. They felt like a family, not just two people who dated, with their gangly 'child' racing on the snowy trails as far as the leash would allow. Boomer loped over tree roots, rocks, and fallen trees, through deep snow and occasional muddy patches. Claire and Matt negotiated the tricky parts of the trails and glowed in the trust that blossomed on the trails and the warmth they felt in their sleeping bag at night. Claire took lots of pictures. She hoped to enthuse the Eco Club members about the trip with a PowerPoint presentation.

Early the last morning, they reluctantly broke camp. It was Saturday. March break was over. Back to Amberton and work.

***

Back at 684 River Road, they transferred Boomer, his crate and their stuff into the house. They lingered in a prolonged embrace. Neither wanted the vacation to be over. "I love you, Matt."

"I love you too, Claire."

They smooched passionately before Claire pulled away. "I'm afraid this is good night."

"Aw, really?" he pouted, his handsome hazel eyes begging to stay.

Claire sighed and kissed him on the cheek. "It's been wonderful."

"I enjoyed it too," Matt said as he walked to the door.

"Safe trip home, Matt."

As his car pulled away, Claire suddenly found herself stifled by her work routine again: reviewing lesson plans, making sure everything she needed was ready to be copied for her classes. Still, she was dreaming about how her relationship with Matt would develop...marriage or...? He had given her a dog and he said he loved her. They'd known each other for years. She had fantasized about Matt asking her to marry him and of course she would say 'yes,' in spite of their issues about work. She'd quit teaching and find something that didn't consume her evenings and weekends all year. She wanted him even if he'd be away a lot.

Buzzing from the wonderful week with Matt, she worked until midnight. Then she let a reluctant Boomer out for a last pee. He was tired and glad to be home.

***

Monday, March 26

Monday after work, Matt came by. He was to leave for Peru the next day. They walked Boomer to the park for a much-needed run. "Looks like he's back to normal," Matt said as the retriever surged off his leash and tore around.

"I wish it were that easy for us."

Claire stopped to watch Boomer play. She stifled a yawn. "I'd like to travel more with you, spend more time with you," she said. Matt put his arm around her. She grabbed his hand with hers and gave it a loving squeeze. For a moment, as he gazed into her eyes, Claire thought he might pop the question. Her breath caught in her throat. Could this be it?

But just as Matt opened his mouth, Boomer and P.C. came barrelling over.

"Hey, boys," Matt said as he broke away from Claire and patted the dogs. He looked up in time to see Gene approaching. "Of course," he muttered under his breath before plastering on a forced smile.

"Claire, Matt, how was your holiday?" Gene asked jovially.

"Fine, Gene. Nice to see you again," Matt said as they shook hands.

Claire felt let down but quickly hid her disappointment. "Our holiday was great," she managed to say cheerfully. "How was yours?"

"I spent the break setting up a couple of simple experiments for the basic learners."

"Dedicated, aren't you?" Matt noted, a little too quickly.

"He's a terrific teacher," Claire agreed with an easy chuckle.

"Me? Nah," Gene said, smiling awkwardly at his feet. "I'm just trying to make my job easier."

Gene's modesty made Matt's jaw clench.

Gene must have noticed. "Claire and I run into each other in the dog park once in a while and talk shop. I hope you don't mind, Matt."

"Not at all, Gene," he lied. Deep inside it was eating away more and more at Matt that Claire had so much in common with Gene, even though he knew it could be totally innocent—for now. He worried that Gene was another good-looking guy Claire could plan lessons with. Like Tyler, Gene was there with her every day of the week, while Matt was stuck traveling.

"Boomer's getting cold, Claire," Matt broke into their conversation. "We'd better get him home."

Claire blinked at him. "Already?"

"I've got that flight tomorrow and what are the chances you don't have prep-work?" he tugged at her arm, hoping she wouldn't detect his sarcasm.

"Oh, all right," she agreed hesitantly. "See you tomorrow, Gene."

"You bet," Gene said. He called P.C. to his side and waved.

The 'see you tomorrow' and the wave ate at Matt. He shook his head and swallowed his feelings of insecurity. Beside him, Claire, so certain he had been about to propose, was suppressing her own disappointment.

"When's Boomer's obedience class?" Matt asked, trying to make conversation after they had walked most of the way home in silence.

"Wednesday nights, for six weeks."

"I wish I could go."

"Really?" Claire said hopefully. "How long will you be in Peru?" After that wonderful week in Algonquin, she was going to miss him.

"The plan is for three weeks."

It might as well be three years, as far as Claire was concerned. "And then?"

"Then I'm here for six days and I return to Mexico for a week."

"Would you come to the obedience class if you're here on a Wednesday?"

"Of course. I really want to be there if I can."

"Okay." Claire heard it, but after the 'if I can' she was less convinced.

"I'll try," he reassured her. "I promise. Mexico's the last trip for a couple of months. I'll be here for the Algonquin field trip in May and for at least one of the club meetings. I want to meet the members before we go. Will you text me about Boomer's classes and how he does?"

"Sure," Claire said. She had already calculated that he could only be at the two last obedience classes. She hoped nothing would 'come up.'

"Can I come in?" asked Matt.

"Sure. But just for a minute, Matt. I have a lot to do. First day back and all that," she smiled.

Inside, Matt took a stance, looked at his feet, then at Claire. "Why can't we have more times like Algonquin, Claire?" he sounded hurt. After seeing Gene again he wasn't handling his insecurity very well. His mood had gone from easy to edgy.

Claire was trying to understand. How was it that he was the one with the hurt feelings? She was the one without a ring.

"I need you and I love you, but when school is on it feels like I don't exist."

Claire exhaled loudly. *Here we go again*, she thought.

"I'm even second in line to Boomer now. And you're doing more and more volunteer work at the school: water polo, the eco club, the Science fair, the grad committee, that teacher in the hospital." He rattled off the list. "I thought at least Boomer would be a project we'd work on together, but you're doing it all. Hell, Gene sees you more than I do."

"Well, stick around and we can do it together!" Claire shot back. Heat flashed in her eyes. A man who was not in love would have picked up on it.

Matt blew out a frustrated sigh and examined his feet again, playing for time. He slowly lifted his head to look at her. "I resent the time you give to Boomer and to your school."

The words struck Claire like a lightning bolt. "You gave me the damn dog!" she yelled.

"Yeah, well…"

"It's always the same fight, isn't it?" she went right up him. "You resent my dedication to the students. Is that worth resentment? I'll tell you what I resent. I resent all the forces out to get me to work less, while the ministry and the board promise parents I'll do more and more to repair all the damage they've done to their neglected, spoiled, uncontrollable, untrained brats, while they tie my hands and provide no discipline." She turned and stormed into the living room. Matt followed, but kept a good distance. "I work hard. I try to remain professional, but the administration overrules me if parents cause even the tiniest fuss."

"Yeah, shit happens, Claire. Get over it. You either love teaching or you hate it. It can't be both. They're not your kids," Matt retorted.

To Claire, that was insensitive. Matt wasn't a teacher. He didn't see it. She glared at him. "While I teach them they *are* my kids. If *my* students arrive in university or college or at a job with high marks and they can't do the work, I look bad and the system looks bad. I want *my* students' marks to tell the truth."

"Claire, there's no formal mechanism for universities to evaluate high school teachers." Matt closed his eyes and shook his head in frustration.

"No, but there's the grapevine and there's ratemydamnteacher.com," Claire shot back. "Maclean's does a yearly article on schools. There's the Fraser Institute. Newspaper reporters write articles with various agendas. And there is integrity."

"That 'rat on the teacher' website is a joke, Claire. It's not maintained. There are dead and retired teachers on it and everybody knows lots of comments come from kids who hate the teacher they're rating," Matt shot back. "Good grief, Claire, do you believe in ghosts, too?"

"Okay, Matt… I get the message… We're made for each other, but our lives are not," Claire said through trembling jaw. She turned her back. "Maybe we shouldn't see each other anymore." She regretted saying it as soon as the words left her lips. But her pride kept her from softening the blow. Behind her eyes the tears were welling up.

"You got it." He slammed the door without even a look back. She didn't watch him get into his car and drive away. She fell into her den recliner, exhausted and emotionally drained.

In the little den, her eyes kept brimming with tears. She hugged Boomer. He wagged his tail and licked her tears. What had just happened? Did she just break up with Matt? Was she so unreasonable to care about her students? Was education really what lots of people seemed to think it was: babysitting? Was it vacuuming kids off the streets, like Naomi Harper was doing? Or was it all of those things? Matt would be away most of the time anyway—even if they were married. Hadn't she told him in January that she was seriously going to look for another career after this semester for all those reasons? for him? She was willing to do that so they could be together. But she could not afford to resign until she knew what she would do and while teaching, she didn't have time to find a new job. How could this have happened after their wonderful week in Algonquin?

Chapter 13

<u>Friends who Care and Obedience Class</u>

Tuesday, March 27

It was four p.m., after a rotten Tuesday. Claire hadn't made it to the dog park and some turkey was leaning on the doorbell. Claire wanted, more than anything, to ignore it and continue watching the chick-flick she had started as soon as she had arrived home from school. Ding dong, ding dong. "Fine, I'm coming!" she muttered as she heaved herself off the sofa and wrapped her fleece robe over her pyjamas.

Hoping for a fleeting moment that it was Matt, she checked the peephole and took a deep breath before opening the door for Shirley and Anne.

"Oh dear," Shirley said wrapping a drab and teary Claire in a tight hug, nearly squishing the box of chocolates she was holding.

"We know you didn't ask for company," Anne said as she pushed Shirley out of the way and went in for her own embrace, "but we're here. We're not stupid. We saw you today. We can tell what happened. You shouldn't be alone right now."

"Oh, guys, I'll be okay…" Claire sniffled into a tissue. She was grateful to have such friends. "Just for a second, I thought it was Matt at the door." She had her cell phone in her pocket.

"Oh dear, we didn't think of that!" Anne's hand covered her mouth.

"No word from 'himself' then, I take it," Shirley said as they moved into the living room.

"No. Nothing." Claire focused on controlling her breathing. She didn't want to hyperventilate or start crying. She had been up half Monday night watching tearjerkers. A lot of willpower, coffee and makeup had helped her keep it together at school, but evidently not enough to hide it from close friends. She told her students she was coming down with a cold. She kept wishing her cellphone would vibrate. Just a text from him, that's all she needed.

"Asshole," Anne said firmly.

"Not really." Claire was shaking her head. "I'm not ready to trade him in. Not yet. It's always the job thing. *He* wants to spend more time with me. *I* dumped *him*. But I didn't mean to… we had a disagreement… it just came out…" she blubbered.

"Right then, pour that wine, Anne," Shirley said, pointing to the bottle of Cabernet Sauvignon Anne had brought, "We'll distract you for a while. It's the least we can do. You curl up on the sofa and we'll pour. Where are the glasses?"

"Cupboard over the sink."

"Was any part of today salvageable?" Anne called from the kitchen. It had been the second day back after March break.

"Not really. I got my instructions for Parent Teacher Interview night. Good times ahead," she said sarcastically.

"None of us look forward to Jack's ideas." Shirley opened the box of chocolates and centred them on the coffee table while Anne brought the wine.

"I could use a laugh, girls," Claire said.

"Well, I got the skinny on the Miss Prady incident," Anne bubbled as she sat on the floor and started checking out the chocolates. Claire perked up a bit.

"When Penworth screwed up the schedule for your substitute teacher?"

"Yep. So, get this. Apparently, Martin Parker hauled the mooning Dwayne Dufresne off my desk, made him pull up his pants and took him to the office. Jack suspended him for 'an act disrespectful of the tone of the school' and kept him in the office for his parents to pick up. Then Martin went back. Brian MacLean was sorting out the class and Miss Prady was cowering in a corner."

"Poor woman," Shirley said sympathetically.

"Luckily she was coherent enough to finger the three kids who had dropped most of the books out the window—including Ricky Penworth—so Martin took them down too. The *two* resulting suspension letters accused them of 'destruction of school property.'"

"You mean Ricky didn't get suspended?" Claire and Shirley looked at each other, their eyes wide.

"Nope. He wasn't doing it the moment Martin and Brian came in so his father said it was just hearsay and there was no concrete proof. Jeff Jenkins, Hervir Malek, and Nicole Gligoric were the rudest with Miss Prady and they got 'malicious opposition to authority' letters. But get this: in the office, Dwayne Dufresne was scared out of his wits when the sniffer dog whose police partner had been meeting with Kristen came out and went straight for his pocket, where they found a bagful of marijuana and a couple of ecstasy pills. The police officer took him down to the station."

"That explains why he missed my class for the rest of that week," Claire said, "and probably the day he said he had to 'meet his mother.'"

"The grade tens are a bad lot this year," Shirley observed, shaking her head.

"Well, there are always good kids," Claire said. "But for some reason the majority in this group don't want to work, are inclined to lie and seem to be proud to go through life doing only whatever the hell they want."

As Anne drained the last of the wine from her glass, she asked, "Speaking of suspensions, did your issue with Maziyar ever get resolved, Shirley?"

"After a couple of visits with Kristen he's behaving a lot better in my class," Claire volunteered.

"For me the answers are: *no* and *maybe*," Shirley replied with a quirky grin.

"Oh? How's that?" Claire asked as she took another chocolate.

"His mother stopped emailing me." Shirley rolled her eyes. "Maziyar was lying to her and she wouldn't believe me when I told her what really happened." Shirley sighed. She was tired thinking about it. "He had treated all his teachers abominably, so Kristen kept up the correspondence with his mother. As for me, after two weeks I got so fed up with the whole running back and forth and up and down to the office about this anal aperture, that I didn't care anymore, and on an impulse I suggested to Maziyar that we call a truce. To my surprise, he agreed. I was curious as hell, but prying doesn't always help, so I didn't." Anne and Claire were all attention. "He promised not to talk so much in class and I agreed not to ask him any questions." She took a sip of her wine. "I did tell him he couldn't play his game apps or text in class. I won. He had to cave."

Shirley stopped and a smile slowly spread across her face. "Later Kristen told me that Martin Parker and Bandhura Abbasi were about to kick him out too. Maziyar was afraid that if there was one more incident Miss Stack would ricochet him to Elgin Falls, and that would make life with his father a lot worse. Good old Dad would be furious to have to drive Maziyar thirty kilometres to school every day."

"Oh, right. Lily mentioned that Maziyar doesn't like being with his father," Claire said. "His father doesn't like him either. He reminds him of his ex and he hates her. So he ignores Maziyar."

"Maybe his mother stopped believing his stories, too," Shirley said. "In any case, it worked to my advantage."

"So it's all over?" Anne asked eyeing the remaining chocolates. Claire gently nudged the box towards her. She smiled and took one.

"Time will tell. So far so good. It's only been two weeks since our pact and one of them was March Break."

"I bet he's listening to your lessons and finding he's learning a few things."

"Or he's listening to his mother."

"Whatever works," Shirley said.

"You're a good teacher, Shirley. Your oral verb drills will help him understand everything he reads in French," Anne said. "My French teacher used to tell us that verbs were seventy-five per cent of the language. I've never forgotten that. They're important in English, too."

Claire stretched her arms high and tried to stifle a yawn. "Hey, know what, girls? Thanks for coming out and distracting me, but I'm ready to drop, and..."

"Are you sure you'll be okay?" Anne asked, her eyes like saucers as she looked at Claire.

"Come on, Anne," Shirley interjected. "I think we've done all we can here for now. Claire needs alone time to heal."

Anne looked at Claire for confirmation. "Yes, yes, go. I'm fine," Claire said, still fidgeting with her cellphone in her pocket. "Now, get out of here. It's a school night. I've got stuff to do. Thanks for caring."

"Yes, Mom," Shirley and Anne said as they took turns wrapping their friend in hugs.

***

Wednesday, March 28

On her way to school the next morning, Claire was headachy. She had worried about Matt, about the teacher interview night tomorrow, about Matt, about her math kids, and again about Matt all night long. To force her mind off Matt, she thought about school. She chose a topic to ponder. Was Timmy Vanderhout on drugs, did he have narcolepsy, or did he simply stay up late playing videogames every night? Brian McLean had told her he slept in the L.R.T room every day and he had asked her to keep him in the Hickenman room until Timmy could stay awake and work. When he came in he always sat down, put his head on the table and catnapped. She decided to email his mom and express her concerns. Once she had sent it, her mind returned to the blow-up with Matt. Then, remembering a study that during adolescence, young people needed more sleep in the morning, Claire wondered why school now started at eight instead of nine in the morning.

It was all piling up for her: the kids, the parents, the system. Could she really choose this over love? She would soon be able to write her resignation letter. Oh, the things she wanted to say in that letter… but what would be the point without Matt?

***

At the end of the day, she remembered a boy in her grade eleven class and popped into Martin Parker's room. Martin was the head of history and his room was the antithesis of the Hickenman room. Everything was neat, clean, organized on solid horizontal shelves, and worked.

"Martin, you teach Serge Leclerc, don't you?" Claire asked.

Martin looked up from the paperwork on his desk and nodded. "Yes, he's in my home room class."

"What's up with him? He's often late and his work is sliding. He's moody and explosive—like when his parents were divorcing last year. He was so much happier first semester. But now, if I ask him anything, he just mumbles a sulky 'fine, yeah, whatever,' or 'no, Miss' and walks off."

"Yeah, I know Serge. I fish with his father. We go back quite a while." Martin said, lifting his face from his work. "Serge's girlfriend, that snippy little Amy O'Leary, wants to break up with him, but she's still using him for pocket money and entertainment when it's convenient. She claims…" and he stressed the word with contempt "…she told Lily Campbell that she is letting Serge down gently, but her strategy is driving him nuts. Serge is more infatuated than ever, but he'd be well rid of her. His father wants him to dump her too, so Serge has it coming from both sides and he's rebelling. Ask Lily Campbell. She knows all about it."

"That explains a few things, thanks." Claire went to Guidance.

***

Lily told Claire that the relationship with his girlfriend was grinding down Serge's sensitive adolescent sense of manhood. He felt used. He was hurt and confused and the whole thing reminded him of his parents' acrimonious divorce.

"Poor kid," Claire said. She could commiserate. Her own heart and ego were bruised, but she had done it herself. Serge hadn't.

Before going home, she checked her voicemail. There was a message from Timmy Vanderhout's mom. She would make a doctor's appointment for him. No more information. No request for an interview. No hint of a follow up. Timmy was on his own and so was she.

On her way home, Claire was back to wondering about Matt. She told herself to get on with her work. Moping wasn't going to solve anything. She had the obedience class with Boomer tonight. Why was it that when Matt was with her she thought so much about work and when she was at work, all she could think about was Matt?

***

After a quick dinner, Claire put Boomer and his crate in the back of her hybrid and drove the familiar route past Matt's apartment in Elgin Falls to the training facility. She didn't look at it. She drove on. Claire arrived at the Deen Obedience School for Dogs early. She wandered around and a green shirted trainer named Jane pointed her to the puppy room. Inside the door there was an area squared off by a blue and yellow picket fence to keep the puppies in when the door was open. There were benches along the perimeter. At one end there was a low table for a demo dog.

Before long, more people and puppies arrived and Jane was busily taking names and breeds. Claire had no idea what was going to happen and held Boomer close to her. She gently rubbed his head, trying to keep them both calm.

"So we meet at another school."

Claire's head snapped up and she immediately smiled. "Gene!" Boomer leapt forward to jump at P.C. who was standing at her friend's side. "What are you guys doing here?"

"We occasionally help out. P.C. is the demo dog this week." He said: "Sit" and instantly P.C. was sitting properly beside him, while Boomer was trying desperately to get Gene to pet him.

"I have no clue what I'm doing," Claire said, glancing around. "Some of the people have bags with treats on their belts. Why didn't I think of that?"

"Not to worry. Here, I've got some extras. Oh, gotta go." Gene checked his watch as Claire put the treats in her pocket. "Things start *on time* around here," Gene said, looking back with a grin. P.C. was at his side. Claire got hold of Boomer and tried to settle him again.

Gene introduced himself and Prince Charles to the class, asked for all the puppies' names and started his introductory spiel. "Like children, given no direction, puppies will make their own rules. Left on their own, dogs live in packs, and as descendants of wolves, they will band together and do what they like. To live in harmony with man, they need socialization and training. If you give them clear signals, they will happily do anything you ask. They're wired to please the leader of the pack—and that's what we'll teach you to be."

Gene looked relaxed and confident as he hit his stride with the class. A true teacher, through and through, Claire thought.

As Gene made his way around the room he gave her a little wink of acknowledgement. "The best learning takes place when they're young, when it's easiest to teach them good behaviour. You'll learn not to reward the wrong thing, such as growling, nipping, pulling and tugging on the leash. The leash is their classroom: when they are on the leash—that is, in the classroom—they should be paying attention to you."

Claire wondered if Gene used his school experience here or his dog training experience at school.

Gene continued: "Dogs want a leader, and we will show you how to be that leader. They may like their siblings in the litter, or their friends in the pack, but if you're a good leader they'll *worship* you." He nodded to another instructor.

Like clockwork, Elena, a full-figured twenty-something, took over. "Our first lesson is *taking food gently*. They have to learn not to bite the hand that holds the treat. *Gentle mouth* is dog-speak for good manners. This has to be their way of life, so you need to practice it with them every day."

At that Gene took P.C. and showed everyone how to hold the treat with the thumb on the flat of his hand. Then everybody tried the *taking food gently* exercise with their puppy, while Elena, Gene and Dave, the third instructor, circulated through the group. Soon Boomer used a gentle mouth and got a clear *yes*, and the treat. Then he did it correctly three times in rapid succession. He liked the *game* and loved the treats. Dave suggested that Claire not pat him on the head so much. "One treat is enough for doing what is expected. The puppies shouldn't think they're wonderful even when they aren't doing anything." With a smile, Dave added, "Praise is to be earned." Claire thought about Ricky Penworth.

"Is that how you teach your classes, Gene?" Claire teased when he came by to check on her and Boomer.

"There are clear instructions, corrections, repetition, and rewards in my lessons, if that's what you mean," Gene replied with a wink.

The lesson progressed to teaching the puppy to *follow the food*. P.C. walked in a circle, following a treat in Gene's hand, but he didn't get it until he had completed the full circle. "This reinforces the *gentle mouth* lesson nicely," Claire thought, as Gene had P.C. do a figure eight. Then the dog owners took a turn. Boomer did well. Soon he did a figure eight too. Claire was proud. She wished Matt had been there to experience it with her. She swallowed her rising resentment and forced herself to focus.

"Puppies have no privileges; they need to learn to behave first," Elena said when the puppies had settled again.

Claire listened. Elena told them how to get the dog to sit and lie down using the *follow the food* technique, letting them smell the treat and follow it as she moved it up or down so they would sit or lie. Gene demonstrated, and every time P.C. did it right, he got a clear *yes* and an immediate treat. If P.C. didn't use a gentle mouth, Gene pulled the treat back swiftly, then tried again. "Rote repetition is important, because it works," Elena stressed.

Claire loved how the trainers worked as a team. While one led the lesson the others demonstrated or observed. They didn't contradict each other. If necessary, they tactfully corrected the owners and their dogs, explained where they went wrong, and the owner was given a chance to do it again as the trainer watched. Claire thought working with dogs might be something she'd like to try when she resigned from teaching in June—if she and Matt got back together, that is...

Claire liked the class and the people in it. They were controlling the dogs with consistency, clear rules, clear communication, repetition, and instant rewards or kind but firm corrections. The success with Boomer proved to her that it worked. She was ecstatic.

"Great class," she said to Gene as they and their dogs locked step. "Best professional development session I've had in years."

"It was," he agreed. "I'm glad you two could make it."

"Me, too." She smiled easily, as she always did in his company.

"Where's Matt? I thought for sure he'd be here."

"Oh." Claire's face fell. "Matt…"

"Uh-oh. Have I stepped in something?" Gene lifted his foot to inspect the sole of his shoe. He sniffed comically.

"No, no, it's fine," Claire said lightly. "We've had a little contretemps."

"Ah, I've been married long enough to know what that means." He gave her arm a reassuring squeeze. "Are you alright?" he asked.

Claire took a deep breath. "Yeah," she lied.

April

Chapter 14

A Suspension, Interviews and the Eco Club

Thursday, March 29

It was seven forty-five a.m., two days since her break-up with Matt. Claire arrived in the science office in a no-nonsense mood. Her colleagues didn't seem to be in the same hurry she was. They were debating environmentally friendly options to solve the world's over-dependence on oil.

"What's your take on getting away from oil, Claire?" Angus asked through a cheek full of bagel.

"Shampoo every morning, guys," she shot back as she rushed through, grabbing a stack of paperwork from her desk. Claire had her grade ten class with Eric Thomson, the boy with Tourette's, coming up. "Sorry, guys, I've got to copy some notes."

Eric didn't only have Tourette's. He was also a reluctant reader. Every day Claire made up large-print double-spaced copies of the lesson notes for him, so he would know exactly what to expect and could follow along. Often he took her notes and copied them in the cafeteria at lunchtime with Samantha.

She would have made copies for Ricky, but he had bought notes from Artie Binton.

Eric was a good-looking boy, Claire thought. With his dark wavy hair, blue eyes and big grin, it was no wonder Samantha Jensen liked him. The tall fifteen-year-old wore the non-torn version of the current trends in clothes. Samantha, science and math interested him; current fashions did not.

After frantically dashing down the short hallway, she was in the lab. As soon as she had put down her papers, Samantha and Marcie came running in. "Miss Hébert, Miss Hébert, you've got to help him!"

"Slow down, girls. Help who?"

"Eric's been suspended. Miss Stack's going to send him to another school," Samantha blurted. She was twisting a strand of her long blonde hair.

"What? What happened?"

"Mr. Abbasi was away yesterday so we had Mr. Bertch for the first half of our math class," Marcie panted. " I guess some of us were being uncooperative. Eric panicked and had a fit of echolalia and tics and he kept repeating what Mr. Bertch said. We tried to explain that Eric has Tourette's, but Mr. Bertch didn't believe us. He thought Eric was being rude and we were lying and it got worse and worse."

"Oh no…"

"Mr. Bertch threw him out and Eric got upset, swore and slammed the door so hard that the window cracked."

Samantha's cheeks were flushed and her voice kept getting higher.

Claire leaned against her desk and shook her head.

"Can you help him? Can you explain it to Miss Stack? Please?"

"There's no time now, girls, but I'll talk to Miss Stack a soon as I can."

"But, what if Eric had more echolalia in Mr. Penworth's office?" Marcie was really worried and Samantha was fighting the urge to cry.

"Okay, okay, calm down. Now, hmm... I really don't think Miss Stack would send Eric to another school, but I promise I'll talk to her. He may have to pay for the window." Putting on a reassuring smile, she motioned for Samantha and Marcie to take their seats.

Claire knew Eric couldn't help it. But if he echoed whatever he said or blurted out a string of expletives to Jack, she didn't know what might ensue. Jack was so unpredictable.

"Samantha...?" Claire looked from one to the other. "Marcie...? Did something happen to set Eric off?"

"I didn't see anything. I was doing my algebra," Marcie said.

"And you, Samantha?"

"I'm not in his math class, Miss H,"

***

Claire was still thinking about Eric as she taught her grade tens the lesson about cells and named the parts and their functions. Most of the kids tittered a bit when she talked about sperm cells valiantly swimming up a vagina and penetrating the ova, but she just smiled.

"Can we try it with a real vagina, Miss?" Logan couldn't resist asking.

"Just answer the questions on the chapter on your worksheets." Claire shook her head as she walked around helping. Those who had finished could go get a microscope and look at a series of prepared slides, or yank out their own hair or clip a fingernail or a piece of their skin or pick up some dust and look at that. A number of them got quite into it, while others decided that once the work was done, it was time to socialize and giggle.

***

One of Jack's unpopular initiatives was to hold Parent-Teacher Interview Night before instead of after mid-term evaluations. Some of the teachers had ordered pizza for those who couldn't go home. Claire loved pizza. As she passed her colleagues in the staff room, the aroma made her mouth water, but she needed to print reports for the parents, swallow some supper and go for a quick walk with Boomer to reinforce his training. She would be back before four-thirty when the interviews were to start.

Boomer got a short walk. Back in the house, Claire checked her cell. She was relieved to see a text message from Matt suggesting that they grab an evening together tonight to talk. His trip to Peru had been postponed and shortened. Damn. Did it have to be tonight? She desperately wanted to see him but couldn't be home before nine-thirty or ten o'clock and then she'd be wiped. She was truly sorry for what she'd said and even more sorry she couldn't see him and texted that and a brief explanation before she returned to school. She wondered how he would take it. Her work had caused all the trouble and now it was keeping them from patching it up. She decided to resign…again.

"Oh shit," she mumbled as she arrived back at the school and suddenly remembered that she had totally forgotten her promise to Samantha and Marcie about Eric Thompson's suspension and possible transfer to another school.

The interviews were held in the cafeteria. Bertha was already busy. Claire wouldn't have time to talk to her before the interviews started. She would be busy with her own appointments: three from the grade ten applied class, seven from the grade eleven biology class and, as expected, nobody from the basic math class. She could tell from the names that most of the interviews would be with parents who wanted to hear compliments about their kids.

The most significant information of the evening came from her interview with Mr. and Mrs. Oliver, Tori's parents. "Miss Hébert," they had asked, "Could you please let Tori and her friends sit near Aisha again? They know they've all been talking too much and they promise they'll behave, but something's up with Aisha and Tori is so worried about it that she can't sleep. They're not sure what it is, but Tori would not be so stressed if there wasn't anything to it."

Claire knew Aisha was vulnerable because she had been cyber bullied first semester. "I'll let them sit together again, as long as they don't distract the others."

"They promised they wouldn't. And please keep an eye on Aisha. She's such a nice girl. Tori suspects some girls in the class have been making fun of her because of her weight or her marks or both. Aisha's been trying to slim down but the constant teasing makes it difficult."

"Thanks for the heads-up, Mr. and Mrs. Oliver. I'll do my best. But I only see them in class and there's a lot of school day when they're elsewhere."

"We're telling all her teachers, Miss Hébert. We understand. Thank you."

When the Olivers left her table Claire was finished for the evening and she was in a frivolous mood when Jack Penworth ambled by.

"Oh, Jack, have you come to talk about Ricky?" Claire asked sweetly and loud enough for Gene to overhear at the next table.

"Uh…What? Well, I," Jack sputtered.

"You're not on my schedule Jack, but I'd be happy to fit you in. Do sit down," she gestured to Jack.

Claire was still emailing back and forth with Ricky's mom. She suspected neither parent would face a parent-teacher interview. Jack could never admit that his son had any problems and Muriel was ineffective in spite of the hovering mother-hen act. In fact, Muriel was dangerous. After seven weeks, Ricky was failing and no classmate—not even Dwayne, Logan or Maziyar—would partner with him because he was absent half the time, annoying when he was present and unreliable in group-work.

Claire remembered Don Patterson's suspicion and was all but sure who was really doing Ricky's work. His mother always knew exactly what was being covered. All his marks came from homework done correctly, but in class Ricky could not or would not answer any questions, had bought his notes and failed almost every test. All that was missing was what Jack called 'concrete' proof. Still, because of Jack's status in the school, Claire felt she had to keep up the correspondence and do everything she could to help Ricky.

"Oh no, we're fine. We're on top of the situation." Jack said, his plump face flushed with the exertion of walking across the room.

"Are you sure?" Claire arched an eyebrow expressively high.

"Oh yes. Don't you worry. All's well with the Penworths." He grinned pointedly before plodding towards the door.

"Nicely done, Miss Hébert," Gene winked and nodded at Claire and put his hand in front of his face to hide his chuckle as he hosted Tariq Tareem's parents.

As Jack squeezed out between the cafeteria doors, Claire couldn't supress the giggle in her throat any longer. "I can't tell you how good that felt," she said to Gene, as the Tareems left.

"Yeah, but it's sad, too," said Gene. "That poor kid… and we can't help him."

***

At the end of the evening Claire found Bertha by the doorway, hosting a group of parents. When they left she asked, "Bertha, there's a rumour that Eric Thompson is being sent to another school. Is that true?"

"I was considering it," Bertha said. "Angus can be impatient and brusque, but all the same, Eric shouldn't have sworn and been so rude."

"Did you know Eric has Tourette's? He can't help his echolalia, his tics, or swearing every once in a while and Angus wouldn't have known that. Angus doesn't teach Eric."

"Eric was involved in a violent incident at a football game last November and I do have to keep our other students and the tone of the school in mind. But Brian McLean, Martin Parker and Bandhura Abbasi and now you have all reminded me of Eric's condition and the efforts his mother is making to help him, so we'll give him another chance. I won't transfer him anywhere for now."

Claire's shoulders relaxed. "Oh good! Thanks so much, Bertha. He's doing very well in my class."

"I'm glad to hear it." Bertha turned off the lights as they walked out together. Claire looked at her cellphone and cringed. 11:00 pm and she wasn't home yet. The weekend couldn't come soon enough. Heck, Claire thought, June and that resignation letter couldn't come fast enough.

***

Monday, April 2

There was a tentative knock on the door of the science office. Claire looked up from her computer to see a group of nervous girls milling in the doorway.

"Hi girls, what can I do for you?" she asked looking over her monitor. The weekend had gone by all too fast and so far her Monday wasn't off to a great start. There was a storm brewing in the grade eleven class, but she hadn't figured it out yet. She had received a suspension letter for Serge Leclerc. Because of his frustration with his on again off again girlfriend, he had started to skip more and more classes and he had been liberally using the *f-bomb* and a string of other expletives around the school. But he went beyond the pale when he swore at Bertha in front of a crowd of students when she spoke to him about shoving somebody in the hall. Bertha suspended him.

Now there were girls at her door. Aisha Ames' friends, she realized. Tori, Maya Li, Danielle, and Janette had been a source of constant support for Aisha as she recovered from the cruel cyber-bullying she had suffered first semester.

"Miss H.," Tori said, "some nitwits in our class are teasing Aisha again."

"I think they're jealous of her marks," Maya Li offered.

"It's hurting her," Tori added. "She's avoiding us. She's skipping our homework sessions."

Since interview night, Claire had been on the alert, but she wasn't at their homework sessions and she didn't go home with them. Of course she had noticed Farah Marie Zahar and Hannah Jessica May sticking their snooty little noses up at Aisha and her friends, who got good marks simply because they always did their homework. But didn't lots of kids do that? Was that bullying or just ignorant snobbishness? Claire suggested to Farah and Hannah that they would have better marks too if they had a homework group, but they didn't want to, and outside of class they got even nastier with Aisha. Now Claire knew why the Olivers had been so concerned and why Aisha needed her friends around her.

***

As Claire was on her way home that afternoon, she saw a sad pair of running shoe-clad feet sticking out from a doorway on the first floor. A slouchy figure in a jean jacket and skirt peered out and stepped in front of her. It was Maxine.

"Hi, Maxine, are you okay, dear? Why are you still here?"

"Miss H., c'n I ask you a queshun?"

"Sure, Maxine."

"D'you think I'm gonna pass math this time?"

Claire considered it a miracle that she even cared about passing math now. "There's a very good chance you will, if you keep working like you have been."

"Really?" Maxine's face lit up with a smile that recalled her grade one picture. "I'm even startin' ta like it, ya know. I never thought I would, but I been goin' to Mr. Gummersahl's Math Club after school. He's nice. He makes us laugh about it.

242

Amir told me about it. My parents keep tellin' me how dumb I am, but I ain't an' I'm gonna show 'em."

Claire fought to keep her tears down. "You're not dumb, Maxine. You just didn't work before. Now that you're working and you're getting help, we all see how smart you are. Amir told me that, too. And getting help from Mr. Gumbersahl after school was a smart idea. He's a wonderful math teacher. Do you want me to talk to your Mom?"

"Nah, Miss, you already do enough for me, you an' Amir. I wanna do it myself, by showin' her an' Pop the marks, in June, like. I want it to be a su'prise for 'em. They won' believe it 'til they see the marks nohow. Thanks Miss."

"Good luck, Maxine. See you tomorrow." Claire smiled as she watched Maxine walk down the hall, her head high and an unfamiliar spring in her step.

Now she wondered if she wouldn't miss teaching next year.

***

Tuesday, April 3

The semester was getting busier. Evaluation week was coming up and the Eco Club activities were ramping up at school. A core group of eight to ten students and Claire usually ran the activities. Their first meeting had been the week after

March break when they had planned their annual *clean up the neighbourhood* campaign for early May. They also wanted to volunteer at a local conservation area to help with spring clean up and planting. The kids wanted to learn about the conservation area and collect volunteer hours for graduation.

As the meeting came to a close, Claire spoke. "Now, one last point of business: we're going to take the club to Algonquin Park for an extended Victoria Day weekend. Okay?"

"Sweet!"

"Awesome!"

"Algonquin! Wow! I've never been there."

All around her the kids bubbled with excitement. "These will explain the plan," she said as she handed out permission forms and information sheets. "Talk to your parents and see if you can go. We'll need an idea as to how many will be joining the trip by Friday, April twenty-seventh."

"What about Mr. Granger?" Sylvia asked. "Will he be coming?"

Claire paused. Matt had worked with Sylvia last year and inspired her to study wetlands. The members liked Matt and the feeling was mutual.

"That's up to Mr. Granger. I hope he'll come."

"Yeah!" the kids cheered then collected their things and made for the door.

"Yeah," Claire echoed to the empty room. "Yeah."

But they hadn't had a chance to talk yet and that might be why Matt hadn't shown up tonight. Where was he? It had been well over six days now and he hadn't responded to her text on interview night.

***

Tuesday, April 10

The Tuesday after Easter, the first day of midterms, Claire had to call an emergency Eco Club meeting at lunchtime. Because of the Algonquin trip, there were suddenly a lot more members—about thirty-five more—including Maxine Young, who was being sponsored by George Gumbersahl, and Serge Leclerc, who had also paid for Amy O'Leary, but she hadn't come to the meeting.

Claire made more copies of the information sheets and permission forms. It looked like the bus would be more than full if all the students submitted their forms on time. Claire would need at least four extra chaperones, five if Matt didn't come. And that was becoming a possibility. She still hadn't heard from him and could only imagine what he was thinking. Had he gone to Peru after all? Or was it time to accept that they were through as a couple? Matt must be as insecure as she was. She refocused. "Do any of you think your parents might want to chaperone?" Claire called to the bustling crowd of teenagers. A number of hands shot up around the room. "Great, have them get these background checks done through the police department. It takes six weeks," she repeated as she made her way to each volunteer with the necessary forms. "Please get them back to me as quickly as possible."

With a bit of luck, she'd get all the help she needed. Taking a deep breath, she turned to a cool dude tapping on her elbow. "Yes, Serge?" She hadn't seen him so animated for weeks.

"What food should we bring?" he asked. Five of his friends who had also joined the Eco Club leaned in. "Can we bring spaghetti?"

"Food's important, isn't it? Sure, but bring canned sauce and a pot to boil it in. " Claire chuckled as the kids thanked her and left, full of excitement.

"What about camping gear?" another smiling face asked.

"It's all in the handouts," Claire assured them. She spent another forty-five minutes answering questions. The kids were excited and Claire was as excited as the kids, even if Matt didn't show up to take that hike up Booth's Rock Trail to the crest over Rock and White Lakes. But he'd said he would. Where was he?

Chapter 15

<u>The Dissection of the Dissection</u>

Monday, April 16

April tenth to the thirteenth had been midterm evaluation days. Matt still hadn't called. Claire couldn't see him anyway. She had been marking and keying marks into the *Gradecalc* program and printing reports all weekend. She was relieved when it was all done, but disheartened about her love life.

Last Friday, Claire had started the chapter on *Climate Change* with her grade tens. When they had read it and understood it she put on a short video and they could play a trivia game about *Climate Change* on the Internet. This morning, the students put their completed homework in the basket on the demo table as they arrived. Claire was sure they'd all get good marks for their work.

At lunch she had marked the assignments and had just stepped out of the science office when she saw Ricky Penworth in the hall. She dashed back in and grabbed his assignment. "Ricky! Just a minute, Ricky," Claire ran down the hall and tapped him on the backpack. "I need a word with you, young man."

He turned around. "What?" he mumbled. "What?"

She showed him his paper. "What's this?" she asked.

"What?" Ricky sulked as he took his earphones out from under his thick mop of hair.

"This, right here," she said, pointing to a paragraph in a different font in the middle of the answer to question six. "It looks like this is a note from your Mom to someone."

"It's not," Ricky said, on the defensive.

"Sure it is. Look." Claire passed him the page. "Look, it's a complaint about a parking ticket."

Ricky's arms dropped to his side and he sighed heavily. His eyes darted from side to side as he said, "Okay. So it's not mine. Who cares?"

"Not yours?"

"Oh, like it's a secret that I don't do my own homework?"

Claire wondered if there was a note of relief in his voice.

"Ricky, do you ever do your own work?"

"No," he huffed.

"Do you even participate?"

"She says it takes too long so she doesn't let me. I just watch TV or play videogames."

Claire didn't know what to say. Even without Don's comment in February it hadn't taken long for her to suspect that somebody else was doing his homework. He was failing even though his homework was always correct. But it shocked her that Ricky would say it to her face. "Do you want me to talk to her for you?" she asked lamely.

"Just leave me alone." Ricky put his headphones back on and took off.

Claire felt sad as she watched him shuffle down the hall in his oversized jeans. She was supposed to know how to get through to kids, but how could she get through to these parents? She went back into to the science office to finish marking the class assignments but couldn't. She couldn't finish her lunch either. On an impulse she headed down to the main floor Admin Office, knocked on Jack's door and invited herself in to take a seat across from him. He looked from his sandwich to her and back again finally sighing and moving his lunch out of the way.

"We have to talk, Jack. Ricky's mother has been doing his homework," she said bluntly, staring him right in the eye.

"What? What are you saying?" Jack sneered.

"Muriel's been doing Ricky's homework all year. Probably longer." She tossed Ricky's assignment on the desk between them.

"No! Absolutely not! She would never do such a thing," he was annoyed and didn't even look at the paper.

"I'm sorry, Jack," Claire said softly, "It's true. Look." She pointed to the paragraph about the parking ticket Muriel was fighting in the middle of the assignment.

"No, Miss Hébert, this is just you trying to lay the blame."

"Blame? For what?"

"For Ricky's lack of success in your class. He complains about you every day in the car on the way home. What are you doing in class when my son is present?" he asked, as if it didn't matter what she did when Ricky was absent. "You're in charge. Can't you handle your classes?"

"I teach the lesson, I explain it with demonstrations or visuals, and I ask questions, but Ricky is often late or absent and when he is present, he does nothing or leaves to go to the washroom. He misses a lot of the lessons."

Jack looked at her and straightened noticeably in his seat. "You mean you let him out of class every day to go to the washroom?"

"He doesn't ask, Jack. He just walks out when I'm busy with other students. And when he is in class, he plays videogames or stares at the walls or the floor. I've talked to him about it." She looked at Jack. His round face was turning ever deeper shades of red. "Ricky won't come for help after school. I've offered it repeatedly." She took a deep breath. "I've asked a couple of good kids, Nathan Bergeron and Sylvia Woodhouse, to help him in class. I thought maybe he'd respond to peers, but Ricky was so uncooperative that after two days Nathan begged me to let him sit somewhere else." Jack was working up to an explosion but Claire faced him squarely. "Sylvia lasted a week. Ricky kept coming on to her. She pleaded to be let off the hook." Claire stopped for a second to let this sink in. "These are the best kids in the class, Jack."

Jack was fuming with suspicion and denial. He sputtered, but no words came out. So Claire continued, "It's impossible to teach somebody who isn't there, Jack, and when he is in class, I can't get anyone to work with him, be in a group with him, or even to sit beside him. He annoys all the kids around him."

Claire took a moment to think. She knew she was about to cross a line. Was she going too far? Would she stop now for any other kid? She dove in: "Ricky is depressed and has no self-esteem, even though you and Muriel constantly give him gifts and tell him how wonderful he is. You're trying to build his self-esteem, but Ricky," she stressed his name, "Ricky gets the truth from his classmates. The mixed messages confuse and depress him."

Jack leaned forward in his chair, his beady eyes unblinking, his mouth agape. "He knows Muriel manipulates his teachers into being easy on him," Claire continued. "She insists on privileges for him and he always has to get the benefit of the doubt." Then she paused and lowered her voice in the hope Jack would take it in. "What scares me most is that the class knows this too and the resentment they are feeling could take a dangerous turn."

Jack Penworth let this flaming red flag flow in one ear and out the other. "How dare you speak about my son this way!" he hissed. "I could have you fired for letting your students do your job for you! No wonder Ricky isn't learning!"

Claire threw up her hands and stood up. As she reached the door, she turned and said, "If I was talking about any other kid in this school, what would you do?"

The silence was frigid as she walked out the door.

***

Claire was relieved that things were calm in the math class after lunch. As she walked around, she noticed Leah Dewaard's notebook. "You don't like fractions, do you, Leah?"

"No, Miss," Leah answered. "Especially the deMONinators."

"You mean the deNOMinators, Leah. Yes, they can be a problem. Look at these magazines, Leah. They're all the same kind, aren't they?"

"Yes."

"How many are there?"

"Five."

"If I take one away, how many are left?"

"Four."

Out of how many in all?"

"Out of five."

"Well, the denominator tells us how many there were—five—and the numerator...the top number... There was a sudden loud noise. Leah jumped... Claire looked up...

The door had flung open and Chester Hickenman had barged in. "You got my text? I need to move those filing cabinets, Claire. Your class works on their own, right?" He didn't wait for an answer. "I need to do it before my next class. It'll just take a minute. You don't mind do you?" Before Claire could respond he had started to push three filing cabinets away from one another to make two individual workspaces along one side of the room.

"God what a racket!" cried Jimmy Church, who was usually noise personified. "I'm off to Harper's room!" and he headed for the open door. Jenny rushed to stop him. "No! Jimmy," she said. "Just plug your ears. It won't be long."

Chester let piles of posters slide to the floor, they disturbed the air, which disturbed the dust and the cobwebs, and then the spiders were running and dead moths were falling from among the posters. "Oh fuck the cobwebs!" cried Maxine, shaking her head and thrashing her arms. "I hate cobwebs!"

Most of the kids got up to see what Chester was doing. Britney was sneezing. Deepak was running amok. Lindsay was plugging her ears and screeching. Maxine was up having a fit because a spider was crawling down her back. Amir brushed the

253

spider off and stepped on it. Maxine thanked him, checked her chair and sat back down to do her math. "Brrr...spiders give me the creeps." None of it bothered Chester. He was used to noise.

Claire saw Joel quietly packing up his stuff and looking at her as he walked out. "Okay, Joel." She nodded to him. "Bring your books back with the others when class is over."

"Mr. Hickenman! Do you have to do this NOW?" she whispered through her teeth, eyeing her panicked class.

"It's okay, Claire, I sent you a text. I'm almost done."

So is my class, Claire muttered, looking helplessly at the upheaval he'd caused and wondering when he had sent the text. Her cellphone was in her purse in the office. Her dislike of Chester and this room was intensifying exponentially.

A half hour after Chester had left, things had more or less settled down again and Kristen Jaworski slipped in. Claire welcomed her. She would have liked for Kristen to see how well the basic math kids were doing. But Kristen looked around. "Wow... this is quite the room, isn't it?" Her jaw dropped.

"Well, yes, I've had better," Claire understated, "Much better..."

Kristen's face became serious. "I need to tell you, Claire, Chester has just complained about you sharing his room. He doesn't like you asking him not to come in to get things while you're teaching."

"HE complained? Do you know what he just did? Look at my class. Only Maxine and Britney are working. All the others were upset by Chester who came in to move three filing cabinets and a couple of tables during my class."

"Move filing cabinets? Really? Couldn't he do that when you're not here?"

"He says not. He says he texted me. I didn't get it. And look. There's only one wobbly little table for me to work at and to put my stuff on." She threw her hands up in despair. "And the dust! And the mould! Look at this coffee cup! The cleaning staff refuses to clean the place."

Kristen was looking at it. "And no wonder...Blech! Hmmm..."

"Every day I carry a box with all the notebooks, pencils, erasers, rulers and calculators back up to the third floor science office after class, so I know where my stuff is for the next day. At first, I kept a watchful eye that my students didn't disturb the mess around them—even though it intrigued them—but I have to tell you that I no longer care what happens to Chester's mess. This mould-infested coffee has been here since February. I'm thinking of analysing the floating fuzz in my lab. And now I find out that among all the inhospitable things he has been doing, he has complained to you about me."

Kristen laughed. I'm glad you still have your sense of humour Claire, and I'm filing this complaint in the circular file where it belongs, but I'm afraid there's not much I can do about

Chester's slovenly habits." With a flourish, she tore up the complaint, pitched it into the recycling and left. "Good afternoon."

***

That night, after her walk with Boomer, Claire was worried about what repercussions would come from her rant in Jack Penworth's office. She thought about Matt. Why did she always think about him when things got rough at school? Feeling guilty that she couldn't see him on interview night, she wondered if he was still upset and would hang up if she called him. She clicked his cell number and waited. It rang four times. No answer. It was ringing for the fifth time. Had he seen her number and decided not to pick up? Was he with someone else? Was he on another business trip? On the sixth ring, he answered.

He did not hang up. In fact, he told her he was glad she'd called. "Just got in from the laundry room," he puffed. "How've you been, Claire?"

"I've been okay. I'm sorry for what I said before Peru. I regretted it as soon as the words left my mouth. I didn't mean it. Really. I miss you, Matt. Friends?"

"I was upset too and stressed. We were both tired after Algonquin and I didn't want to go to Peru. I knew how much I would miss you. I miss you now."

He hadn't called her *Clarikins*, and she wondered if that meant anything. She wondered what on earth he could be stressed about. He loved his job. She told him about the kid and parent X. She didn't tell him it was the V.P.'s son. Matt could tell she needed a diversion. "Hey Claire, want to come to the U.K. with me for three days to see the real Prince Charles' reed bed at Highgrove?" It was the sort of distraction that would do her a lot of good right now. "Want to drop everything and come along, Clarikins? We leave Sunday night." It was typical Matt. He was already joking, and now he'd called her 'Clarikins,' so she knew he wasn't mad anymore. He didn't expect her to go on his fantasy jaunt to the U.K. She had classes to teach and the Amberton Science Fair coming up.

But it was Matt's way of telling Claire he was still interested. And he knew she was too. It helped to laugh and forget the Penworths for a while.

***

A half hour later Claire was in her nightie about to relax on the sofa with Boomer and her evening glass of sherry. She had worked hard on every aspect of the next day's grade eleven lesson, preparing point-by-point instruction sheets for it with questionnaires for the observations. She was proud of her work. It was a lesson plan she could keep for future use. The students would be dissecting foetal pigs and filling in observation sheets as they went along. She had made beautiful clear diagrams and if they followed the steps, the kids would have a good note at the end.

Claire knew some of the kids were looking forward to the dissection part, while others were dreading it. So she suggested to the apprehensive ones that they could observe and take notes, while the keener biologists did the actual cutting.

She was relaxing in the knowledge that everything would go smoothly with the foetal pig dissection the next day. Better yet, she was feeling a renewed confidence in her relationship with Matt that she hadn't felt for a month. She was taking her first sip when the doorbell rang. She grabbed her robe and checked the peephole.

"Matt!" she gasped, as she opened the door. There he stood in his deep blue viyella shirt and light jacket, a sheepish grin spread across his handsome face. "What are you doing?"

"I had to see you," he interrupted. "I thought you'd given up on me."

Claire felt her face blushing. "I wanted to see you, too. Come on in."

Matt stepped in and she shut the door. They held each other long and tight.

"What we said three weeks ago…" she started. "Do you want to talk about it?"

"Ah, we were both stressed. No. I want you." He grabbed her by the arms and kissed her on her lips, her neck, her forehead. They went into the living room. Claire's eyes closed and her heart thumped as she melted against him, his hands sliding to her thighs. She had missed him so much. She wanted him. For a while they just held each other. Claire took his fingers from her breast and licked them. She put her hand between his thighs. She felt him swelling. She put his hand back and licked his earlobes. Then his warm hands were feeling her legs, probing her buttocks, moving up, lifting her nightie. With his teeth, he pulled down a spaghetti strap and kissed her shoulder, her breast, her nipple. In one swift move Claire threw off her nightie. Her hands roamed under his shirt tenderly rubbing his chest. He tossed his clothing aside. She licked each nipple for a moment. He relished in the sound of her breath catching in her throat. He took her hand and they lay on the rug facing each other. Their love surrounded them. Claire felt so good, so safe, so protected. The passion lingered as they rolled and lay panting, ecstatic on

the soft rug until Boomer came in and jumped on them, wagging his tail and licking their faces.

"Boomer!" Claire gasped, playfully pushing him away.

"He's happy I'm here," Matt said, kissing her again.

"So am I, Matt," and she kissed him a long kiss back.

***

Tuesday, April 17

"That's it, we're done, Serge!" Amy O'Leary shouted in the science hall. "No way am I going camping with you!" The entire class was ready to go to the lab for their much anticipated pig dissections. "Do you hear me, Serge?" she shouted, "It's over."

"Amy please, you don't mean it," Serge pleaded pitifully. "You love camping!"

"I do mean it," she countered loudly. "An' I hate camping. 'Sides, I'm going out with Alex Pattison. He's in grade twelve and he plays basketball. I been seeing him since exams."

"Like we didn't all know that," Mick Taylor, the class rebel, snickered it loud enough for Amy to hear. Serge heard it too.

Serge looked around and realized the entire class was staring at him. Anger blazed in his eyes as he grabbed Amy by the arm. "Why are you doing this to me? Why now? Why here?"

Amy tore away shouting angrily, "Ha! Now you know how it feels, you insensitive clod!"

Right now, Serge was anything but insensitive. All his classmates were in the hall and heard it. Farah Zahar and

Hannah May giggled and whispered as Serge struggled to choke back the tears. "But I love you," he shouted pathetically. Amy fled down the stairs.

For a moment Serge just stood there, turning around and around, hitting his head with his hand. It was the calm before the storm.

When some of his friends tried to approach him, Serge, hurt and furious with embarrassment, pushed them away. He turned and stomped towards Claire's lab.

"Fuck!" he yelled, clenching his fist to his head." Fuck! Fuck! Fuck!"

Letting loose his considerable emotions, he lashed out at his surroundings, kicking in a few lockers on the way. He entered the lab. He shoved Farah and Hannah out of his way. They ran screaming to the back of the room. He turned, wild-eyed and utterly out of control. On the lab demo counter he saw the six plastic wrapped foetal pigs Claire had set out a few minutes before. He grabbed one and slammed it sharply onto an edge. The bag exploded, the pig split open, and the formaldehyde splashed everywhere as pieces of piglet went flying. Blind with rage, Serge grabbed another one and then a third and swung one into the corner of the lab bench and the other on one of the desks. Then he stamped his foot on the slippery porcine pieces. More formaldehyde and bits of piglet spewed about, hitting some of the girls watching in the doorway.

Alanna McPherson heard the noise and saw the violence of Serge's outburst from the back of the room and even she was alarmed. By now Hannah and Farah were with Alanna cowering behind the lab desk at the back.

Artie Binton had followed Serge in. Knowing his friend's rage would eventually dissipate, he waited patiently, motionless in a front corner. As the smell of the formaldehyde filled the room he calmly opened the windows.

In response to the girls' continued caterwauling, Serge stopped momentarily and stared in their direction. Then his anger got the better of him again and he smashed a shelf full of glassware on the floor. Sean Jacobson and Kariem Jazrawi, who had been transfixed in the hall, entered the lab to try to tackle him but when they saw the flying glassware they decided against it and ran to get Claire. They bumped into her and Gene and Angus rushing towards the noise in the lab.

As quickly as it had started, Serge's rage ebbed. The whole outburst had taken no more than three minutes. Suddenly, Serge was standing there, deflated.

"Miss Hébert! Serge's lost it! Amy's just broken up with him in front of everybody! He's gone bonkers. He's smashed our pigs!" Danielle Duncan cried. She had been looking forward to the dissection lesson.

"Settle down," Angus called out as the three teachers entered the room. Just past the doorway, they stopped and let their eyes scan the damage. "Yikes," Claire said as she sidestepped a puddle of intestines on the floor. Serge was a statue in the middle of the lab, surrounded by the destruction he had caused.

"All right, it's going to be okay," Claire said calmly. "All of you wait in the hall." Some obeyed while others seemed frozen in fear. Alanna, Hannah and Farah and some other girls had to be escorted out of the lab by the back door. Artie stayed on his stool, watching his friend. In the hall, Kariem filled in Jimmy Hu, who was wondering what all the fuss was about because he hadn't put his hearing aids back in after lunch. Claire was patient with them all.

Gene stood by the door, checking each student for injuries as they filed by and assessing the damage in the room. Serge saw Claire. For a moment their eyes met. His tantrum had run its course, but the emotion was still flashing heavily around him. To Claire, he looked like an automaton bereft of power, about to crumple into a passionless heap.

"Come on, Serge," she urged gently. "Let's get you out of here."

As the boy moved towards her and into the hall, Angus got on the P.A. and asked for a caretaker to clean up the mess of mangled flesh, bones, formaldehyde and shattered glass. Then he and Gene went into the hall to help Claire.

Serge didn't stay. Numb, and blinded by grief, his heavy shoes plodded ever faster down the hall and down the same stairs Amy had taken and out of the school. Claire, her hands full of the emergency, realized that she would have better success with Serge when he had calmed down, so she turned back to the kids in the corridor. Some girls were whimpering while others were animated and chatting expressively. In a corner a little way off, Aisha Ames's friends were standing around her protectively. The chaos was subsiding. Farah Zahar and Hannah May had recovered and they were gawking onto the room, their cellphones out and snapping pictures.

Now Claire's luck nosedived. Kristen Jaworski, who had Serge on her list, was away at a conference. Jack Penworth was the only V.P. in the school. In the office for a break, he had heard the P.A. call with the screaming in the background and decided to rush up to the third floor to check on the situation. Jack rushed like a slug. He used the rickety old elevator, which moved as if it had all the time in the world. He was still fuming about Claire's rant yesterday about his ex doing Ricky's homework, Ricky's work habits and his attendance, as he puffed along the hall. In his mind this confirmed what Ricky had told him on the way home: Claire was a bad teacher.

He found Claire calming the students, mostly the girls. He saw the messed up foetus body parts and all the broken glass and puddles of formaldehyde. He noticed the smell. He glanced around the room. Other kids and some teachers had come out of classrooms to gawk. Chin Ho arrived too, but sent the others away and left when he was satisfied that Claire, Angus and Gene had the situation in hand. Shaking his head, Jack muttered, "Gawd, what a mess! Miss Hébert, I'll see you in my office after school." He nodded sternly and departed without lifting a finger. It wasn't needed. Moral support might have been appreciated, but Jack didn't know what that was.

Angus and Gene left for their own classes when they saw Jethro Mason, the caretaker and his assistant Ivan Kowalski, arriving to clean up the room. They worked methodically, sweeping up pieces of piglet and putting them in a garbage bag. Then they gathered the shattered glass. After picking up the big pieces with gloved hands, they meticulously looked for dangerous slivers that could have flown out of the main damage zone. Artie pointed some out. The formaldehyde smell was no longer a concern. Angus, Sean and Kariem were closing some of the windows Artie had opened to let out the stench.

Jimmy Hu, having put in his hearing aids, was now in full hyperactive mode, running up and down the hall. Claire asked Kariem to calm him. Twenty minutes before the end of the period, as Jethro declared areas of the room safe, she let a few kids at a time go in and sit at their desks. Ivan Kowalski had closed the rest of the windows.

As they worked, Jethro listened for classroom gossip. He eyed the class suspiciously. After many years at the school, he was wary of teenagers in groups, or 'packs' as he called them. But this class was now sitting in stunned silence and it intrigued him. Artie was still on his stool by the windows, quietly keeping an eye on Serge who was now in the parking lot, sitting on a car in the sunlight, having a smoke to calm down and mull over his new lonely unloved status. All his family problems had flooded back to haunt him. Claire could see him out of her window wiping his face with his black leather sleeve. She felt sorry for him.

When Jethro and Ivan had finished, there were words of "Thank you, Mr. Mason! Thank you Mr. Kowalski!" from the subdued students. Claire would have to rearrange the dissection groups because there were now only three foetuses for the exercise. She decided to postpone the dissection exercise until tomorrow and use the little time left to discuss the importance of self-control and anger management.

"Does anyone have any comments about what happened?" Claire asked a subdued class.

Several did.

"What are we going to do now, Miss?" Tori Oliver wondered. "Three of the pigs have to be thrown out. We were looking forward to this lesson."

"Not me! I don't like cutting animals open!" It was Maya Li Chu.

"Me, neither!" said Alanna McPherson, looking around to see if anyone would agree with her.

"Well, some of us were!" retorted Danielle Duncan, the future oncologist.

"Okay. Let's ask ourselves another question then," said Claire, aware that for the first time she was working without a lesson plan. "Does being jilted by his girlfriend—no matter how cruelly—give Serge the right to destroy things in our classroom?"

"Come on, Miss H.! That was awful what Amy did to him! Like, he didn't have no choice!"

"Choice? Choice to do what?" Claire picked up on a key word.

"She broke up with him an' embarrassed him in front of ever'body, you know? Like, anybody woulda been pissed and exploded!"

"Yes, and we all feel very sorry for his embarrassment and his heartache, don't we?"

All heads nodded and some said, "Yes, Miss."

"But he did he have a *choice*." Claire stressed the word. She looked at the class and

noticed blank faces looking at each other. She gave it a minute. Then, "To help figure it out, let's divide the situation into two parts: Serge's emotional break-up with his girlfriend which hurt *him*, and his reaction to it which hurt *us*." She folded her arms across her chest as she walked in front of the class. "We didn't do anything to him. Did we deserve what we got? Could he have shown more self-control? Should he or *could* he have reacted differently?"

"No way, Miss!" the majority chimed together.

"Does anyone have a different opinion?" Claire asked, noticing Aisha Ames shaking her head slowly.

"Aisha?"

"I think he could have run off and skipped classes until he felt better," she said in a soft voice, looking down at her desk. "He was hurt and probably ready to cry. Skipping class isn't a good thing, but maybe this would have been a good time for it, you know? Then he wouldn't 've broken anything and we could do our dissection lesson. It wouldn't have been easy, but Serge just exploded. He didn't show any self-control at all. I understand why he did it, and I sympathise with him, and I feel sorry for him because of all the trouble he's in now and how hurt he is..."

Several kids gawking at her interrupted at this point saying, "Do we have that kind of self-control though? Does anybody? Is it fair to expect Serge to control himself when we don't?"

Claire now noticed Farah and Hannah giving Aisha a particularly snippy look that said, what do you know?

Aisha didn't respond. Claire watched her withdraw like a frightened turtle back into her shell. She had had her say and didn't anticipate any respect from her classmates. It was the first time Claire had seen her fear, even with her friends around her. Claire watched as Maya tried to put a protective hand on her shoulder, and noticed that she shook it off. Claire made a mental note to ask Lily Campbell to have a talk with Hannah and Farah.

"Good point," Claire answered, keeping an eye on Aisha and catching another key word. "Self-control is something you have to work at, people. It doesn't just fall out of the clear blue sky the moment you need it. You need to cultivate it, to nurture it, to think about it, to work at it, to practice it. What else could Serge have done differently?"

"He could have gone to see Miss Campbell in Guidance," Danielle said.

"Yup."

"He could have run out of the school and just skipped, like Aisha said," added Elisa Rollins, who had had her own run-ins with Hannah and Farah.

"Yup."

"He could have ... er... I forgot what I was going to say... oh yes ... he could have gone home," Rebecca Chow said, blushing.

"Good."

"He could have gone to the cafeteria to see his friends and talked to them," Danielle Duncan suggested.

"OK. So you all see now that even though he didn't have many options, he did have some choices besides the one he made."

"Yeah, but it's so hard!" Ahmed Yousef said. "Like, I got a girlfriend too and I know how hurt I'd be if she did that to me! And now he's in so much sh-- er trouble!"

"I never thought of separating his breakup and his reaction," Tori Oliver said, thoughtfully. "You're right, Miss H. If he'd been able to separate his reaction from the break-up with Amy, he'd be here now and we'd be dissecting pigs."

"So you see the benefit of self-control or self-discipline."

"They keep you out of bigger messes than you're in!" Kariem said from between Jimmy Hu and Omar Samil.

"If you all try to learn to cultivate your self-control, we'll all be able to thank Serge for this lesson when he comes back. It's one of the best things anyone can learn." She looked over the class for questions. There were none. "Now, how are we going to treat Serge when he comes back?"

"Oh, we'll be nice to him, Miss, don't worry!" Kariem and Omar said together. They were glaring at Hannah May and Farah Zahar as they said it.

"That's good. Thanks, people." Claire was thinking that this class today had gone well after all, and maybe the class would help Lily straighten out Hannah and Farah.

"Where's Serge now?" Sean asked.

"He's sitting on his car. I think he's crying, poor guy," Danielle replied.

Artie, who had a secret crush on Danielle and hadn't said anything during the entire discussion, volunteered, "I'll go and talk to him, Miss. I'll tell him what we said in class. I know what he's going through."

"Thanks, Artie. Tell him we care."

***

At the end of the day Claire had to go and see Jack Penworth again. She was tired. She was dreading it. But she was also in a careless, *who-gives-a-shit* kind of mood. She was now confident that she was a good teacher. Today's class proved it. Still, in the science office, she procrastinated. She straightened her skirt, touched up her makeup and made sure her desk was in order and her lesson plans were done. Finally, she gritted her teeth and headed down to confront the unpleasant consequences. "Here goes nothing," she told herself.

Claire walked slowly, feeling like Serge would when he came back, wondering what would happen, and wanting to postpone it and get it over with at the same time. She decided to let Jack do all the talking. There was no point in baiting the bear.

Jack was at his computer, his beige, rounded, rumpled back to her. Claire knocked on the open door. He swivelled his chair and looked at her.

"Come in, Claire. Sit down. How are you?"

271

"I'm fine, Jack," she said, smiling tightly. "Just busy as usual. It's been an exhausting day."

"Oh?" Jack had his usual defensive look on his face. His office door remained open to the main office where five students were serving ten-minute detentions and three secretaries were still working. This made Claire uncomfortable. Jack didn't notice. "You're having some difficulties in your classes, Claire," he started as he leaned back in his chair. "Last semester and at preliminary report time, there were complaints from parents about low marks, and this scene today was terrible."

Claire wanted to say: *REAL marks,* but she controlled herself. "Yes, Jack."

"You always send students to the office for a discipline form, Claire. Why don't you send them to the cool room?"

Claire wanted to interject: *The cool room doesn't work. It's a total, time-wasting disaster like most of your ideas, and only makes more work for teachers.* But she didn't say that either. She said, "Nobody has ever sent anyone there when I'm on duty. They send them into the hall."

"Why don't you flex just a little? As for the fracas today, there are already calls from Mrs. Zahar and Mrs. May. Farah and Hannah took pictures of the mess."

So you think that's my fault too? Did you forget that cellphone photography is not allowed in school without prior permission?

But she said, "Farah Zahar and Hannah May dramatize everything until it's a third rate soap opera." Then Claire whispered, "Sorry, Jack."

"Claire, if you have problems with Hannah and Farah, you need to document that."

Claire thought: *You must think teachers have all day to document every bloody thing every kid does just in case they have a meltdown some day and we need to prove to a halfwit like you why they have been sent to the office.* But aloud, she said: "Yes, Jack."

"Claire, you need to learn to control your classes better. When there are kids in the lab, you need to be there."

Yeah, based on what I see of your son, you're an expert. Claire remained tight-lipped, but she couldn't stop her thoughts. "Yes, Jack."

Jack interrupted her thoughts. "Have you thought about the quality and detail of your lesson plans? Is there something missing that could keep the kids' attention more focussed? Are you using the Smart Board?"

Oh God, here he goes again, thought Claire, but she was on autopilot and said, "Yes, Jack."

Claire was furious inside, but hoped it didn't show. Jack hadn't asked about who did what or why. When he arrived she, Angus and Gene had the situation pretty much under control. He didn't ask any questions about the incident then and he certainly wasn't asking about it now.

"I have to tell you that if your classroom management doesn't improve, there will be consequences, Claire."

Oh, shove it up your wazoo, she thought, but she said, "Yes, Jack."

Claire was dumbstruck, but her mind was raging with all the things she couldn't say. Did Jack even know about Serge's situation? Did it interest him that nobody got physically hurt? Did he appreciate that she and her colleagues were right there handling the situation? Did he care that she used the rest of the class time to let the kids vent and used the teachable moment to discuss self-discipline and anger management? Did he care that the dissection activity would still take place? Did he know that she sends just as many students to Kristen Jaworski, and she never complains? She wanted to tell Jack to do his job, but she knew that would guarantee her a swift transfer to the board's equivalent of Siberia next September if she weren't already on the short list.

"The clean-up is going to cost a few hundred dollars," Jack said, tapping his pencil on the desk. "We'll need a special cleaning team with expertise in chemicals, blood, and body fluids. That will come out of the science budget, Claire."

What? Claire thought. *Jethro and Ivan have already cleaned it up.* But she said, "Yes, Jack."

Claire shifted uncomfortably in her chair, her eyes wandering all around Jack's office.

"And I'm also tired of your grousing about my son. I expect better results for Ricky in the future. You're dismissed."

"Yes, Jack. Thank you, Jack." At least it was over. Jack turned his chair back to face his computer. As she left, she saw the stunned looks and open mouths of the secretaries and the students on detention as they watched her leave.

***

Wednesday, April 18

As Claire expected, the next day Serge was back in class. Although he deserved some level of punishment for wrecking the pigs and breaking the glassware, Claire, knowing the situation in his family and the cruel incident with Amy, quietly let him in with Artie, no questions asked. He and Artie now sat together. She didn't want the office—especially Jack Penworth—any more involved. As a Leclerc, Serge fell under Kristen Jaworski's part of the alphabet. Claire had emailed her about the incident, including that she could handle it herself. She explained that the whole class was aware of his losing his girlfriend and they felt his pain. In fact, most of the kids were going out of their way to be nice to him. Kristen complimented Claire on a situation well handled.

The foetal pig-sectioning lesson went exceptionally well. All the students were subdued and worked intently.

Nobody socialized or wasted time. There wasn't a cellphone or videogame to be seen—even from Elisa Rollins and Alanna MacPherson. Word got around about Miss Hébert's 'interview' with Mr. Penworth—perhaps he had left the door open on purpose—and although there were a few whispers here and there, "Miss Hébert's in big shit" and "Miss H's gonna be fired," the students concentrated on their task.

The complaining parents' princesses were not in class. Farah Zahar and Hannah May were too 'traumatised.'

In the end, Claire was pleased. "If this is the effect that smashing some stuff around the lab has," Claire later told Matt, "I should let them smash something every day," she joked.

Chapter 16

<u>Bullying Goes Both Ways</u>

Friday, April 20

At the end of the day, Claire found Gene standing over his desk in the science office, holding his head in his hands. "Are you okay?"

"Yeah, I suppose." He lifted his head. Dark circles shadowed his eyes and his brow was furrowed.

"You don't look it. Gene. Are you sure you're alright?""

"No matter how many times I ask my grade ten general science class to stop, there's somebody playing videogames or texting. I'm always confiscating cellphones but it keeps getting worse, especially when a new gadget or game comes on the market. I wish the blasted Tech Committee would come up with a policy or something. They all have a bloody phone now."

"I know. It drives me nuts, too. I want them to learn. Want a coffee?"

"Thanks." Gene plopped down in the comfy chair, shaking his head. "I don't want them to miss the instructions before an experiment, Claire. There are safety issues—in science and in woodworking." He cleared his throat. "I'm hoarse." He took a roll of lozenges out of his pocket, offered one to Claire, and popped one into his mouth. "I have to repeat everything for those rude, sharp-tongued gamers. They think they're so smart, but they slow everything down, making every class more arduous for the good students." He shook his head.

"You could announce they'd won twenty million on Lotto Max and they'd miss it," Claire said, passing him his coffee.

Gene didn't laugh. "This grade ten course doesn't have a lot of experiments, so I made up some extras, from cute to spectacular, to keep their interest—or so I thought—Bertha's interesting lesson plans and all that."

"I know. If we could count on everybody in a class being cooperative long enough to hear the instructions, we could make more lessons fun. My grade tens are just as bad."

"Exactly." Gene sat forward in his chair, glad to talk to someone who sympathised. "I love to supplement my courses with hands-on stuff. It's the best weapon against boredom. If I could be myself in class, we could have fun." Gene took a deep breath. "But the kids won't let me. I can't do real stuff that pops or explodes or lets off a smelly cloud when I have to be a security guard."

"You don't have to tell me, my friend," Claire laughed. "The techies hardly ever listen. And then they complain that they're *bored.*"

"I absolutely hate that word coming out of a teenager's mouth," Gene said. "It means 'you're not wowing me so I'm tuned out.' I've considered stopping all experiments, but that'll punish the kids who listen too."

"The system really does let the good kids down." Claire shrugged her shoulders and checked the parking lot. "When do *they* get a spot in the sun? Techies, slow learners, kids with syndromes, kids with learning differences, disinterested kids who act out, they're the ministry's greatest concern."

She turned back from the window and looked at Gene. "You're wiped, Gene. Go home and have a good weekend."

"A rest's as good as a change, eh?" Gene muttered as he wearily stood and reached for his jacket.

"That's what they say," Claire said it as cheerily as she could and patted him on the shoulder. "Go take your girls to a movie."

Just as Claire reached the door, the intercom on the science office wall scratched to life. "Miss Hébert? Can you come to Miss Stack's office, please?"

Memories of her interview with Jack Penworth after the Serge Leclerc incident jammed her mind. Claire wanted to say *No way, José*. "Be right there," she said instead and went down to the first floor. In the copier room, Claire quickly made copies of her lesson outlines for the following week, so she could plunk them in Bertha's hand when she asked for them. She slipped them into an envelope and knocked on Bertha's door.

"Hello, Claire. How are you?"

"Fine, Bertha, thank you." *Here we go with the pleasantries again,* she thought. *As if she gives a hoot…*

Bertha jumped right in. "Sit down, Claire. I need to speak to you about what happened in your biology lab last Tuesday. Jack briefed me about it."

How could Jack brief her on something he didn't see and hadn't asked about? Claire thought. "Yes, Bertha, I'm so sorry about what happened. One of my students had a very upsetting experience…"

"Yes, yes. Jack told me all about it." Bertha waved her hand dismissively. "But I have phone messages from Mrs. Zahar and Mrs. May. Their daughters… what are their names?" She rechecked her notes… "Oh, yes… Farah and Hannah came home with cellphone pictures of the mess in your lab. What do you have to say?"

"It's regrettable." Claire spoke fast so that Bertha couldn't interrupt her. "But after Jethro and Ivan cleaned it all up, we talked about anger management and the kids have now completed the dissection exercise… and they did very well."

Bertha ignored the good news. "Don't change the subject, Claire. I have Mrs. May and Mrs. Zahar to contend with. What am I supposed to tell them? The damage, the mess." She lowered herself into the chair behind her cluttered desk. "Those girls were traumatized. Their mothers had to keep them home for two days. They missed the dissection. What can I tell them? They want to know how it came to be that such a violent individual was in the same class as their daughters."

Claire wanted to remind Bertha that it was the administration who made up the class lists, not she, but stopped herself. "Hannah and Farah tend to exaggerate everything, Bertha. They're spoiled princesses. There was nothing more for them to be upset about than for the girls who stayed. Farah and Hannah were with Alanna MacPherson watching from behind a counter at the back of the room, far away from the fuss and we escorted them out the back door into the hall until it was all over. Poor Serge…"

"Never mind Serge. The girls are the subjects here. Pictures of the mess in your lab are all over the Internet. What will the chairman of the board think? Why would anyone be so upset in your class? Do your lessons catch their interest?" She straightened her back and raised her chin. "I would like to see your lesson plans for the next couple of weeks."

"Certainly," Claire said through a tense smile. "I have copies of next week's lesson plans right here." She plopped them in Bertha's hand. Bertha hadn't expected such rapid compliance and was in no mood to be conciliatory. On the other side of the desk, Claire was too tired and angry to be rational. She consoled herself with the thought that Bertha didn't like teachers whom she imagined were smarter than she. Claire wasn't worried about showing Bertha the lesson plans. They were up to date, if not quite complete—much to Matt's dismay…

"Let me know your thoughts when you've had a chance to review those," Claire said as she stood to leave.

Open-mouthed, Bertha looked at the envelope in her hand and back to the door, which was just closing.

***

Claire needed to see a friendly face. She found Shirley still in the French office. Claire fell into a chair and let out a huge sigh.

"Don't worry, Claire," Shirley sympathized. "Bertha is famous for forgetting things. It's one of her best qualities."

"Don't we all know it," Claire fought back a yawn.

"I've taught Serge. I know how explosive he can be when things are bugging him," Shirley said. "He's had to cope with his parents' venomous divorce, and he's doing better with it than most. He's a good kid who will be embarrassed and very sorry it happened. He'll respond to quiet understanding without rehashing everything."

"That's what I thought. But I didn't get a chance to say it…" "Who does with Bertha?"

"Only Jack." They laughed.

"If I know Serge," Shirley said, "he'll want to turn a new leaf. The teacher who lets him have a fresh start will succeed with him."

"That's what I'm doing. Thanks, Shirl. I value your friendship. By the way, how is the Naomi Harper situation going? It's been a bit quieter down the hall from the Hickenman room."

"I'm happy to hear that. Bertha is getting a long-term occasional teacher qualified for French Immersion to teach the grade eleven *Littérature* class for the rest of the semester. Naomi will be teaching the *Sociologie* using the French text from now on and continue the Entrepreneurship in English. The *Littérature* class has been moved to another room."

"How on earth?" Claire stuttered, her eyes bulging out incredulously.

"The kids got their parents to complain to Bertha," Shirley whispered, as if the walls had ears. "Some wrote letters threatening to go higher up."

"I guess that's the only way to get Bertha to act. How did the kids get the idea to get their parents to complain? I'm an inquiring mind," Claire said with a wry smile.

"I'm sure I have no idea," Shirley said innocently, but as she turned her head away, Claire saw a wide grin. "I'm quite happy with it. Mme Moreaux starts Monday. She did a fine job with them in grade ten last year."

"I heard some of them gave her a hard time."

"Yes, but the good kids told me she was very helpful and with the power to pass or fail them, she'll do fine with those battered grade elevens."

"They'll be happy to be away from Naomi."

"You can bet on that. Marthe knows *La Sablière* and the grammar, and is eager for a chance to teach for a few months."

"Fantastic. One problem solved, and God only knows what tomorrow will bring..." Claire said with a sigh as she got up.

"Only forty-two days until my retirement," Shirley said as she quickly buttoned her jacket. "But who's counting?"

***

Monday, April 23

At lunch hour, Maya and Janette came to the science office looking for Claire.

"Miss Hébert, Miss Hébert. It's Aisha!"

"What's happened, girls?"

"The snots are at it again! They've been picking on Aisha. One minute they're nice and tell her she's pretty, the next moment they yell at her that they hate her clothes and mock her. They may say sweetly that they like her makeup, but then they shout out that she should tear out her hair to look better. I don't know how she stands it, the pictures and the things they have put on the Internet about her. It's awful. We tried to protect her, but she still heard it."

"Oh no, not again," Claire said as she rubbed a hand across her forehead.

"Now Aisha's doing strange things," Maya continued. "We're supposed to be her friends, but she's been avoiding us all week."

Oh no, Claire thought, I spoke to those girls about Aisha just a few weeks ago. And Lily Campbell spoke to them the other day. Did we make things worse?

"Last Wednesday, the last day she came to school," Janette said, her voice squeaking with tension. "Aisha gave me back the friendship bracelet we made for her in February. It had all our birthdays and birthstones on it. When we gave it to her we all swore we'd be friends forever."

"She gave each of us something, her favourite sweater, her favourite earrings, the framed picture they took of us all on the ski trip," Maya said. "We haven't seen her since."

This was true. Claire had assumed Aisha had the flu, and she'd been away this morning too.

"My father's a sociologist," said Janette, "I told him about the bullying last semester and showed him the bracelet. He told me it could be a sign that she's thinking of doing something really bad. He looked worried."

A sign of impending suicide, Claire thought. At school people like me, who don't know her that well, wouldn't know

285

anything was wrong. Out loud, Claire said, "Does she get along with her parents? Her siblings?"

"Uh-huh, we think so." The girls looked at each other. "Mr. and Mrs. Ames are nice. They helped her a lot last semester. She has no brothers or sisters."

"Could she be depressed?"

"It's more than that, Miss H.," Maya insisted, fighting tears. "There is something mega not right. We know it. Aisha liked the Weight Watchers Club. We all had a ball on the ski trip. We were best friends and like, everybody thought she was okay. We did everything together, until this week…" Maya fidgeted with the bracelet in her hands. "…this week she suddenly quit everything and stopped speaking to us. I don't know if I should call Aisha's Mom."

"Thanks for telling me, girls. I'm going to call right now. You two go to class," Claire said, as she turned to her student directory. The girls continued to stare at her, wide-eyed. "It'll be okay," she said firmly. "I'll let you know."

***

What Claire learned from Mrs. Ames shocked her. Aisha had been photographed in a cubicle in the girls' change room after swim class the week after Easter. There had been a traffic jam of girls in there, some getting changed after their gym class, others getting ready for after school sports. Two pictures were

286

taken from under a sidewall of the cubicle, another one from over the top. All three were photo-shopped to look *hilarious* or, in the opinion of sane adults, *terribly embarrassing.* They had been posted on the Internet along with a degrading epithet stating that she was 'open for business.' The pictures had been there for three days before Aisha realized why so many students had been snickering at her. Hannah and Farah, who had been mocking Aisha in class for weeks, had told her that her *brainy* friends were in on it.

With that, Aisha's world imploded. She refused to leave her room. Aisha's parents called the school. Since then the administration had been quietly trying to get to the bottom of it. The bullies posted their lack of success on the Internet, causing even more laughter among the student cliques.

"For a week Miss Stack and Mr. Penworth called suspects out of class to ask them to admit it or tell on the culprit," Aisha's mother told Claire over the phone. "When that didn't work, they called the police, who tracked down the kid who had posted everything and got the Internet service provider to remove the offensive pictures and epithets."

"Thank God for that," Claire said, her mind still reeling.

"But the photo-shopper/Internet-poster was a boy. He couldn't have been the one who took the pictures in a busy girls' change room."

"Right, not unnoticed," Claire agreed. "The photographer had to be a girl."

"And whoever her friends are, they're tight-lipped," Mrs. Ames sounded bitter, paused and took a deep breath. "…and protecting the little bitch…sorry."

"Oh no, don't apologize on my account," Claire assured her.

"In the meantime, Aisha is at home with us. We've tried to persuade her that horrible as this is, it doesn't have to be the end of the world. Interest in her will fade and in time she'll overcome it. We'll move to another city or country and change our names if necessary."

"Surely it won't come to that."

"I hope not, but what else can we do? Aisha is in a terrible state. I'm taking time off work. I can't leave her alone like this."

"What about her friends?" Claire asked.

"Tori, Maya, Danielle, and Janette have tried to visit, but we've turned them away. Until we know for sure who's done this to our daughter, we just can't take any chances. She's not safe in this day and age."

"Is anyone?"

***

That evening, Claire had the television on as she was rinsing off her dishes after dinner. Matt was on his way to Mexico, so she had eaten alone.

"…A student from a local high school is said to be in serious condition this evening…" the newscaster said. Claire shut off the tap and stared at the screen.

"Oh my God," she gasped, bringing a tea towel to her mouth. Across the television set, an unconscious person was being wheeled to a waiting ambulance. Even without seeing her face, Claire knew it was Aisha.

"…suicide attempt. It's believed that the girl has been the victim of an intense cyber bullying campaign. Pictures of her, taken in a school locker room without her consent were posted…"

Claire watched in horror as the doors to the ambulance shut. This couldn't be happening. She had just talked to Aisha's mother hours ago. She stumbled to the sofa and let herself fall into it. Boomer immediately jumped on her lap.

"Oh, Boomer, how can this be?" Claire watched the newscast change to a weather story and rubbed the dog's head. Then she remembered that Bertha had done nothing about the photos Hannah and Farah had taken of her messed up lab last week.

***

Tuesday, April 24

Kristen Jaworski, whose husband Steve Lawson was the school police officer, led the school reaction. Claire, her

289

colleagues, and other kids who had been bullied or persistently teased, got together and planned an assembly against bullying. Claire thought it would do them all good to be busy for Aisha. They set about contacting experts, organizing, and planning. The faster they could present a strong anti-bullying program the better.

***

Danielle, Janette, and Maya had been calling the Ames house without any luck for a week. Now they decided to go in person and asked Miss Hébert to come with them for back-up.

"Look, girls," Mrs. Ames said irritably, "Aisha was told that you four took part in the bullying."

"What?" Mia gasped, frantically looking back at Claire who was standing behind them on the lower step of the front porch.

"No, no way," Janette blurted. "We love Aisha... She's our friend."

"Who could have told her such a thing?" Danielle asked, the tears welling up. "Tell her, Miss Hébert. We'd never hurt her."

Aisha's mother looked past the girls to Claire and raised a questioning eyebrow. "I cannot imagine these girls being part of a thing like this, Mrs. Ames," Claire said firmly. "They've been beside themselves with anguish. They've been protecting and supporting Aisha all semester."

Mrs. Ames nodded, slowly. "Well…"

"We would never do anything so mean," Maya gushed, now in tears. "We're helping Miss Hébert and Miss Jaworski plan anti-bullying assemblies with other bullying victims."

"That's true," Claire confirmed. "We're hoping to present them Thursday or Friday."

Mrs. Ames turned in the doorway to look at her husband. Mr. Ames nodded. "We took them all skiing," he said, "and they all seemed like such good friends. Let's give them one chance, Alice."

The girls all sighed and wiped their eyes. Behind them, Claire smiled and nodded.

"They'll help, you'll see."

"Alright," Mrs. Ames said, smoothing a hand down her hip. "You may visit her, two at a time, but only when there's a nurse present, do you hear?"

The girls nodded enthusiastically. "You can count on us," Maya said. "We're Aisha's friends."

***

Friday, April 27

Both assemblies were successful. A strong anti-bullying message was sent. Even students who usually chatted through an assembly were quiet. This stunt had hit teacher and student alike, most because they didn't like bullies, a few because they would soon be caught. Both assemblies ran overtime, the second one well past the end of lunchtime.

Claire had to skip lunch and rush through a milling crowd of students in the hallway to get to her math class. What was going on?

As she reached the Hickenman room, she had figured it out. Jack had forgotten to get on-call teachers for her—or any other teacher—while they had to be in the auditorium and the programs had each run about twenty minutes overtime. Students, who usually remembered no rules, did know that class was cancelled if a teacher was more than ten minutes late. Half the school was loose in the halls.

Claire stepped into the empty Hickenman room and put her box on the wobbly table. She sat and took what felt like her first real breath in the past week. Aisha had been on her mind non-stop. Aisha was still on her mind as she surveyed the vacant seats and crowded walls. With a shudder, she got up, grabbed her box and marched to the cafeteria to find Aisha's friends. She had questions.

The girls were sitting in the far back corner of the cafeteria, chatting over their open books. "Girls, about Aisha... Was there more than just teasing about her weight last semester?" Claire sat down at the end of the table.

"Oh, yeah. The grapevine was full of it," Maya said, pushing away her books.

"She was totally catfished," Janette interjected.

"Catfished?" Claire asked, utterly confused. "What does that mean?"

"Some jerks went into a chat room for overweight kids Aisha used to frequent and pretended to be a girl who was overweight and suicidal. Aisha wanted to help her."

Maya nodded. "It went on from September to mid-November. Aisha told her how she felt about her own body, how she thought she'd never get a boyfriend." She wiped away a tear. "She got too involved. But she thought she was saving the poor girl's life."

"Then somebody tipped her off and she saw her own letters being made fun of in another Internet chat room along with people's crass comments. Is that when she realized she had been duped?" Claire guessed.

"Yep, Aisha's parents told us the police found the computer it came from. It turned out it was a couple of Amberton football players and their cliquey cheerleader girlfriends who did it," Maya explained. "They were jealous of Aisha's marks."

"There was more than one photo-shopped picture this time, right?" Claire wanted to know.

"There were two from the change room that went viral." Janette looked disgusted. "They also photo-shopped 'before' pictures of fat people from weight loss ads and put Aisha's face on them. There were five altogether."

Tori had been silent until now. "When it all started last semester, Aisha was totally caught off guard. She had no idea why it was happening and it hurt."

"Did anybody here help her?"

"No, not until she figured it out and told her parents in November."

"Right, of course," Claire nodded her head. "When they caught the kids, the guys were suspended for three days, had their school Internet privileges withdrawn, and they were taken off the football team—when the season was over."

Tori shook her head. "Those jerks got a slap on the wrist for hurting Aisha to the core."

"Don't forget, Caitlin Somers got sent to Bellington Secondary," Danielle added.

"Oh, right. How could I forget that?" Tori said bitterly.

"Aisha's parents helped a lot," Janette said thoughtfully. "But Aisha would have done a lot better than a *C* average on her January exams if all that hadn't happened. And now this. What will all this do to her university application next year?"

Claire wished she had a good answer.

***

Claire and Chin Ho had been helping student participants prepare for the Amberton City Science Fair since October. This year the exhibition was being held in the Amberton District High School gym on Saturday, the week after the midterms.

"Great projects this year, eh, Claire?" Chin Ho commented as they stood back and admired the setup in the cafetorium. All that was left to do was to welcome the public when the doors opened in ten minutes.

"Lots of participation. Which projects do you like best? I bet Shirley would vote for the handheld that teaches French slang."

"Jack Penworth would like the robot that can do your work for you," Chin observed with a smile. "He likes to push buttons." They were both glad to have something positive to focus on for the day, after an emotionally draining week.

"I agree. But, as the advisor to the Eco Club, my vote goes to the student who researched and demonstrated a new natural way to clean sewage water."

"I see Matt's influence on you, Claire. I saw him in Bellington a while back. We had coffee. We talked about his work at Ecohydrelco."

"Really?" Matt hadn't told her.

"He definitely knows a lot about purifying water,"

She checked the time on her cellphone and made a move towards the doors. As she pushed them open, Matt was standing in the hall. "Well, speak of the devil," she said and kissed him on the cheek.

"Devil I might be, but you'll notice I am on time."

"For once," she laughed as they joined Chin.

"Matt, good to see you again!" Chin said as the men clamped hands.

"And you. How's the Science Fair looking?"

"You have some competition, sir," Chin said, pointing towards the water purification table.

"Really?" They were admiring the stalls, chatting with the participants as parents and the interested public started filing in the doors. The students had to be ready to explain and answer questions about their projects. When the people left, they could leave a ballot indicating their choice for first, second, and third prize in a box at the exit. The judges would use them to help make their decision.

Matt agreed that the boy who had learned how to clean sewage water should win first
prize.

"Of course you do," Chin teased. A student at the far end of the auditorium caught his eye. "Looks like I'm needed," he said as he broke off at a brisk walk.

"You sure do love your sewage water," Claire teased Matt.

"Nah, I love YOU!"

"Thanks… I think …" she laughed.

"When you're done here, let's go for a nice late dinner."

"I'd like that." Claire was happy. It would be their first date in a while.

Matt left after his tour of the room, to allow Claire to focus on the students. With a light kiss, he promised to pick her up at the end of the evening. From the corner of her eye she saw him joining Chin Ho in an animated conversation before he left. She was glad they seemed to get

along, as she admired the biology displays from the other participating schools.

At the end of the day it was announced that the solar panel had won first prize, the growth hormone study got second, and the third prize went to the student with the natural sewage water clean-up system. Claire knew Matt would call foul—she was looking forward to teasing him about it through dinner.

***

After a nice meal and a romantic walk through the moonlit park with Boomer, they found themselves on Claire's front porch and… just as her hopes were rising and she was about to invite him in for a nightcap, Matt's cell vibrated.

"Damn," he said with a strange look on his face as he quickly tapped a response.

"What's up?" Claire asked, already pretty sure she knew the answer.

"Got to go to Denver in the morning."

"Early? Just like that?" She raised her eyebrows.

Matt looked into her eyes and felt himself melting, "Afraid so. Really early, Claire. Sorry, I have to go home to sort out a few things and pack."

"You mean you can't come in because *you* have to *work in the evening*?" she said a bit snidely. She gave him a quick peck as he turned to go to the car.

Suddenly his leaving felt insensitive to Claire. Why hadn't he explained? He hadn't even said he'd love to come in, but... She was disappointed and it felt as if he was keeping secrets. And why would he do that? It made her wonder how she was going to survive five days with him on the fieldtrip. Her imagination was working overtime...

May

Chapter 17

<u>Sometimes Not Caring *is* the Way to Go</u>

Tuesday, May 1

Gene wasn't at school this morning and Claire had missed him at the dog park the night before. Claire was sure he had said he would be there. "Where's Gene?" she asked Don, Chin and Angus that morning before running off to her first class.

"Didn't you hear? He got swarmed on the parking lot after school last night." Angus said. "Some kids came out from behind shrubbery, took bricks and some lumber to his car, smashed it and tore the seats out as he watched."

"Holy crap!" Claire dropped her handouts on her desk. "Is he okay?"

"He was rattled, but he ran back to the lab and took cell pictures of the kids. He even got a video after he called 911." Don said.

"Unbelievable. The hoodlums! I hope they throw the book at them!"

"We all do," Chin agreed. "First Paul gets run down and now Gene is attacked. What's next?"

"Do you think there's a connection? Between Paul's accident and the attack last night?" Claire tried to absorb the possibilities.

"Who knows?" Chin said pensively. "The police will figure it out."

"They haven't found the hit and run driver yet." Claire said cynically. "How is Gene?" She was gathering her copies.

"His doctor put him on stress leave for a week or two to get over the shock and fright. The union advised him to see Henry Smyle, the board psychiatrist, for at least one session," Angus said.

"Uh-oh," Claire shook her head and raised an eyebrow. "I've heard about that guy."

Chin looked at her over his spectacles. "Now, now, Claire."

Angus watched him leave with a wide grin on his face.

***

Friday, May 4

Claire stood nervously on Gene's doorstep with Boomer. She wanted to come earlier in the week, but knowing how Matt felt about Gene she felt a bit awkward going to his home. Gene had rested for a week and now he had invited her to come for a visit. Claire and Boomer had walked over. Gene was a great work friend but she had never been to his home or met his wife.

"Claire?" the petite brunette asked as she looked up at Claire.

"Natalie, how nice to finally meet you." Claire pulled the leash to keep Boomer still.

"I'm very happy to meet you too," she said as Natalie invited them in. "And this must be the famous Boomer." She held out a hand for the dog to sniff.

Claire smiled and blushed as she looked around. The house was warm and inviting, with signs of kids and life everywhere.

After giving Boomer a quick pat, Natalie showed Claire to the living room where Gene was in a chair with P.C. at his side. After some happy sniffing, Gene managed to persuade Boomer to lie down beside P.C.

"I'll get some tea," Natalie said as she excused herself to the kitchen.

"How are you, Gene?" Claire asked tentatively.

"Still pretty rattled, I guess. I have six more weeks with those jerks."

"Have you seen Dr. Smyle yet?"

"Yeah, that's what rattled me the most." He smiled weakly.

"Oh?"

"I told him my concerns about the porn, the texting, the sexting and the Internet games the students are playing in class. He kept asking why that bothered me so much and why did I give a damn?" He imitated Henry's gestured incomprehension with his hands. "I told him it was because the class needed to learn some basic science to get their credit and to get ahead in life and the cellphone activities of more and more students are slowing that down and sometimes even preventing that. He kept repeating that it was just a job and strongly implied that it didn't matter, which I took as meaning that in his opinion my—our— profession is insignificant."

"I don't understand his angle," Claire said, shaking her head.

"He tried to persuade me that I wasn't there because I cared about kids, but because I got the shit scared out of me when they swarmed me."

"Well, you can see his point there. You were sent to him because of the swarming, weren't you?"

"Technically, yes. But it was more than that. I wouldn't have been swarmed if I hadn't stood up against the misuse of technology in my class. I naively hoped to get some pointers to help make things better in my classroom. The issue of discipline and the swarming are interconnected." His hands began to shake and he stopped to take a deep breath.

"So it was the techies? Tariq and the kids who always play games in class?"

"Of course it was. Who else? I'm new to the school. They're the only ones who could hold a grudge against me. The police have arrested them and released them into the custody of their parents. The police used the videos on my cellphone to counter the lies the kids told them and to make their case with the parents and the judge. Ironically, for once I was happy to have a cellphone in the lab."

"Bertha has given them four-day, in-school suspensions," Claire scoffed. "That's it, can you believe it?"

"Sadly, yes. I can." He sighed and patted P.C. on the head, as he collected his thoughts. "My insurance company is going to replace the car, but my rates are likely going up. I'm a high school teacher and to them my vehicle is at a greater risk now. Bertha considers the case closed."

"All because you wanted Tariq and his friends to stop wasting everyone's time and learn something."

"You should apply for Henry's job, Claire," Gene chuckled.

"Tell her the rest," Natalie said firmly as she came in with the tea.

"Yes, dear, I'll get to it." He took the cup she offered and selected a cookie. "I told him I wasn't dealing with widgets, but with real children and that's why I give a damn. I told him it's my job to teach them science and they won't get their credit or graduate if they don't pay attention."

"So he asked you if you wanted somebody to make your job easier, isn't that right dear?" Natalie said. "It sounds as if he doesn't care much himself."

Gene got up and paced and gesticulated in front of the window. "I shouted at him: 'Hell, no!' but then I realized … 'Well, maybe I do want my job made easier by having reasonable discipline enforced with sanctions that are not cruel but more than a joke and that teach them respect for others—so students who do want to learn can reach their potential. I want people to do their bloody jobs.'"

"What did he say to that?" Claire asked.

"He said one person can not change the system. It sounded so pat. He wanted to know if I think anybody cares whether I sink or swim in my job. Or that anyone gives a shit if little Johnny or worldly Mary passes or fails science."

Natalie's eyes shifted to the floor. She'd heard it before.

"Henry got in my face and I didn't like it one bit nor did I like what the man was saying. 'Let them play the games,' he said. 'Work with those who do pay attention,' he said. 'Gene, you can't fix the entire education system and it's not in your job description,' he said. Then he sat back in his rollaway chair, with that smug grin, hands joined at the fingertips, thinking he'd made his point."

"But they're people's kids," Claire said, her face flushing. "How many young people have been caught with dubious ethics in the last few years? Knowledgeable people are tracing more and more crime back to how much kids can get away with in school."

"What will happen to society when they learn—at school—that they don't have to do anything at their job and they don't have to follow rules or show up on time and they can just do whatever the heck they want and still get paid even if they get caught?" Natalie asked.

"According to Henry, that's not my job. Their parents are supposed to do that." Gene mimicked Henry's nasal voice.

"But the parents aren't doing it," Natalie said, so incensed that she almost spilled her tea.

"Do you know what his answer to that was?" Gene asked, looking straight at Claire. "He said, 'Their kids may well fail, lose their jobs and become thieves, druggies or welfare bums and the system will deal with them.'"

"That's our tax money up the pipe!" Claire said, throwing up her hands and closing her eyes. "They'll reproduce and make more generations of parasites." She gave an apologetic look
in Natalie's direction but she was watching Gene.

"But, according to Henry, that's not our responsibility." Gene paced across the room and looked at Claire, imitating Henry, pointing his finger at her. " 'Trying to save the world is going to drive you to a nervous breakdown—and sooner than you think. I'm here to save *your* life, not theirs.' That's what he said!"

"Now I understand why some teachers try to be pals with the kids and water down their courses," Claire said. "They've seen a Henry."

"I'm a team player," Gene said, tapping his chest. "If I don't fight it, I'm part of the problem, and I won't be able to live with myself. I'm a teacher because I love kids. I want to inspire them if I can, but if not, at least teach them good work habits so they can succeed and graduate and lead productive lives."

"Tell her what he said to you then, Gene," Natalie smiled encouragingly.

"He repeated that I was there because the kids had scared the hell out of me by wrecking my car. I tried again to tell him that that was only the half of it and that the other half was because of some of the spineless, namby-pamby administrators in our schools today. That if breaking rules had *real* consequences—as it does in the outside world—and if kids knew that they had *real* tests and exams to pass," Gene had to take a breath, "then they'd get some *real* self esteem and just *maybe* I wouldn't have been swarmed. And do you know what he said to that?"

"One person can't change the system," Claire and Natalie chimed in unison.

Gene stopped where he was and gave a hearty laugh. The ladies joined him. "You got it!" Henry had a face on him that said: *nobody can possibly argue with that.*

306

"And that's when you left, isn't it, darling?" Natalie said.

"'Is that your fall back line, Henry?' I asked him sarcastically. I knew this guy wasn't going to help me, in fact, he sounded like a big part of the problem. The fact is, I do know one person can't change it, but the system will only get worse if everybody follows advice like Henry's. I stood up, picked up my jacket and left. To me the session was over. I may be an idealist, but I try. I'll rest up, get back in the ring and take my chances."

"You will!" Claire cheered. She watched Natalie walk over to her husband and put her hands on his shoulders. She was so supportive. If she had been swarmed, Claire wondered, would Matt have cheered her back to work? Would he have stood by her, knowing she was doing the right thing? Or would he have persuaded her to walk out? Would she have had the courage and conviction to go back, like Gene? Up against present odds, was fighting the good fight worth it?

***

Monday, May 7

The following week, Gene was back in the science office, ready for class. "A friend gave me this old cellphone," he told Claire and Chin. "It gave me an idea that could put an end to my *torture by technology*—for a while, anyway. I don't care what Bertha thinks if she finds out. She can turkey-trot me to another school if she wants, but I intend to try it this Wednesday."

"What are you going to do?" Claire saw mischief in Gene's twinkly eyes.

"I'm going to turn it into a lesson for my worst offending grade tens," he said. "You have a spare when I have my tens, Claire. Come and watch at the back door if you want. Just don't let them see you." His glasses moved up and down as he wiggled his eyebrows mischievously.

"I'm intrigued," Claire said, rubbing her hands together. "It sounds like fun!" Chin just smiled.

***

Wednesday, May 9

During her spare, Claire followed Gene to his grade ten science class, excited to see the show. Claire stayed by the back door of the lab. As he entered the front door of the lab, Gene stopped Justin Menzies, a smart, reliable boy who usually sat at the front.

"Justin, I need your help," Gene whispered to the boy. Claire listened.

"Sure, sir," the boy nodded, looking up at his teacher.

"I need you to help me teach the techies a lesson," Gene said softly. "I want you to take this old cellphone and play a game on it during class."

Justin smiled. He looked at the thing with trepidation. "Which game?"

"Any game, it doesn't matter. Just as long as it looks like you're playing."

"OK," Justin said. "So, I can just pretend to play?"

It dawned on Gene that Justin might have to pretend. He didn't play videogames—he paid attention in class. "That'll be fine, Justin. Now, I'm going to yell at you, but I won't be mad. I'll just be acting. You understand?" Gene looked at him hopefully.

"Yes, sir," Justin nodded with a big grin on his face.

"I'll give you lunch money for a week," Gene said. "I just want to make an impression on the folks who always play games in class."

"I'm in, Mr. Putnam. I hate what they did to your car. It'll be fun. And you don't have to give me anything." Justin was excited to be part of the ruse. "Lots of students are tired of waiting for kids who never pay attention and who have to be told what we're doing before they tell us
that they have no clue."

"Our secret?" Gene asked.

"You bet, sir. Don't worry sir." Justin gave Gene a high five and entered the classroom, cellphone in hand.

"Just be yourself, Justin."

The bell went. The videogame players coming in were confident that they had taught Mr. Putnam a lesson earlier in the month. They swaggered into class, their fingers flying over their cellphones. Gene began his lesson, reminding them to put away their cell phones. Two minutes later, he looked at Justin, playing on the cellphone. Claire watched silently at the back door.

Gene grabbed the cellphone from Justin's hands. "I'll take that, young man," he shouted. "You know you shouldn't be playing games in class."

"B ... b ... but ..." Gene had moved so fast, Justin really was startled. But Gene had picked the right student. Justin could act. Justin stood up and looking like he was about to cry, stammered, "B... b... but sir..."

"I'm going to teach you a lesson, Mr. Menzies." Gene gave him a quick wink as he walked to the demonstration desk and took out a hammer and flamboyantly slammed it down beside the handheld game on the demo counter. As he did it, he watched the regular techies to see their reaction. A few heads went up nonchalantly, but they went back down, so Gene shouted. "Justin, this is what I will do with cellphones or handhelds that are being used during lessons from now on." As he said it, he slammed the hammer down hard a second time, this time on the cellphone.

The scrunch of the cellphone caught the techies' attention. Claire saw the expressions on the faces at the back of the class and had to step away from the door. She was doubling over as she stifled her laughter. But Gene's continued hammer blows got her back into position.

Gene hit it again. Pieces flew. "How..." smash! "Many..." bang! "Times..." thump! "Do I have to say..." bang, bang! "No tech gadgets on in my class?" With a final swing, the cellphone was shattered.

"Holy shit!" a kid shouted at the back of the room.

"I tol' ya. He's off his rocker," another responded.

"What the hell?"

Gene gave it one more blow. As the last bits of the cellphone settled on the ground, he looked up to see a room full of staring eyes and gaping mouths. He pointed the hammer squarely at Justin.

"Is that clear enough, young man?" he asked, his chest heavy with the effort.

Justin nodded nervously, pretending to be scared.

"Who's next?"

"You can't do that, sir!" some kids at the back shouted. Gene raised an eyebrow. "Oh? I happen to think I just did."

"We'll get you fired!" Tariq said.

"Go ahead. It'll make my day!" Gene shot back.

He tossed the hammer back into the open drawer. The students in the front row jumped.

311

"Now, get to work. Chapter ten…"

Without so much as a word, the class turned their attention to their books.

***

Thursday, May 10

Bertha heard about the destruction of the cellphone and called Gene into her office for a tongue-lashing.

"Whose cellphone did you destroy?"

"Mine."

"Did you return from stress leave too soon? You should be setting a good example for your students and control your emotions."

"I wouldn't have such emotions if the kids did their part in the education process as prescribed in the Education Act."

"Do you need an anger management session?"

"I don't think so, Bertha. Do you? My classes were already much better today, now that I have control over the games." With that, Gene left her office.

Later, he told Claire, "Sometimes not caring *is* the way to go. You just have to know what *not* to care about."

Chapter 18

Insecurities, a Gift and Tori Solves a Mystery

Monday, May 14

Three days before their departure, Claire had a meeting with Eco Club parents to collect the outstanding money, remind them to hand in the permission forms, find out who would help chaperone and give everybody the final program for the trip to Algonquin Park. The club members were excited. Matt was there as promised. He worked beside Claire handing out the lists of clothing, equipment, and groceries required for the trip. Serge was not. There would be no spaghetti. He needed the money back to help pay for the damage he had done in the lab.

Now that Claire knew Matt was coming, she called for four volunteers—two men, two women—to assist in chaperoning. Four parents jumped at the opportunity, waving their police-check papers.

After a short question and answer session everyone mingled.

While Claire was glad Matt was there, her self-confidence had taken a beating. After over a year of happy

313

times, out of the blue they'd had two serious quarrels in the last two months and had only been together twice since the last one, less than an hour after she had been sure he was about to pop 'the' question. It had felt like a break-up. She had to admit to herself that the times they had been together since then had been pleasant, but she still felt like a yoyo.

Everybody treated them as an item and in love, and they were right—to an extent—but Claire felt like a fraud because of her insecurities. She obsessed about it. Why should she give up her profession for a man she wasn't sure of? After high school, where they went 'steady' for three years, he had gone to Queens and she to McMaster University. He had never written or returned a call. Maybe he had just gone out with her until something more convenient turned up. He had married Jennifer, hadn't he? Claire blushed when people looked at them working together. Was he just a good friend? Or was he more? She looked at him. Who were his friends? In high school, she had known them all. He was jealous of Gene and the only time she had seen Matt with another man other than his Ecohydrelco colleagues, was at the Science Fair when he
had gone off to talk to Chin Ho.

She watched him. He was making himself useful and looked as if he didn't have a care in the world. What were his true feelings? How could he procrastinate for so long? Would he ever propose? Where did he go after the Science Fair when he got that text and he wouldn't come in? Would he ever stay in one place long enough to settle down? At thirty-three, Claire's reproductive clock was ticking. She was glad that they wouldn't be in the same tent or yurt on this trip. Too much time together could be uncomfortable.

Matt had introduced himself to volunteer chaperones Josh and Ryan, while Claire chatted with Hester and June. There were guidelines to be followed. Claire gave them each a copy of the booklet with the board policy on mixed gender, overnight trips. The room buzzed with excitement. As the evening came to a close, Claire found herself discussing the plans a bit awkwardly with Matt.

"The final canoe trips will be popular, don't you think? It's good to end on a high note," Matt said. He was getting excited about the trip.

"It'll wear them out for the ride home, too," Claire added with satisfaction. "I hope we'll see some wildlife this time.

"Don't worry. The kids won't disappoint," Matt said with a laugh.

"No, I mean there should be fawns, bear cubs, and moose calves by late May." Claire wasn't quite as relaxed as Matt seemed to be.

"I hope so. It'll be quiet without Boomer. You'll get some pictures this time, I'm sure." Matt said with an easy grin.

"The spring flowers will be out and the trees will be fully leafed. I love that fresh green," Claire said.

Matt looked at her. "It'll still be pretty wet from the spring runoff."

"It'll be muddy then. I loved mud as a kid. Are 'boots' on the list?"

Matt checked the clipboard. "Yup. They're on."

They chatted on like good friends, not really connecting deeply. Then Matt helped Claire clean up. It was almost like old times. Claire wondered if perhaps Matt thought they had solved their problem that night on the living room rug.

***

Tuesday, May 15

"Hey guys! Look what my Dad gave me." Ricky Penworth was running toward a clump
of his classmates at their lockers down the hall from Claire's lab.

Darryl and Walter sauntered over to see Ricky's gift. It was the latest igadget and he had it in a brand new case. Ricky pointed out that he had loaded it with apps. Walter and Darryl had to admit to themselves that they were envious.

"Nice kit, Ricky. D'ya know how ta use it?" sneered Walter.

Before Ricky could open his mouth, Darryl snatched the cellphone and ran around the corner towards the science hall.

"Come an' get it, lardy-buns. Come an' get it, ya stinking ball o' pig-shit."

Walter ran around the corner too. Ricky puffed after them, face red, eyes tearing up with the effort. "Give it back, turd-heads!"

Logan Stanley and Dwayne Dufresne got in his way. "Ooooh … you called them *turd-heads*! Is that the best you can do, you son-of-a-prick?"

"Too bad, Ricky! Too bad," taunted Justine Jones and Karla Kozak.

When he finally caught up to them, Logan yelled, "Hébert's coming, Ricky. Why don't you tell on us, scrotum-face?"

Not to be outdone, Dwayne added, "Oh, I'm scared! Are you going to tell your daddy on us?"

"Don't worry. He'll fix it," taunted Darryl, shaking the cellphone just beyond his reach.

"Should I call him? Maybe he can help you... again," Logan mocked.

Claire heard it as she was unlocking the lab door and shook her head. She was starting to admit to herself that it was hopeless. Between Ricky and his parents, there was nothing more she could do for this boy to succeed in science or socially. These people would never change. She could no longer afford to care about Ricky.

If he came the last week of class asking for an assignment to make up for all the work he hadn't done, she intended to refuse him, she told herself. She knew Bertha would somehow manipulate her into passing him and she dreaded the vain attempt at a fight she would put up to keep Ricky in grade ten science for another year—away from the kids who hated him and had taunted him for years.

Muriel would object, Jack would be indignant, Bertha would give him the marks, and he would be a junior where the same unhappy saga would play out—perhaps with a violent end this time. These people made their own trouble.

It frustrated Claire that Muriel wouldn't risk him doing his own work. It told Claire—and Ricky for that matter—that even his mother had no faith in him. Worse, Ricky learned that passing was the only goal, whether he learned anything or not.

Claire felt terrible for Ricky, because if he had any clue at all—and his guidance file said he did have normal intelligence—school for him must be some kind of hell, never understanding the work and always knowing that every last one of his classmates thought he was the spoiled class dimwit. On the other hand, maybe he just never thought about it. It had been his life for so long.

The way Claire saw it he should be given paper and a pencil and put back into grade six or seven, whatever level he could handle without help. Then he should be allowed to do his own work and to progress at his own pace until he gained some

318

motivation and self-esteem. For anyone else, she might suggest home schooling, but with Muriel around that wouldn't work. He needed professional help. After that, he should choose his own way—probably a vocational school. Skilled craftsmen are always needed and they make a good living.

Still, Claire obsessed. She hated giving up. What could she have done better? Where did she go wrong? Her common sense reminded her that she had wasted enough time on Ricky and that she should concentrate on the students he had deprived of her time and who had a chance of passing.

"Boys!" she yelled out the door. "That's enough! Get in here!"

***

Pressured by the Ames, Bertha and Jack had interviewed every girl they could think of in trying to get someone to admit to photographing Aisha in the change room the month before, but no one would admit to it. Stepping up the pressure, the police had interviewed all the friends—both sexes—of the fellow who uploaded it to the social network but their efforts led nowhere. Even with the promise of immunity, there had been no luck. Bertha and Jack were running out of ideas and out of time as they met a solid brick wall.

On the advice of her police officer husband, Kristen Jaworski walked the halls listening to the kids' gossip and making small talk. Steve was sure somebody would eventually drop a clue. But before long Kristen too was drawn away by other duties. Final exams had to be scheduled and a graduation needed to be put on. The official search for the photographer had tapered off until somebody stumbled across her by accident.

Aisha Ames had not been to school since the photo-shopping incident and all her teachers were concerned. For the three weeks since her suicide attempt, she had been under observation in a special unit in the hospital. The board was paying for a child psychologist to help her. The weight she had lost skiing was not returning. She was refusing to eat.

Aisha's teachers sent work to the hospital for her and offered to tutor her when she felt better. They would arrange for Aisha to take her final exams privately in an empty classroom or at home with a teacher volunteer whenever she was ready if she wanted it. Several teachers had already volunteered. They'd do it during their holidays if necessary.

Aisha's parents were investigating a transfer to a high school in another province for her senior year. But how do you get away from the Internet? Home schooling was another option. Aisha's parents were not wealthy, but they were angry enough to hire a lawyer to apply to have Aisha's right to privacy enforced, write a cease and desist order and start a legal fight with the board over the lack of control over student-owned technology. The board's Technology Review Committee's work had come to a halt while the *Ames issue* was being resolved.

In spite of the seriousness of the incident with Aisha the board still had a problem banning cellphones because many parents wanted to be able to contact their children at the drop of a hat. Others, like Jack Penworth himself, had given in to their children begging for a cellphone or a tablet. The Ames had little hope of ever getting the board to ban cellphones without a major legal battle—even if a lot of the teaching profession agreed with them.

Aisha's friends missed her. Two of them came to the hospital after school every day. But Aisha was still suspicious that they had played a role in the bullying. She was listless and refusing to eat and didn't want company and she screamed at them to go away whenever they came. The girls didn't give up.

Paul Fraser visited Aisha in the hospital. He was now well enough to go around and help young patients with elementary math and he had heard about the cyber bullying and wanted to see if he could help Aisha. He had taught Aisha math in grades nine and ten and she trusted him. When he explained to her that he could not imagine that Tori, Danielle, Maya and Janette could possibly have participated in such tyranny and that it was most likely a lie fabricated by some of the clique girls, Aisha relented and let her friends visit.

She started to eat again. The nurses encouraged the girls to bring things to distract Aisha and make her laugh: magazines, DVDs, puzzles, the laptop, computer games, her charm bracelet. One day at a time.

Paul, anxious to see if he could remember it, started to tutor Aisha in grade eleven math and later, with Claire's and her friends' help, they worked on her biology. "You're helping me remember my skills," Paul told her, rubbing his left calf as he adjusted himself in his wheelchair. He was walking better after the attentions of his therapist, but he still had a way to go. His memory, much to his chagrin, was still iffy and headaches and dizziness sometimes kept him in bed. Still, he was pushing forward, determined to get back to his life.

"Thanks for the lessons. I enjoy your company, Mr. Fraser," Aisha said one day when he had a headache and she had gone to visit him. "Are you going to be okay?"

Paul smiled. The caring girl he had known was coming back. "Me? Oh, I'm fine. Getting hit by a car isn't going to stop me." He hooked his thumbs in his pyjama top and pulled. Aisha smiled. "And you'll be fine too, Aisha. We're not going to let the jerks get us down."

"No, Mr. Fraser, we won't."

***

During the last ten days of classes, when the news about Aisha had faded at school and the assembly had temporarily curbed the bullying, the school grapevine had gone on to other things and Tori found out who had taken Aisha's picture in the change room. The news gave Aisha's recovery a big boost. Now

322

that she knew who the enemy was, more of her fears and insecurities were disappearing.

"How did you do it?" the girls asked.

"I infiltrated their stupid clique. The teachers and big fat Miss Stack couldn't do that. I talked to Alicia Jonasson and Heather Walton."

"But they're not *in*-girls, Tori. They're silly clique wannabes," Maya said.

"Exactly. Weak links," she winked. "The dumb '*in*-girls' gossip in front of them and they all know who did it. Heather and Alicia were stupid enough to think I was a member. It wasn't
long before they let it slip."

"So who was it?" Aisha was blushing but Maya and Danielle were dying to know.

Tori looked at Aisha, who nodded. "Maziyar Bizhani got the pictures from Karla Kozak's cellphone. She'd loaned it to Stella Grachin. Karla is Maziyar's cousin and she dared Stella to take some pictures of somebody in a change booth as an initiation for getting into the clique." Tori's thin face flushed with anger. "Karla isn't even a member. That tells you how stupid Stella is. Stack and Penworth probably can't find her because she doesn't even know she did it. When she gave the camera back, Maziyar was there and he saw the so-called fun they could have with the pictures. Everyone already knows that Maziyar photo-shopped them and put them online."

Tori's expression was downcast as she turned to Aisha. "I had to pretend I didn't like you, Aisha, or they wouldn't have talked. I'm sorry."

"Don't worry about that, Tori. I'm just glad you found out," Aisha said. She gave Tori a reassuring hug. "Thanks so much! You guys are the best friends ever."

"Okay, so what happened when you told Miss Jaworski?" Danielle asked.

"Miss Jaworski wasn't in her office."

"Dang! You mean you had to go to Penworth?" Aisha gasped.

"Yup, I went to Penworth's office and told him. He looked shocked. His eyes were open wide and his chin just hung there."

"I wish I'd been there to see that!" Janette and Maya giggled.

Just then, a nurse came in to check on Aisha and offered them all some cookies and juice.

When the nurse had left, Tori continued. "He wanted to know how I did it, so I told him." She stood back, her head high.

"What did he say?"

"What did he do?"

"He took me to see Miss Stack. Boy, was she surprised," Tori said with a snicker. "I think she'd given up on ever finding out. She said, 'I cannot believe that a student could do what we and the police could not,'" Tori mimicked the principal. "They were totally embarrassed. They knew I was right." The girls all laughed at Tori's rendition of Bertha's voice. "She wanted to know if I was absolutely sure of it and then she said they would take it from there and I shouldn't play detective anymore and concentrate on my exams."

"Didn't they even thank you?"

"Well, sort of, but when I asked them if they would take the information to the police, they hesitated, saying they didn't want to accuse the wrong person—let's face it, Stella probably had no idea—and they didn't want to hurt you anymore, the clique girls could have been lying, I could have imagined it, and the old *those things are to be left to adults*—yadda, yadda, yadda."

"There are legalities to keep in mind that you would not understand, Tori," Danielle and Janette said, mimicking Mr. Penworth.

"Yup, they said that, too." By this time the girls were laughing heartily. Then Tori became serious again. "But it was like the brush off. It made me really mad but I was afraid to show it, so I just said, 'Okay, Miss Stack,' and left. I know better."

Aisha was dumbfounded. Danielle, Maya, and Janette were disgusted when Tori had finished her story. They had spoken to their parents about switching schools along with Aisha in September. For a brief moment Tori considered it too.

But then she applied Claire's lesson of separating the components of a problem: Aisha was feeling better. That had been her goal and she had achieved it.

Chapter 19

The Algonquin Trip and Ricky's Comeuppance

Thursday, May 17

The Eco-group was leaving for Algonquin on the Thursday before the Victoria Day weekend. It was a sunny and warm morning in Amberton. By eight a.m. the parking lot was a cheerful circus of kids and bags with Claire, Hester, June, Matt, Ryan and Josh as ringmasters. The driver was masterfully loading the gear into the hold and, as each bag was loaded, its owner boarded the bus. Bertha was there, looking important for the parents.

Of course, one girl's parents had to drive home to find her medication and her healthcare card. Another had left her groceries and sandwich lunch at home on the kitchen table. A third had to have the driver get his suitcase out again because he'd packed his cellphone in it and he wouldn't survive if he couldn't text his friends and take pictures on the bus. The driver responded to such requests with admirable patience. Slowly the havoc dissipated.

When Claire was satisfied that everyone was accounted for and every kid had his or her luggage, healthcare card, health information, clothes, boots, tooth brush, tent, sleeping bag, towels, packed lunch, and groceries, the driver closed the door. Parents formed a line to wave goodbye to their offspring who were climbing over each other to wave and tap on the windows. The line stepped back as the bus made its way out of the parking lot at eight thirty-seven a.m.

On the bus, between questions from students and volunteers, Claire and Matt were able to grab a few moments. They reminisced about their trip in March, and their hopes for this trip, avoiding sensitive issues on a bus full of teenagers. They were relieved to finally be in the bus, leaning against each other for a few hours. Both had been busy for weeks and had missed each other. Boomer was in Doggy Daycare at the obedience school.

They arrived at Algonquin just after six p.m. The gates were usually closed around six but Claire texted ahead and Adam, one of the rangers, knowing a bus of high school students from south-western Ontario was coming, stayed to register them. They drove to the Rock Lake campground. Everyone was excited to get off the bus and get moving. Claire assigned the campsites. Two groups got it wrong. Another group suddenly realized they had brought a blow up boat instead of a tent and had to be dispersed into other tents. They thought the boat might be fun, but they hadn't brought the pump to inflate it nor the oars. Matt admired the way Claire calmly sorted it all out. The nights in Algonquin were still cold but the days were getting longer and warmer. Ryan, Matt and Josh urged the kids to take advantage of the fading light to pitch their tents. The chaperones helped the two groups who had set up on the wrong sites move their tents to the correct ones before they'd need flashlights. It was all done with lots of energy, shouting, and laughter.

Finally, campfires were lit and sticks were being cut to roast hot dogs. Hester and June set up a picnic table with buns, mustard, relish, bacon bits, cheese, drinks, and the boxes of fixings for s'mores. After the meal, everyone settled down and told stories until the fires had burned to embers, when Josh and Ryan poured buckets of water over them. By eleven o'clock, thirty-four exhausted but still giggling kids had crawled into sleeping bags and six weary adults retired to theirs.

***

A half hour later, thinking everyone asleep, Claire and Matt sneaked out and met beside a little copse of trees.

"Would you say that was a successful day?" Matt asked.

"I would. We haven't lost any," Claire answered. "Would you?"

"Yup! I'm amazed at the way you handle things: the scuffle between Martin and Eric; Wendy's tears when she realized she'd forgotten to charge her cellphone. You're good at this, Clarikins. You really are."

"I don't always feel that way, but things did go well today. It could all go wrong tomorrow. That's what makes teaching interesting—you never know what'll happen next."

"Never a dull moment, eh?" Matt put his arm around her as they looked at the sky. "Have you ever seen so many stars?"

"Last March when we were here to reconnoitre."

Matt turned to face her and put his other arm around her. "I love you."

"Be careful," Claire whispered. "The shrubs have ears. Juvenile eyes may be watching us with cellphone cameras poised through tent flaps. Before you know it, they'll be tweeting about us."

"I don't care," Matt said, pulling her into a snug embrace. "I've been thinking. When school's out we're going to solve our work problems." He had noticed Claire's face when he had received the text to go to Colorado. She had looked hurt, but he hadn't been able to explain because it had been for a confidential interview with an Ecohydrelco contact in Denver who worked as an advisor to Bellington University. In Colorado, Matt had made it to second base in a plan to change his job, but nothing was sure yet and he didn't want to get Claire's hopes up. The fact that Gene wasn't on this trip reassured him that they were just colleagues who shared an interest in dogs.

Claire sensed his reassurance and responded with a deep questioning look as her lips found his. She pressed her breasts against his chest and felt him swelling against her.

"What was that?" Claire pulled away suddenly and tilted her head to the side.

"Well, if I have to tell you…" Matt jibed.

"Not that!" Claire slapped his chest lightly. "Shhh…"

This time Matt heard the rustling behind her. Sylvia Woodhouse stepped out of the trees and nearly had a heart attack at the sight of them in the shadows. She thought it was a bear.

"Sorry, Miss H.," she whispered when she recognized them. "I was looking for the washroom." She turned her head from side to side, her long hair swinging.

"It's alright," Claire said, her cheeks flushed. "We were just saying goodnight…Don't you have a flashlight?"

"They're reading with it in the tent," Sylvia smiled, knowingly. "Don't worry, Miss H., I didn't see anything."

"Thanks." Claire smiled as she switched on her flashlight and pointed it at the path towards the facilities. "You see that light over there? Head for it."

With a little wave, Sylvia dashed off into the moonlit night.

"Didn't I tell you?" chuckled Claire, still blushing. "Adolescent eyes and ears. We're lucky it was just Sylvia."

Matt laughed. "We'd better hit the sack. We have our thirty-four kids to organize tomorrow."

Claire gave him a long goodnight kiss. "I'll wait for Sylvia to make sure she gets back alright. See you in the morning."

"I can do that for you, Clarikins. You go to bed," Matt offered.

"No, I'm responsible. I'll do it." Claire would not pass the buck.

***

At seven-thirty the next morning, Hester and June went about shouting, "Wake up time!" When the first bunch was up and dressed, Josh, Matt and Ryan shouted like drill sergeants to get the rest of the sleepyheads up. "There's a schedule to keep, folks. Get some breakfast and decide who's cooking supper for your group."

"What are we doing this morning, Mr. Granger?" Maxine Young asked. It was obvious she had never been on a trip like this before.

"There's a talk about *Algonquin in the Spring* that starts at nine-thirty sharp at the Visitor Centre and then we watch a forty-minute documentary about the work at the park. At eleven-thirty we all return to the campsite for chilli con carne. Do you like that?"

"Yeah, I guess so," Maxine said, as she ambled back to her group.

After the documentary, Adam, who had given the talk, warned them all that the bears were coming out of hibernation and would be hungry. "The females have cubs and will be protective of them and very aggressive if you go near them. Also, keep your camp absolutely clean. The bears will smell any food you leave out or in your tents, and come for it, so absolutely no snacking at night in your tents and all garbage goes into the container. Do not go anywhere without a buddy. Miss Hébert has some bear-bells, which she is now handing out for you to wear as you walk or hike to warn bears humans are coming. The good news is that the bears don't want to see you either, just your food. They'll leave if they hear you coming. But they'll take you if you insist on bothering them. The key is not to surprise them. Any questions?"

There were no questions.

***

After lunch there was a choice of hikes, each with a guide to explain the history, ecology and biology of the area and answer questions.

After the afternoon hike, the kids had some time to themselves while the designated cooks got a burger supper ready. Many were tired from the fresh air and exercise and some had scrapes from the hikes. Claire had a first aid kit and cleaned and patched up the worst ones; then hamburgers, campfire stories and into the tents like the first night—only faster.

Saturday was a repeat of Friday, with a shorter presentation from the rangers and longer hikes. Again, the kids were there with bells on—literally—to ward off the bears. Sunday and Monday there were guided canoe trips instead of the afternoon hikes. The presentations were hands-on native craft sessions.

Nine kids went canoeing on Sunday, twelve on Monday. They learned to paddle and portage as a team and to prepare and eat camper's dried food. The canoe trips gave them lots to talk about: the canoe that tipped; relieving themselves in the woods; what to use if they forgot the toilet paper; how lumpy the trail food was; how gross it tasted; portaging and dropping things; wildlife they thought they saw but could not photograph; how hungry they got; how many blackfly bites they got and where; who caught a fish and how they cooked it and ate it; and how much their muscles ached after the whole escapade.

Those who did not go canoeing got experience animal tracking, rock climbing, carving, beading, Indian life skills and using natural fibres for making rope or baskets. A few kids rented equipment for trout fishing, but the proviso from Claire was that they had to cook and eat the trout they caught or release it. There was no way to take a trout home other than in a photograph. Most did one or more of the workshops. The kids who opted for workshops had crafts to show: wooden carvings, ropes, several baskets and a lot of half-finished items. Maxine made a basket. There wasn't a face without a smile, especially Maxine's. She loved the experience and the holiday from her parents.

***

Monday, May 21

The last afternoon everyone had a few hours of spare time. The kids invented their own extra-curricular activities: smooching behind trees; capture the flag; throwing rocks in the lake; telling lewd stories and jokes; nature photography; exploring; snoozing; texting; games on their cellphones, all that teen stuff.

"Well, how about that hike?" Matt said as he tossed the dregs of his coffee into the low burning fire.

"Alright!" Claire answered, jumping up. "I've been looking forward to this for months."

"Where are you off to?" Hester asked.

"Booth's Rock Trail," Matt said. "Er...are you guys okay with that?"

"Nice spot," Ryan nodded. "Gorgeous. Have fun." The others nodded.

"WE will," Matt said with a wink. "Ready, Claire?"

"Sure am." She grabbed her camera and hung it around her neck. "Bear bells?" she asked as they made their way to the edge of the campground.

"In your pocket if you want to get pictures of wildlife."

"Good thinking. We don't want to scare the deer away."

They followed the trail along the edge of the rise, curving away from the lakes, heading for the lookout. After about twenty minutes a twig snapped behind Claire and she stopped, and tapped on Matt's shoulder. They tilted their heads and looked at each other. They didn't have any food. When no bear appeared on the trail behind them, they went on. The trail was rocky, but it was a beautiful uphill walk and remembering that they would not see any animals if they talked, they were very quiet. Again, Claire heard something. She signalled Matt and they hid by some shrubs. After a few minutes, they saw Maxine. "What are you doing, Maxine?"

"C'n I come with you?"

Claire looked at Matt. Matt looked at Claire. They shrugged their shoulders.

"Sure, Maxine. Come on. But keep up and don't talk. We're trying to take pictures of animals."

"Okay, Mr. Granger."

"Shhh!"

336

A half hour later, about two-thirds of the way up, Claire was able to take a few pictures of a doe and a newborn fawn, using her zoom. Maxine had never seen one and was open-mouthed. As they went on, Maxine took pictures of the landscape and the view over the lakes behind them with her cell.

After a hike of about fifty minutes, they were close to the top and approaching a clearing when Matt tapped Claire on the shoulder and pointed to a spot about thirty metres ahead. A sapling was swaying back and forth, but there was no wind. All three stopped while their gaze explored up the tree and they saw a little black bear cub cradled in branches eating fresh green foliage. Aiming her zoom lens, Claire took pictures of the cub. It moved up a branch. Claire took a couple of steps over to get a better view of the cub higher up the tree. Suddenly she lost her footing and fell, slid and rolled thirty feet down the slope to the rocks, brambles and grass below. Her screams brought the mother bear running. Matt scrambled down the bank almost as fast as Claire fell. Maxine was screaming at the top of her lungs as she followed.

"Oh Claire! Claire! Wake up," Matt said frantically a few minutes later as he kneeled down and gently held her shoulders. "Come on, Claire, open those beautiful eyes." His own eyes
flicked up and around, searching for the bear. "Come on…"

"Wha?" she finally mumbled. "You okay? Where's Maxine?"

"Oh, thank God!" Matt bent closer to her face and looked into her still slightly crossed eyes. "Don't move," he said as he rolled up his jacket and carefully put it under her head. Then he looked around and saw Maxine hanging onto some roots halfway up the bank, frozen with fear. The mother bear was pacing along the ridge, followed by her cub. Matt helped her down.

"I'm so scared of bears, Mr. Granger!"

"Me too, Maxine, me too."

"Ouch!" Claire reached a hand up to feel the large lump that was already forming on the back of her head. "What happened?"

"A big stone gave way and you became part of a rock slide," he explained lamely, his eyes on her and simultaneously watching for Mama Bear. "You'll be alright. Don't worry."

"The bear?" Claire's eyes flew open. "Holy cows, Matt, where's the bear? Where's Maxine?"

"It's okay. I don't see the bear anymore and Maxine's right here," he said, as he wiped
the hair back from her bruised forehead. "Where does it hurt?"

Maxine hovered over Matt's shoulder, trembling and chewing on her thumbnail.

Claire closed her eyes and moaned. "Everywhere."

Matt checked her arms, her legs and her ankles and found lots of bumps, scratches and bruises. Then Claire tried to move and screamed in pain. "Ouch! My tailbone!" Matt helped her

into a more comfortable position on her right side.

Shaken, Matt sat on a rock to collect his thoughts. He couldn't carry Claire or Maxine up the steep bank or through the brush below. If he left them here to get help, the bear or some wolves or a coyote might show up. He had to stay. Finally, he thought of his cellphone. Shit. After five days, the battery was dead. "Claire, do you have your cellphone?"

"Jacket... pocket..." she moaned.

Matt gently patted her pocket on her upper side, to see if it had the cellphone in it. Drat. It was in the lower one. Oh dammit, she's lying on it, he thought. He hoped the cellphone wasn't broken, and not wanting to move her, he gently tugged at her jacket to pull the pocket out from under her hip. "Got it!" he exclaimed as she screamed in pain. "Please God, let it not be broken," he muttered to himself as he stood up. "Let it work."

There wasn't much battery left and the reception bars didn't look encouraging but there might be enough for one call. Should he call 911 or one of the chaperones and have them call 911? If he called 911 it would be farther and he'd have to explain where they were, and he wasn't sure there would be time to explain that with so little power. Algonquin was such a big place.

Then he remembered that the chaperones had all exchanged cell numbers. His list was in his back pocket. He called the one who had the best cellphone.

"Ryan, it's Matt. We've had an accident and Claire is hurt, down at the bottom of the rock face off that trail…" The phone went dead. Oh God, what was he going to do now?

"My cell's working, Mr. Granger," a soft voice behind him said. "You can use mine. Here."

Matt gratefully accepted Maxine's phone and re-dialled the number. This time he finished the message for Ryan. "Booth's something or other, about forty-five minutes—maybe an hour—up from the camp."

"Booth's Rock Trail, Mr. Granger. It's called Booth's Rock Trail."

"Booth's Rock Trail. We'll need a board to get her up the bank, Ryan. Maxine's here, too… No she's not hurt, only Claire. Can you call 911?" Matt didn't hear the answer. Claire was drifting in and out of consciousness from the pain and now Maxine's cell died too.

"You should have told him there are bears around, Mr. Granger. I don't like bears."

"What did he say?" Claire asked weakly.

"He said to sit tight. They're on their way," Matt fibbed. He hadn't heard the reply. "Now all we have to do is sit back and wait."

"Easy for you to say," Claire mumbled. "I think my coccyx is broken."

Matt laughed out loud. "God, even with a broken butt, you amaze me." He knelt down and kissed her on an unscratched spot on her forehead. She was shivering. Maxine put her jacket under Claire's head so Matt could cover her with his warmer jacket. "Just rest, Claire. Maxine'll keep watch."

He walked around and found a sapling lying on the ground. He used his pocketknife to cut it to make a strong pointed stick he could use against any animal that might show up. He kept Maxine busy collecting some of the soft grasses that grew along the bank and packing it around Claire to keep her warm and make her more comfortable. The minutes crept by. Matt started collecting stones and branches to make a fire if it got dark. Maxine helped to find wood but stayed close to Claire.

A few metres away, Matt almost stepped on Claire's camera. The display was cracked, but she might still get her pictures. Matt looked up to the darkening sky and as he worked he wondered how they would get through the night. He had some matches in his pocket for lighting the evening bonfires and was soon ready to light a fire.

After what seemed like hours but was only about forty-five minutes, they heard voices from above. "Miss Hébert! Miss H.!" Matt saw a long row of worried young faces, peering over the ledge. The kids had beaten the adults up the rise.

"Here!" Matt yelled up. "We're down here!"

"They're here!" Maxine yelled, waking Claire and looking up at the line of campers who had come up the trail. There had been no time to organize everyone. The word had spread like wildfire and they had all come. "We're coming down," some of the boys shouted.

"No, wait, STOP guys!" Matt yelled, his hands held up to stop them. "The rangers will need you up there!"

Finally, Josh and Ryan came into view, huffing with the exercise of racing up the trail.

"The rangers are on the way with first aid," Josh yelled down between huffs. "They've got a board, some ropes and blankets."

"Thank God," Matt said as he fell to his knees beside Claire. "Hear that, Clarikins? Ranger Adam is on his way to rescue you."

Claire smiled weakly. "My hero." She reached a shaky hand up and pressed it to Matt's cheek. He turned his head and kissed her palm.

"Ooo-ooo-ooooo," some of the kids snickered from above. Matt waved them off and stayed by Claire's side until Adam and Dan arrived with the truck. Adam lowered himself with a rope and together he and Matt gently placed her on the backboard, on her side, with a rolled blanket under her head. He put one icepack on her head and another on her coccyx. They immobilized her with blanket rolls and strapped her securely to the board so she wouldn't move when they hauled her up. Dan,

Ryan and Josh were at the top, working the ropes. The kids helped pull and cheered when Claire finally reached the top. Matt was bewildered at the heartiness of it. Finally, Maxine, Matt and Adam were all back up the bank and Matt couldn't get near his girlfriend for all the concerned kids hovering over her. "We gotcha, Miss H.," four boys said as they lifted the board onto the truck bed. Matt quickly climbed into place beside her.

"Well done, boys," Matt said as they slowly started down the trail.

Claire smiled at him. "They've got me. Ouch. I can feel every root—ouch— and bump the truck hits. Ouch." Then she passed out.

The truck drove them to the ranger station where an ambulance was waiting.

***

It was half past eleven when a cab dropped them off and Claire hobbled back into the camp with Matt's help. The doctors at the hospital had given her the all clear to spend the last night in the park. She'd be uncomfortable no matter where she was and she insisted she'd be happier at the park.

"Here they come!" one student yelled.

"Are you okay, Miss H.?" another asked. "You're walking kinda funny."

"We're so glad you're back!"

All around the camp, heads were popping out of tents. Claire smiled through the pain pills, waving an inflatable doughnut. "I'm going to be fine, guys. Go back to sleep, you've had a long day."

As Matt was about to help her into her tent, Hester stopped him. "Don't take her in there, Matt. Adam and Dan thought she'd be more comfortable in a yurt, so they brought one over for you. That way you two can be together and more comfortable."

They walked to the yurt in a nearby campsite. It had a floor, a table, a chair and beds with foam mattresses. "Wow! I must thank them for this. That was wonderful of them." Hester gently helped Claire onto a bed. Matt plopped down in a chair. He was glad he didn't have to leave Claire's side.

"What's the prognosis?" Hester asked.

"Broken tailbone and lots of bruises," Claire said from her prone position on the mattress.

"But they gave me this..." She waved a doughnut cushion.

"Aren't you lucky?" Hester joked. "Seriously though, you were lucky. It could have been so much worse."

"I know. I could have been a bear's dinner." Claire shook her head, but stopped when she felt the yurt spinning. "How did things go here?"

"Great. The activities kept the kids busy and entertained." Claire had planned a special campfire and had invited Adam and Dan. Adam had obtained special permission for them to have some fireworks at the beach, since it was the Victoria Day weekend and the ground was wet. "The fireworks were a huge hit and the kids told stories until dark. The stars were beautiful."

"Good," Claire said, letting her head fall to her pillow. "That's exactly what I wanted."

"Are you going to be okay?" Hester asked.

"Yeah, there isn't much the doctors can do for a broken tailbone. Painkillers and this trusty doughnut—that's about it."

"Good drugs and a good night's rest should help," Hester said, backing out of the yurt.

"Thanks, Hester," Matt said, shutting the door. "We'll see you in the morning."

Matt sat back on his heels and let out a long breath. "I'm wiped," he said.

"It was quite a day," Claire said, her eyes half-closed. "You should go sleep."

"I will." Matt hesitated. "I don't know what I would have done today if…if things hadn't worked out." For the first time, his chin quivered.

"Oh, Matt." Claire reached out a hand. "I'm okay."

"I know. I know that. Logically. But, what if I'd lost you, Clarikins? What would I have done? You mean the world to me, you know that?"

"I know," Claire tried to reassure him, her voice trailing off in the fog of the pain meds. "I love you too…"

"You're amazing, truly. You planned this whole trip, charmed the rangers into doing the canoe trips, and the fireworks—in a provincial park, no less. I'm proud of you—of the work you do." He paused and looked at the roof of the yurt. "You deserve more from me. I'm going to make some changes…"

Claire's soft snoring interrupted him. Matt waved a hand in front of her closed eyes. She was fast asleep. "I'll tell you about Colorado another time, I guess," he said softly before kissing her cheek. "Maybe when your ass is healed."

***

Wednesday, May 30

A week later, at the end of the day, Claire was in her lab on the third floor, holding on to the desks, limping from workstation to workstation, trying to set up for the next day. After a week off, she had gladly returned to work. Her first day back had been productive, even with the ache in her lower back.

***

346

"Whoever thought running track indoors was a good idea?" Tommy Rizzo complained to Logan Stanley as they made their way around the third floor of Amberton High for the seventh time.

"Ugh, just do it," Logan puffed. "Coach doesn't want us to miss a practice just because it's raining…it's too close to the finals."

The two kept pace with each other as they usually did when there wasn't a clock on them. Both were strong athletes who had trained hard during the year. They all had to do twenty laps.

"Come on, ya ninnies!" Ricky Penworth jeered from the window where he was waiting for his dad to finish a meeting. "Pick up those heels!"

"Fuck you, Ricky," Tommy fired back. Ricky had been playing on his last nerve for weeks—distracting them in class, being an asshole for Miss Hébert's substitute while she was away on the Eco Club trip, and now heckling.

"Just ignore him," Logan advised. "He's a loser."

"He's a pain in my ass, that's what he is."

As they rounded the corner, Ricky's lame taunts faded from their hearing. Three more turns, though, and they were right back at Ricky's favourite spot.

"Run, twinkies, run!" Ricky screeched. "Nice fucking shorts!" He pointed to Logan and Tommy's track uniform shorts and laughed. His own baggy cargo shorts were riding well below where the waistband should be.

"Pull your pants up, you waste of oxygen!" Logan huffed as the two again ran out of sight.

As Tommy and Logan finished their last lap—well behind all the others, having been distracted by Ricky's taunting—they came to a halt by the stairs, where Ricky now stood, smirking and blocking their way.

"Move, shithead," Tommy barked.

"Make me, pizza-face," Ricky taunted, hitching his oversized shorts up and snorting loudly.

Tommy and Logan looked at each other. If they ran for the stairs, he would grab them. If they went the long way down the other stairs, he'd be after them and push them down those stairs. They needed a surprise. Tired, they walked away, pretending to ignore him, then turned and made a sudden run for it—one on either side of Ricky, heading for the stairs. It didn't work. Ricky grabbed their shirts and swung them into each other, tearing their uniforms.

"You fucking asshole!" Tommy yelled.

"That's it, turd-face!" Logan said, his sweating face beet red.

Ricky stepped forward, his flabby chest puffed out, and took a swing at Tommy who evaded the attempt. As Ricky's hand caught nothing but air, Logan lunged forward and shoved Ricky hard with both hands.

Ricky tried to regain his balance and pull up his shorts at the same time, giving Tommy and Logan an advantage. Ricky had to hike up his shorts repeatedly as he stepped right and left blocking the narrow stairs and trying to land a punch. Tommy and Logan were dancing in front of him. They landed a few minor blows, but not enough to knock him down or make him run away. Ricky couldn't defend and attack and hike up his pants at the same time, so he kicked Logan in the shin. In a flash Tommy saw an opportunity and pummelled him. Ricky was down, but still between the boys and the stairs.

Catching his breath, Ricky sat up pulling out a key chain and swung it hard. The keys scraped Logan across the temple, narrowly missing his eye. Ricky stood up, still swinging the keys.

"Nooo!" Tommy roared, attacking Ricky with all his might. Logan, blood dripping down his cheek, came back—all their loathing for the pathetic, pretentious Ricky fuelled their anger and they pummelled him mercilessly.

With every punch, Ricky shuffled backwards. But in the heat of the fight he didn't realize he was inching closer and closer to the edge of the stairs. At the precipice he took a swing at Tommy, missed and lost his balance just as Logan turned and gave him a good solid kick in the side. Ricky twisted backwards, hit his head on the wooden railing and rolled down the marble steps to the landing thirteen steps below.

"Holy fuck," Tommy muttered.

"Shit!" Logan confirmed.

"We gotta split, dude," Tommy grabbed Logan's shirt and pulled him back from the steps. "Come on, man, let's bolt!"

Logan strained back against Tommy's grasp to look down the stairs. "Dude, he's out cold...Oh God, he dead?"

"No way. We're not that lucky. I'm outta here," Tommy replied, running down the stairs. Logan followed.

Frightened, they stepped over Ricky. Tommy looked back quickly as they rounded the corner. "Ha! He's pissed his pants, man!"

"Seriously? Oh man, he's such a fucking wuss!" They jeered as they continued to run down to the first floor and out the door into the rain without changing out of their torn track and field uniforms.

***

Claire let out a long breath as she threw the last dirty towel into the garbage. She had survived the day and didn't feel too bad, considering. "Ah, more paper towels," she said to herself as she noticed the roll was out. As she waddled back from the broom closet at the end of the hall, a couple of rolls of towels in hand, she heard moaning and snivelling at the bottom of the stairs behind her. Had a pair of lovebirds broken up? Did somebody need some reassurance? Curious, she hobbled around the corner to the stairs. Nothing. But the moaning was louder.

She went to the railing and looked down. At the bottom of the stairs, on the landing, she saw Ricky, his head and his nose bleeding, one arm obviously broken, and his torso in an unnatural twist.

She lurched forward and immediately had to stop. Pain shot up from her coccyx. Clinging to the railing, she eased herself down the stairs. Arriving at Ricky's side she unrolled half the roll of paper towels, slowly got on her knees, and carefully put a wad of towels under his head. She laboured her way back up and wet more towels and applied them to his head and nose. She called 911 on her new mobile. She called the office. Jack was not in the building. He had forgotten Ricky after his meeting. She met Jethro on his rounds and told him where Ricky was and that the paramedics would be coming.

Returning to the second floor landing, Claire checked if there was anything more she could do for Ricky. The awkward twist to his back worried her. She'd let the paramedics decide how to move him. Meanwhile, she tried to keep him conscious and responding. He was drifting in and out of consciousness. Paying attention had never been his strong point.

Ten minutes later, police, fire engine and ambulance arrived.

"Stand back, Ma'am," a young E.M.T. said as they swooped in and took over. "You haven't moved him?"

"No…no, I've just been trying to keep him awake and stop the bleeding," Claire said as she stood back. Her hands were shaking as she gestured with the third roll of paper towels.

"Well done," the E.M.T. said as she took a penlight out of her shirt pocket and started checking Ricky's eyes. "Have you notified his parents?"

"No, I…I…" Claire fumbled with her cellphone. "I'll call them now."

As she dialled Muriel's number, the paramedics carefully shifted Ricky onto a backboard.

"Hello?" Muriel answered tersely.

"Muriel, it's Claire Hébert…"

"Oh, Claire, I can't talk right now. I'm in the middle of a meeting here," Muriel sounded annoyed. "Call back later? Thanks…"

"No, Muriel, listen," Claire cut her off. "It's Ricky. There's been an accident."

"Wha…? What are you saying?"

Claire could hear people talking in the background. Around her, the E.M.T's were getting Ricky onto a gurney.

"Ricky's hurt. I found him at the bottom of a stairwell and called the paramedics." She waited a beat, hoping the information would sink in. "They're taking him…" she covered the mouthpiece of the phone and yelled to the E.M.T's, "Where are you taking him?"

"Amberton General."

"Amberton General, Muriel, Emergency," she relayed to Muriel. "I'll call Jack's cell now and let him know. Okay?"

Claire didn't wait for her to respond. That could take forever and the paramedics were already moving Ricky to the ambulance. She dialled Jack's number and waited while it continued to ring. When he finally answered, she repeated the same conversation with him. Then she waddled to her car to follow the ambulance to the hospital.

***

As she made her way through the doors to the emergency ward ten minutes later, Jack caught up with her and grabbed her arm.

"You knew this was going to happen, didn't you?" he demanded, his face flushed and his mouth grim. "How did it happen? Were you there?"

Claire turned. "No, Jack, I wasn't there. I was working late and needed some paper towels, Jack. On my way back to the lab I heard sounds in the stairwell. When I looked, I found Ricky moaning at the bottom. He was semi-conscious and bleeding."

"Oh God!" Jack moaned. "But how did he get there? Why was he there?"

"Sorry. I have no idea," Claire said. "I was down the hall in my lab. I didn't hear anything or see how he got there."

"Mr. Penworth?" a stalwart nurse in green scrubs called from down the hall.

Jack blinked at Claire, then suddenly turned his head as he realized someone had called his name. "Yes!" he yelled back. "I'm Jack Penworth."

"Come with me." The nurse gestured towards the door behind her. "Your son's awake. You can see him—but only for a minute."

Jack looked back at Claire. "Go on," she said, shooing him along.

Just then, Muriel arrived in a flourish of tears and incoherent mumblings. Jack grabbed her hand and pulled her along the corridor behind the nurse. Claire followed and stood in the doorway as Ricky's parents rushed to his side.

"Mom? Dad?" Ricky said weakly as soon as Jack and Muriel came in.

Jack looked over his son then looked to the doctor expectantly. "Mr. Penworth, we're going to run some tests, get some x-rays. We suspect Ricky has a concussion, a broken arm, and possibly some broken ribs."

"Oh God," Muriel muttered as she took Ricky's good hand in hers.

"As you can see," the doctor continued, "he's got lots of swelling and bruises on his face— torso, too—and a bad lump on the side of his head. We'll know more when we see the x-rays, but he's lucky. His back's going to be okay, thanks to that teacher who found him and didn't move him."

"All this from a fall down the stairs?" Muriel asked.

"They swarmed me," Ricky said, his voice weak. "They came out of nowhere."

"Who?" Jack demanded. "I want names."

"There was a bunch of them, I don't know how many." Ricky looked towards the door as Claire shuffled in. "The only ones I remember are Logan and Tommy." Claire's stomach sank to her knees.

"Logan Stanley and Tommy Rizzo did this? You're sure?"

Ricky looked to Claire. "Yes." The corner of his mouth twitched slightly and his face darkened.

"They're in your class too, aren't they, Claire?" Jack turned towrds her.

"Yes, they're in Ricky's class," Claire stood as tall as she could. "They're good kids…"

"Good kids!" Muriel shrieked. "Do good kids beat up an innocent boy?"

"Well, we don't know the full story yet," Claire ventured.

"I told you, they jumped me," Ricky said. Claire shook her head. She knew Jack and Muriel would believe anything he said, especially now.

"This is your fault!" Muriel turned and pointed a finger squarely at Claire.

"Whoa, what?" Claire stepped forward, jarring her coccyx and wincing with the pain. "How on earth is this my fault?"

"You've been turning everyone in your class against Ricky all semester. He told me."

"I have done no such thing!" Claire roared.

"Now's not the time," Jack said, stepping between the two women. "We'll discuss your classroom management problems later. Go home, Claire. You've done enough here." Somehow to Claire, this didn't sound like thanks.

"Found your injured son, called the ambulance and took care of him until they showed up, you mean?" She snarled the words. "Yeah, me and my busted coccyx have done more than enough." She turned and waddled carefully out the door. "You're welcome, by the way," she said over her shoulder.

Chapter 20

Amberton's 150th Anniversary Celebration

Thursday, May 31

May 31th was the hundred and fiftieth anniversary of the founding of Amberton, and as part of the festivities; the school community had planned a concert with the massed bands and choirs of all the district schools. It would feature individual school groups: jazz choirs, trumpet trios, and string ensembles. Each school had its star soloists. The schools had advertised the concert for weeks.

"So who's organizing all this?" Matt asked as he and Claire and the doughnut arrived at the Amberton Concert Hall to volunteer. They had planned to attend as guests but had been roped into helping at the last minute when some volunteers had bailed.

"There's a music committee. Each school has a rep and Jake McAlister, our head music teacher, is organizing our musicians. He's been great—letting the kids choose their favourite pieces from a list. It's boosting their confidence."

"That's quite an undertaking," Matt said as he took her arm and they gingerly started up the front steps. It had been ten days since her roll down the hill. The bruises were almost healed and she was walking better but the tailbone still hurt and he worried about her. "And amazingly, you weren't involved in the planning of it... I thought you did everything... until now," he teased.

"Ha ha, aren't you funny?" Claire rolled her eyes and smoothed a hand down the front of her shift. "It might seem like I run the whole school sometimes, but believe me, there's a lot more going on that I'm not involved in."

"It must be a bitch trying to get kids to practice for something like this," he noted as they passed a trumpet trio warming up in the hall.

"The music kids have been excused from classes to practice in groups for a week and yesterday they came here for a full dress rehearsal."

"They must have loved that!"

"Yes, their teachers keep them alert and on time." Claire arched her neck to look down the hall. "Look, there's Paul Fraser. He's on crutches," she said pointing and waving. "He's being mobbed by kids!" For Paul, the ebullient welcome from students was good medicine.

"Hi Claire," Paul said as the enthusiastic crowd dispersed to their music groups and he
and Deirdre could see them. "Good to see you again."

"You too, Paul, and wow! You're walking!" Claire said with a warm smile as she hid her doughnut. She quickly introduced Paul and Deirdre to Matt. "You're looking great, Paul."

"Thanks. Our kids are in the concert." His eyes sparkled with pride. "We made a deal. They would practice their instruments for as long as it took me to do my exercises. We all got better. They're still nervous though." He looked around at a world he'd missed for months. "It's nice to have a night out to hear a concert and watch the kids."

"I'm sure it is," Claire said. "What about next year? Are you coming back?"

"Well," Paul cocked his head to one side, "I can't leave you girls and old Gumbersahl to do battle with Bertha and the bootlicker all on your own, now can I? Especially now that Shirley's retiring?"

"See," Matt elbowed her, "I'm not the only one who thinks you do too much."

"A broken record, that's what you are," Claire rolled her eyes, flapped his butt with her doughnut and smiled back at Paul.

"Didn't mean to start a domestic, as the kids say," Paul shrugged, leaned against Deirdre and chuckled. "Oh, and sorry about your little roll in the park, Claire," he said with a wink. "We'd better go find our seats, Deirdre."

"Enjoy the show," Matt said. Paul's spirits were high.

As they headed to the stage area they came across Gene Putnam leaning against a wall, checking his cellphone. "Hey, Gene!" Claire said warmly. "What are you doing here?"

"Same as you, I imagine," Gene smiled and held out a hand to Matt. "Got McAlister's bat signal for help. Hi, Matt, good to see you."

Matt shook Gene's hand absentmindedly and reminded himself to keep smiling. "You, too," he said flatly. "Looks like we're in for a busy evening."

"Sure, but with Claire here it should be bearable."

"Oh yeah, some help I'll be," Claire chuckled. "As long as no one requires me to sit or actually sing, I'll be okay."

"Oh yeah," Gene guffawed. "The broken behind!"

Matt's hand tensed around Claire's. "Her behind is..."

"Healing," Claire jumped in, swinging her doughnut. "Right?" She looked at Matt directly. "It's fine."

"Yeah, right, fine," Matt muttered. "Let's get the show on the road."

"Why not?" Gene smiled, gesturing for Matt and Claire to walk with him. Matt had been hoping he'd go in the opposite direction.

"Heard anything about Ricky, Claire?" Gene asked as they walked. Around them a swarm of elementary kids was flocking to the staging area, all a-twitter.

"Yeah, he's resting at home," Claire said over the din. "He has a broken arm, pulled back muscles, a big lump on his head and bruises. His ribs are fine. But the Penworths think he'll need to take the rest of the year off to recover."

"Oh, please!"

"I know, right? A few days, a week, I get. He was beaten up pretty badly, but the whole rest of the term? It's just another excuse."

"Do they let him get away with everything?" Matt said, trying to get into the conversation.

"That and then some," Gene confirmed. "I don't know what happened that day, but I have a hard time believing Ricky was completely innocent."

"No chance in perdition," Claire said, sidestepping a running flutist. "But, it was Tommy and Logan's word against Ricky's. They didn't have a hope. They're in Penworth's half of the alphabet."

"It's a shame the school will be losing them," Gene concurred.

"They've been expelled?" Matt asked.

"No, but they've been 'transferred' to Elgin Falls High," Gene said, with air quotes. "They're only allowed inside Amberton for their exams, then they're off the roll. Come to think of it that may be why Ricky doesn't have to do his exams. He won't have to be in the building when Tommy and Logan are there."

"Meanehile the police are still investigating," Claire added. "It's maddening. Jack and Muriel blame me. All I did was try to help."

"Ridiculous!" Gene exclaimed. "You're the best, Claire. A good, solid teacher who cares."

"Yes," Matt agreed. "She is the best." His chest puffed out slightly.

"Now, now, boys, my head will get too big." Claire laughed off the compliments as they arrived at the staging area.

"Oh, I'm over there," Gene pointed to a group of overly excited junior high students. "See you after the show!"

"Break a leg," Claire said as she waved him off. She turned to Matt and looked him square in the eye. "Ready for this?"

Matt took a deep breath. "How can I not be? I'm with 'the best' aren't I?" He was glad Gene had left.

They moved through the buzzing crowd of seven hundred and fifty young performers to take their places amongst the kids, volunteers and teachers. When their turn came, the kids proudly took to the stage and performed their program in front of parents, grandparents, friends, and neighbours from all over Amberton.

The adults heartily applauded every piece of the program and although there were delightful little glitches, it proved the merit of the music program, which was always threatened by budget cuts.

The audience left with music in their hearts and minds, Claire and Matt manned the door, asking everybody to sign a petition to keep the funding in place for the music programs in the coming years. As the crowd thinned, Claire excused herself to the washroom while Matt manned the door, pen and petition in hand.

"Good show, eh, Matt?" Gene said heartily a few minutes later. "Wasn't it wonderful?"

"Sure was," Matt said, pretending to look for Claire down the hall. "Really good. The kids did well."

"I was just talking to Claire," Gene said, pointing over his shoulder at the nearly empty hallway.

"To Claire?" Matt arched a questioning eyebrow.

"Yeah, I just saw her in the hall. I mentioned coming back to my place now that…"

"Excuse me?" Matt's eyes bulged. "You invited Claire back to your place? You've got some kind of nerve, you…"

"Whoa there," Gene said, holding his hands up in front of his chest. "Calm down, Matt. You've got this all wrong, my friend." Just then, Claire approached. Gene turned to the sound of her shoes clicking on the tiles. "Claire, er…save me here, will you?"

Matt looked furiously from the back of Gene's head to Claire's confused face.

"What on earth?" She saw what was happening.

"I was just telling Matt that I wanted to invite you *both*..." he emphasized the word, "...to my place for a nightcap. Natalie will have the girls down, but she'll still be up."

"Natalie?" Matt's jaw dropped.

"Yes, Natalie," Claire said, looking Matt dead in the eye. "Gene's adoring wife." She watched Matt's face turn red and his shoulders droop and shook her head. *Men*, she thought to herself. *Boys, more like.* "Thanks, Gene," she said, taking Matt's hand. "But it's been a long day. Another time?"

"Sure," Gene said, shaking off the tension.

"Yeah, another time," Matt reiterated. He sheepishly held out a hand as Gene went to leave. "Er...so sorry, Gene."

Gene looked at it for a moment, then took hold. "Good night, Matt. It's been interesting."

"Hasn't it though?" Claire said through a smile as they watched Gene's form retreat down the steps. Then she walloped Matt with her doughnut and they both cracked up.

June

Chapter 21

<u>A Grad Celebration and a Red Line</u>

Since March, Claire and Anne had spent many a lunch hour supervising the planning of the Graduation Ball. The administration had approved the budget, notified the police of date, time and venue and asked for officers to be on duty at the dance. Only then had Claire and Anne invited interested grad students to form a Grad Committee. For six weeks, the teen decision-makers argued and debated and finally decided on the theme, the menu, the D.J., the music, the decorations, the level of dress, the designing and printing of tickets, the cost of admission, the 'gown exchange closet' and the photographer—all under the auspices of the teacher advisors.

Of course, there had to be authority figures present. This year, the grads asked for their own school group, *Kids Against Drinking and Drugs* (K.A.D.D.), to be frontline observers and bouncers at the dance. They had to invite the administration—no choice there—and had prepared a sign-up sheet for teachers to volunteer as chaperones.

The Grad Committee decided to save money and ask the art department to make paper flower arrangements for the tables and regularly went to inspect their progress. Several classes were put onto the project and in a couple of weeks they had created flower arrangements for the tables and metres of garlands to adorn the pillars in the room.

Ticket sales were slow at first. Early in May, Claire and Anne had to warn the committee that the grad celebration would be cancelled on May 31st if they hadn't sold a hundred and seventy-five tickets by then. They needed to sell at least that many to pay for the venue. Announcements were made and on May 30th, the last day of sales, the last minute people came through and sales went well over the required number. By closing time they had sold two hundred and seventy-three couple tickets for the dance. The celebration was on.

***

Friday, June 8

The afternoon of the dance many third and fourth year students skipped classes to get ready for the celebration that evening. Hair appointments, tuxedo fittings, limousine rentals, corsage deliveries, shoe shopping, organisation of accessories and bling, all were happening that afternoon. The airwaves were crammed with phone calls and texts to coordinate apparel and plans for all night after-dance parties.

Claire had planned a review for her leftover grade elevens who came that day. The less studious students skipped to enjoy the riverside parks. The serious ones stayed home to study. Seven kids in the middle came for help. They were lucky. Claire went from one to the next and the next and back again, helping each one with whatever they needed. Claire was gratified to know how hard they were trying to learn the work for their finals.

***

After school Claire sent Boomer into the yard and got herself ready for the dance. Matt had enthusiastically agreed to volunteer with her as a chaperone. He would be picking her up at five-thirty. Matt enjoyed a good meal and Claire loved a formal dance, so tonight was made for them, or so he believed.

At the sound of her doorbell, Claire rushed down the stairs, still fastening her earrings. She opened the door to see Matt, once again in a tuxedo. There was a tinge of self-satisfaction in his bearing. "You do get a lot of use out of that tux," she teased with a big smile.

"Well, when you look this good…" he said as he let his hand glide across his chest, "…there's no point leaving it in the closet." His smile was contagious.

Claire laughed and pulled him in for a kiss.

"You're looking ravishing yourself, Miss Hébert." He pulled her back in for another smooch before she turned away.

"I'm not quite ready yet," she tried to say through locked lips.

"You look perfect to me," he said as he spun her out and looked her up and down. Her sunny organdie gown in a colourful floral print on a misty green background fit her like a glove. She slipped on a pair of matching pumps to complete the outfit. In her clutch, she carried her freshly charged cellphone. It would be needed. Matt had his in his pocket. He frisbeed her doughnut into the open car window. Both of them knew it could be fun, but were also aware that they would be working.

***

Matt dropped Claire at the front door of the Amberton Arms Inn and went to park the car. Claire made small talk with students and the other chaperones while she waited for him to return. She hoped the dance would be beautiful and without incident, for the grads' sake, but she knew that was wishful thinking.

There was a lot of support for the chaperones: the *Bouncer Club*, as K.A.D.D. was informally called, was the frontline of correction for unacceptable behaviour. If the bouncers couldn't handle it, a teacher or a volunteer chaperone would step in and failing that, there were Bertha, Jack, and

Kristen, with the police as a final recourse. It gave bad actors many chances to alter their behaviour before serious consequences were applied. But it didn't always work. Nothing works every time with *homo sapiens adolescens*.

It was a bright and sunny but refreshing June evening. Claire watched the guests arrive: limos disgorging handsome young men in rented tuxedos, clumsily taking the hands of luscious young ladies in stunningly stylish gowns of every colour. Claire didn't recognize some of her students. They had covered their youthful faces with so much makeup. She didn't recognize their behaviour either. They were polite. They carried themselves like adults. It was the giddy giggling and the juvenile joking level of their conversation that gave away their youth.

"Hi, Miss Hébert," a belle in a yellow dress said excitedly.

Claire looked into the made-up face. She looked at the flowing black curls and the bling. "Ummm…" she played for time.

"It's me, Maxine, Miss H.," the girl gushed as she rolled her lined eyes and giggled.

"Oh my goodness," Claire said. "Maxine! I didn't know your hair was that long." Claire looked around, wondering if Maxine had a date. She imagined Amir's terrified face and hoped he hadn't been bullied into an evening with her.

"Extensions!" Maxine said, twirling a lock. "D'ya like it? My aunt did it. You know, it took more than, like, four hours this afternoon to get it done, Miss." Maxine's radiance was as real as her tresses were fake.

"It's lovely, Maxine. You look gorgeous. Who's your date?"

"Serge's meeting me here." Maxine blushed gently.

"Serge, really?"

"Yeah, I invited him 'cause I know how hurt he was when Amy dumped him. I known him since the first semester I failed math. We were in the same class. We both wanted to go to the dance and we both needed dates.

"That's wonderful, Maxine, and so sweet of you."

He's getting me a corsage. Nice eh?"

Claire nodded.

"An' I got this dress from the Grad Committee's Exchange Closet." Maxine leaned in and lowered her voice conspiratorially. "Free! D'ya believe that?"

Claire smiled proudly. "It looks like it was made just for you," she said. "I hope you and Serge have a great time tonight, Maxine. You've earned it."

"Yep," Maxine beamed as she spotted Serge walking in. "An' I'm gonna graduate next year, Miss. Nothing's gonna stop me no more."

"I'm sure you will, Maxine." Claire was confident that Maxine would be in the successful group next year. She was working well in all her classes.

Serge looked handsome and nervous as he arrived with the corsage. Maxine didn't know how to put it on, so Claire pinned it for her, while Serge clowned with her doughnut. "Thanks, Miss." She beamed.

Matt arrived as Maxine and Serge went inside. "I parked the car a bit farther away. That way we won't be blocked in," he said, assuming he wouldn't need it until they left.

"Shall we go in?" Claire tried to steer Matt towards the door, but he was too busy looking around at the young guests. He wanted to get an idea of what today's adolescents looked like when they were all dressed up—especially the girls.

The kids arrived in limos. The staff arrived in their own vehicles, some of which looked like junkyard rescues. The grads looked better than their teachers. A few of them were pompous, snubbing their teachers with a conceited, self-satisfied air. This was their Grad Dance and they acted as if they alone had accomplished the unachievable. Ironically, the dance came before final exams, so that everybody could celebrate, but not everybody would graduate.

"Let's go in, Matt."

Kristen Jaworski soon followed with Steve Lawson. It couldn't hurt to have an extra cop around, especially a tall and handsome one dancing with a Vice Principal. They surveyed the throng of student guests. There was nothing amiss... yet. Claire and Matt watched as Kristen and Steve made their way to their table. The chaperones—admin, staff and volunteers—were all seated at three round tables, each in a corner. From there, they could keep an eye on most of the goings on, including the fun in the photo booths. The fourth corner was the marble foyer entrance.

***

Frank Cechi was finally first in something. He was the first to be ejected. Like many others, he'd been smoking dope and drinking with friends before the dance. He was sick at dinner. Two members of the bouncer club escorted him and his embarrassed girlfriend to his parents' car.

"Here we go," Claire said.

"Where? What?" Matt's eyes had been following a chatty group of girls led by a very elegant one wearing a hijab walking to the punchbowl.

"Oh, you missed the first one? That was Frank Cechi and his date being escorted out by bouncers."

Before the evening was out, a number of guests were drunk or stoned. Claire helped to escort some to their parents' cars and Matt drove one reeling reveller home, worrying all the way that the kid would vomit in his car. The kid's father's car had been impounded.

"How do they manage it? There's been something happening almost every twenty minutes," Matt said, returning from yet another trip to the front foyer.

"It's been pretty regular, hasn't it?" Claire said.

"Where the heck's the weed coming from?" Claire was wondering out loud just as Kristen and Steve arrived for a chat.

"It's around. There are pushers in the bushes and we don't control the outside of the premises here," Kristen said.

Steve nodded. "But the police do. They've asked a few kids hanging out at the doors to leave. They do, but they sneak right back or send replacements."

"Bertha just sent a boy to the hospital with possible alcohol poisoning," Kristen added. "They don't seem to care what they consume."

"What was the commotion a few minutes ago?" Matt asked.

"Oh, they arrested some guy for streaking through the foyer. He got loud and violent when the officers covered him up and took him away."

Suddenly a dishevelled Ethan Boyd came running over. "Miss Jaworski, Miss Jaworski! Mark Compren's barfing in the washroom and he looks awfully drunk. He hit me and chased me out. He was rambling about something. He's not making any sense, Miss. He's very sick. His eyes look funny."

Steve Lawson immediately headed for the men's room. Matt followed. They found Mark by a puddle of vomit, mumbling incoherently. He fought the men as they tried to clean him up a bit, offered him water and tried to prop him up so they could talk to him. Somebody called for Bertha, who was calling ambulance on her cell when Mark had another violent fit, spouting gibberish sprinkled with threats and things like "kill 'em", "hit 'em again", "gotta get away from them," and "they can't find out." The men couldn't control him. He started to vomit again. He seemed to be having a nightmare and to be extremely angry at something. Mark's parents were not home. The officers who had just returned from the police station said it looked like an anxiety or a paranoia attack and took him to the hospital. They gave Bertha a sneer that said: there is no discipline at this school.

"That's the supervisor's son, Matt," said Claire when he got back.

"Whew! I wonder if he knows what his little boy has been into," Matt scoffed.

"Probably drugs, alcohol—not both, I hope," Kristen said.

As much as possible, bouncers, volunteer chaperones, staff and police tried to move the rowdy behaviour out of the earshot of the kids enjoying the dance. But teens are perceptive and love to gossip. They heard. It would all be fodder for the school grapevine and on social media sites tomorrow.

At one a.m. the last dance was over and the remaining guests applauded and made their way to the door—some to other parties. Tired and happy that the hours of working and observing were over, the chaperones meandered to their cars. Claire and Matt returned to her house, where they had their own wind down.

***

Monday, June 11

Early the next Monday, Bertha Stack, upset at the behaviour of more than a few grads at the dance, and influenced by the police officers, decided that anyone who had had to be disciplined by the police would not be allowed to attend the graduation ceremony or receive a scholarship. She and Jack decided to keep it quiet, so they mailed letters to the families of those Amberton students who had been taken home or to the police station for bad behaviour.

***

The day they received the letters, Claire happened to be there as the first parents barged into the main office at eight-thirty in the morning. Inconvenienced by the letters, they were already irate when they arrived. Claire's class had a guest speaker, so she had brought the attendance to the office, and was able to linger a short while to talk to Bernice, the Bookstore Barracuda, who was enjoying the developing storm. They recognized three of them as parents of potential scholarship winners.

"We want to see Miss Stack NOW!" the parents shouted at Bertha's stunned secretary, Sylvia Dawson, shaking the letters in her face.

"I don't know anything about your letters," she gasped. She had typed them, but it was not her job to edit or memorize the contents. "Do you have an appointment?"

"We don't, but we are going to see Miss Stack NOW!" they shouted. "Get the principal out here at once!"

"I'm sorry. Miss Stack isn't in yet. Please remain calm." Sylvia said, her voice
trembling. "Please take a seat. She'll be here any minute."

"The principal is late, eh? What an example! School starts at eight-fifteen," somebody mumbled.

"I heard she became a principal because she couldn't handle her classroom!" another parent, who was also a teacher, shouted. There was some mumbling among the parents at this comment. Sylvia watched and listened to it all with concern and interest.

At eight-forty, Bertha slugged in and was immediately startled by the angry mob of parents. Bertha invited the unruly crowd into her office to keep some semblance of calm in the outer office. At least classes have started, she thought. "Miss Dawson, please call Mr. Penworth and ask him to come in right away," she asked her withering secretary.

From inside her office the indignation and shouting could still be heard.

"I want an explanation for this!" a fuming mother bellowed. "My daughter is qualified to graduate and I intend to make sure she does!"

My daughter came to the dance with a student from Elgin Falls. Why didn't he get a letter? He's the one who brought the booze. Why is *she* punished for what *he* did?" Bertha was doing her best to keep some semblance of control.

"This is the school's fault! My son's a good boy. He deserves to graduate, Miss Stack." Claire, Bernice and the secretaries were wide eyed hearing it all.

"My son was in a group with Mark Compren, Miss Stack," Mrs. Boyd snarled. "Did Supervisor Compren get a letter? I don't see him here. Ethan said Mark was drunk as a skunk at the dance."

"That dance should have been better chaperoned, Miss Stack. There shouldn't have been anyone from another school there," said an incensed businessman. "I'll be calling Supervisor Compren."

Jack Penworth arrived. He took one look at the enraged throng of parents and was tempted to sneak back out, but one of the parents nabbed him.

"What the hell's going on in this school, that kids are accused of taking drugs and drinking at a graduation dance and they can't get their scholarships? My kid didn't do any of that and he loses his scholarship? I don't think so!" an angry father spat in Jack's face.

"Hmmm ... er ... Excuse me, please. Miss Stack wants a word with me."

When the parents saw Mr. Penworth standing beside Miss Stack they calmed down a bit. Bertha whispered something in Jack's ear.

"Please excuse us for a moment while we have a quick conference, ladies and gentlemen," Jack said.

The two of them went into the principal's private washroom for a few minutes. When they came back red-faced, they announced, "Your young people will be able to come on stage, wear their gowns and receive their diplomas, but scholarships will go to the runner up." Many parents left, but the parents of the scholarship revellers were still furious.

"That's rubbish!" a woman shouted.

"Wrong move," a man growled. "Miss Stack, you have no control over this school or the students, and you are either ineffective or—as in this case—totally over the top. If you cannot satisfy us —and by this I mean that our kids should be able to get their scholarships—I shall be going to the chairman of the board."

After the parents had left, a trembling Bertha shut the door to her office.

**

Friday, June 15

This morning, from the anonymity of board headquarters, Supervisor Compren intervened and declared that anyone at Amberton District High School allowed in the auditorium and wearing a gown must be given the privilege of crossing the stage to receive his or her diploma and scholarship.

That was it. Bertha was beaten. She hadn't made the punishment public, so she was glad to be able to save some face. By lunchtime the staff room was abuzz with it.

**

Tuesday, June 19

The second week of June, the teachers were breathing a sigh of relief. Classes were finished. They could finally see the light at the end of the tunnel. The weather was cooperating— sunny but not so hot that sweaty exam-writers stuck to their desks.

In Claire's lab, there would be two students at every lab table, the rest at the tablet chairs. The day before the exams, Claire had arrived early to space the chairs far enough apart to discourage cheating. Caretaking couldn't block the cupboards in the lab, so Claire again donned rubber gloves and scraped out gum, boxes of leftover snacks, old grey-green mouldy sandwiches, broken ballpoint pens, broken games, calculator covers, empty snack wrappers, rotting apple cores, banana peels, gum wads and gossipy notes from the shelves.

When would these kids learn not to leave notes lying around with names of people they hated, things their peers did, plans for revenge or where the next party would be held, a who's who of people who had crashed a party or slept together and when and where, and what they thought about it? Claire wondered.

"Damian Stoker was with Cait Somers last weekend…they hooked up at a rave in Bellington… they got stoned," was one note that caught her eye. She wondered when that had all started again and how their mothers would react if they found out. It was all in two of six crumpled notes, carelessly left on the shelves and the floor for anyone to find. "It truly is a jungle in here," Claire thought as she absentmindedly stuffed the notes in her pocket. Her mind flitted to Paul Fraser who was home now but still getting daily physio. "When would the police find the *effing* hit and run driver?" she thought. But there were no witnesses. She replaced a wobbly stool with a stable one.

The admin had sent the usual memo to staff. Teachers had to tell the kids every topic on the exam and the kinds of questions for each topic. Claire had a short multiple-choice section; some diagrams to be identified and labelled; and finally a choice of paragraph answer questions based on all ten units they had covered in class. They only had to answer eight questions out of the twenty, as long as they didn't answer more than one question per unit. Even Ricky—if he had read half of the notes he had bought from Artie Binton—and if he wasn't at home convalescing with his right arm in a cast—even Ricky could have passed it. Now, they would never know. Jack had decreed that Ricky wouldn't have to write any of his final exams.

***

That night at the dog park, Claire found the wad of notes she had stuffed into her pocket.

While Boomer chased the ball, she read them to Matt.

" 'OMG, can you believe Becky's hair?' this one says." Claire shook her head as she and

Matt laughed at the drivel the notes contained. "I guess you have to know the context."

Then she read: " 'I don't know how Damian...' " Claire's voice suddenly trailed off. Her smile faded as her eyes scoured the page.

"What?" Matt asked, his own giggles subsiding.

"Holy jeez, Matt, listen to this... 'I don't know how Damian S. can live with himself. We were supposed to be in Mr. F.'s math class. Now I have a lousy mark cause Abbasi doesn't explain stuff like Fraser does. Julie P. told me it was Damian that hit Mr. F. in the parking lot...' It's unsigned. Holy *shit*, Matt, I have to get this note to the police!"

She showed the note to Matt. He agreed. They jogged back to #684 River Road as fast as they could. "Put Boomer inside. I'll drive you."

Rushing to the police station, Claire was a nervous wreck. "Whom do I talk to?" She looked at Matt wildly, her hands shaking. Matt wrapped his right hand around hers and tried to steady her as he drove. "You'll be fine. Breathe slowly,

Clarikins. Ask for the detective working on the Paul Fraser hit and run case."

"Right," Claire said. She straightened her shoulders and breathed deeply as they screeched into the parking lot.

Claire ran into the station with Matt following. She identified herself and asked for the hit and run detective. "I have some evidence he could be interested in," Claire said excitedly.

"I'll get Lieutenant Wajowski for you, Ma'am."

"Thank you." Too excited to sit down, they paced as they waited.

Lieutenant Wajowski came out a while later. His neat shirt stretched over a solid paunch. Claire looked at the badge clipped to his pocket and the stern look in his eye. "Sorry," he said, reaching a hand out to each of them, "I was on a call. What can I do for you, Miss?"

"I'm Claire… Claire Hébert. And this is Matt Granger.

"Miss Hébert, Mr. Granger." He looked them in the eye and nodded.

"Are you the officer investigating the Paul Fraser hit and run accident from last January?"

"I'm Chuck Wajowski and that's one of my many files," he said, his eyes narrowing.

"I'm a teacher at Amberton District High School and I found a note in my classroom after school today—it may be of interest."

"Hmmm… Is that so? May I see it?"

"Of course." Claire handed him the scribbled note and watched him read it.

"This does look interesting, Miss Hébert. May I keep it?" the detective asked as he folded the scrap of paper back up.

"Sure," Claire said. "Paul Fraser is a friend and colleague. How is the investigation going?"

"We found silver paint on the caretaker's car and we know it came from a new Corolla—this year's model. But with no license, and no witnesses, and thousands of silver Corollas in the area, it's impossible to determine which one may have hit Mr. Mason's car and run over Mr. Fraser. The best tip we had was that a student may have hit Mr. Fraser with his father's car, but we..."

"His mother's car. That was me," Claire interrupted, proudly. "In February I overheard a conversation between two students and reported it."

"Well, we talked to the boy. He admits he drove his mother's new silver Corolla that day." Mr. Wajowski shook his head. "But he insists he hit a tree on Elgin Falls Road. The car didn't have any paint marks on it that could connect it to the Mason car. It had a little damage right of centre on the front bumper and a broken headlight, but nothing more. The paint we got was from the dent in Mr. Mason's red Civic is from this year's model of a silver Toyota Corolla, but that doesn't prove that it was the Stoker's silver Corolla that hit Mr. Fraser. Silver's a popular colour and the Corolla is a popular car. We have third lead, but we still have some work to do on that one so I can't talk about it." He held up the note. "Or, this note could be the answer we're looking for, unless the girl's got it wrong or she's setting him up. We have to talk to her and find the source of the rumour."

"I hope it helps, Lieutenant Wajowski. Have a good evening."

"Thank you, Miss Hébert. You too."

***

Wednesday, June 20

The next day, the grade ten exam started at nine o'clock. At eight forty-five Claire was ready and opened her door. It had been a month since her fall and she happily left the doughnut at home.

For exam days, she put a sign on the door, reminding the kids that no backpacks or technical devices aside from calculators, were allowed, but that they should return their science text and bring pencils and an eraser, two pens and whiteout. Then she locked the back door to the lab and screened everybody as they entered at the front.

"But I don't have a locker," Karla Kozak whined as she arrived. "I have to bring my backpack in."

"Everyone got a locker in the first week in September," Claire said, blocking the doorway with her arm. Karla was lying. Karla knew that Miss Hébert couldn't check up on her because she couldn't leave the room. "You are not coming into this room with that bag," Claire said firmly. The students lining up behind Karla groaned.

"Come on, Karly," someone said from the back. "Get rid of the damn bag."

"Yeah, Karly, come on, you're holding us up."

Claire arched an eyebrow and waited for Karla to crack.

"Fine!" Karla finally said. "I'll put it in Maziyar's locker. You're mean, Miss Heebert."

"And proud of it," Claire muttered as Karla stomped away.

After ten more kids had filed in, Halfa Sadat, who never gave any trouble on purpose, but was absentminded and a follower, arrived with her backpack. She obeyed when Claire sent her back to her locker with it. Claire turned to survey the room. They were all chatting. Everybody in her grade ten class had decided that the usual order of things was over. But all the exam papers were still on her desk, face down, so Claire didn't say anything.

The exam started at nine a.m. sharp, no fuss. Justine Jones and Adi Safavian rushed in late and Claire accommodated them with seats and exams. Dwayne Dufresne, the weakest kid in the class after Ricky, was typically ten minutes late and did

386

not disappoint. Claire did the attendance and called it in to the office. Everyone except Ricky was present.

During the exam, Claire had ample opportunity to use her standard exam answer.

"Does _____ mean _____?"

"I cannot answer your question at this time."

"What does this mean?"

"I cannot answer your question at this time."

"Is this the right answer?"

"I cannot answer your question at this time."

Out of twenty-eight questions asked, only two could be answered. Claire sharpened a few pencils and lent out her eraser.

Every little while, she walked up and down the rows to see how far along the kids were on the exam. And there it was: Darryl Howard had his smartphone on one knee. Claire saw the glow from the screen on his face and, looking over his shoulder, saw the Wikipedia logo just before he turned it off and pocketed it—too late.

She stood beside Darryl and held out her hand. "The phone," she said through clenched teeth. "Now."

Darryl slumped in his seat, gave her the phone, and glued his eyes to his desk. Claire drew a red line across the bottom of the part of the exam that he had done. "I'll only mark your paper below this line."

"We'll see about that," he retorted. Claire knew *we* would, if the Howards got involved. The obliging and ingratiating Bertha would have the final word. At least he was one of Kristen Jaworski's responsibilities.

After the first forty-five minutes, students who thought they had finished could leave. The first one to go was usually the one who got the lowest marks. In Ricky's absence, Dwayne Dufresne filled the position. The world can be a harsh place, Claire thought, as she watched him leave. She hoped he did better in his other subjects. She suspected she knew how he would earn his living

The real science aces would be last to leave the exam. They knew how to work. And they were. Sylvia, Marcie, Samantha, Nathan and Brendan wrote to the bitter end, having used every last second to squeeze in all the information they could.

"What did you think of the exam?"

"Fair," Nathan declared.

"Easy" Sylvia said, " but if I interpreted something different from you, would I lose the marks?"

"Don't worry, Sylvia. If I see your logic and it's correct, you'll get the marks. You guys are great. Good luck on your other exams and have a wonderful summer." They returned the good wishes.

***

Alone, Claire sighed as she looked at the exams. She had a pretty good idea what all the marks would be. The exams in ninety-eight per cent of the cases determined the results to one or two per cent above or below the class mark. Claire had already put the papers in alphabetical order. She slipped the last five exams in their places.

In the staffroom, she slid the cards with the first batch of questions through the Scantron machine before going home to mark the rest. She was bored before she even got there. Their cursive writing resembled the stumblings of drunken chickens. It would take her all afternoon and most of the evening to slush through the clumsy writing and mutton-headed mistakes in thirty-three exams. One day soon, Claire thought, the exams would be set on a computer, done on a computer, and marked on a computer. She could hardly wait.

Maziyar had done well.

***

It was eight-thirty and Kristen Jaworski's office was open. Claire knocked. She wanted last period off to check out some second hand lab equipment at the board's warehouse. Kristen understood.

"Go ahead. I won't give you an on-call today," she joked.

"Thanks, considering it's exam time and there aren't any on-calls," Claire smiled as she returned the banter. "Oh, by the way, I got a very nice thank you card from Maziyar Bizhani. I couldn't believe my eyes." She pulled the card from her briefcase. "I'm going to frame this one."

"Well, look at that," Kristen said as she read it. "You can be proud of that. He even apologizes for his bad acting at the beginning of the semester! You turned him around."

"Well, not alone... and how far? You helped and so did Shirley."

Kristen smiled. "The little monster has changed for the better in Shirley's class too but for me he still has his issues—his photo-shopping exploits and his superior attitude. But you and Shirley won him over in your classes with your meaningful lessons. He responds well when he realizes he has a teacher who explains things he needs or wants to know in clear language and doesn't mask knowledge with games or projects all the time. That's you two."

"That *was* us two," Claire said with a smile. "Shirley's days are numbered."

"Ah, retirement." Kristen sighed wistfully. "I'm dreaming of it already."

"I'm glad that you have many years ahead of you," Claire said. "The system needs Vice Principals like you, Kristen." She thought of Anne and Gene and other colleagues. "The system will collapse without good leaders like you."

***

Later, when Claire was preparing the lab for the grade eleven exam, there was a timid knock. Opening the door, she was surprised to see Aisha Ames and her friends. Aisha was looking healthier and happier than Claire had ever seen her. She was so overjoyed and speechless that before thinking about it she gave Aisha a hug. She couldn't hold back the happy tears.

"How are you, Aisha?" she finally said, sniffing and wiping her eyes.

"I'm much better now, thank you, Miss Hébert. They gave me some medication and I've been seeing a therapist. I wanted to come and see you and thank you. I really appreciated the lessons you sent to the hospital." She was smiling as she looked at her friends. "What really helped were my parents, Mr. Fraser and my friends. I really do have friends here that I can trust."

"I'm glad," Claire said.

"My parents offered to send me to another school in Bellington or even to move to another province, but Janette's dad, Mr. Chang—he came to visit me too—said that I would always be afraid of the popular girls if I did that."

"It's wise to face your fears, Aisha," Claire said.

Aisha nodded. "We talked about good people and people who make stupid choices. I feel strong enough to face it now, and my parents agree that if I want to, I can keep coming here."

"We're her friends and we want her to stay," Tori said.

"We won't let this happen again," Maya chimed in.

Claire considered the girls thoughtfully. "You know, I believe you! I know what you did too, Tori, fingering the culprit. That was amazing. Maya told me."

"You!" Tori said, looking at Maya and pretending to be shocked.

"Yes, I thought somebody should know what a good detective you are, even if Miss Stack and Mr. Penworth don't think so. We know you were right and we know we can trust Miss Hébert."

"Thanks for that vote of confidence, girls." She shook her head for a moment. "I can't get over the fact that you're here, Aisha. I'm so happy!"

"I've come to write the exam."

"Really? Here? Now? With your class?" a dumbfounded Claire said.

"Yep, there's nobody in this class that I'm afraid of anymore. And I know the work, remember? You sent me the lessons and Mr. Fraser and my friends tutored me."

"Well, come on in then. We start in twenty-three minutes. I'm so glad, so glad." She dabbed her eyes with the tissue again.

The girls sat down at their desks, waiting for their biology final to start.

Claire looked at them and knew that these girls would support each other through thick and thin for life.

Chapter 22

<u>Another Excellent Year</u>

Thursday, June 28

The students had vacated the building for the summer. For five days the teachers had outlined and marked assignments for *credit recovery* kids and prepared for next semester: cleaning out closets and filing cabinets, discarding the year's memos and refreshing bulletin boards—except, of course, Chester Hickenman, who never refreshed anything.

Credit Recovery was a contrivance to help some kids who were borderline because of legitimate family situations (37% – 47%) pass a course. The window was officially open for a few days. Teachers would find or create an alternative version of a project or an assignment that the failing student had missed. Then if they completed it satisfactorily by the end of the last credit recovery day, they would be given fifty percent.

***

Credit recovery finished, all staff members had to be available, preferably on site, preparing for the next school year. Shirley was retiring and didn't have much left to do and Anne was all caught up, so they came to Claire's lab, where there was always something to sort, scrape clean, repair or throw out.

"How many credit recovery kids did you have, Claire?" Shirley asked as she deadheaded the geraniums.

"I was lucky. All my kids except four passed on their own steam."

"Even Maxine? Wow! I'm impressed," Anne said as she wiped down a microscope. "I had three and guess who the third one was?"

"Ricky Penworth!" Claire and Shirley said together, laughing. "Who else?"

"He was one of mine too," Claire said.

"His parents wouldn't let him come to school so he got special permission to do his credit recovery projects at home," Anne said.

"I know. His right arm is broken and he hasn't got the balls to type on his computer with his left," Claire said.

"So Muriel got permission to help him," Shirley said. "Guess who fixed that…"

"Who else did you have, Claire?" Shirley asked.

"Farah Marie Zahar and Hannah Jessica May were recommended by Bertha because of the 'trauma' they suffered the day Serge Leclerc smashed the foetal pigs, and Darryl Howard because he was *so* sorry he was caught cheating. "

"Oh God … And who were *your* lucky credit recovery winners, Anne?"

"Alicia Wazberg was recommended by Jack Penworth against my better judgment—but whose judgment isn't better than Jack's? —to appease her parents because I didn't give her any notes. I don't know how many other ways I could have explained that I'm not the one who's
supposed to take the notes."

"And…?"

"Dwayne Dufresne, the drugster."

"Good God, few of these kids really qualify," Claire snorted. "They're supposed to have legitimate personal reasons for their low marks."

"Bertha wants the school to look like it does miracles, girls," concluded Shirley.

***

It was early in the afternoon and Anne, Gene and Claire were again working in the lab for the September start-up before the holiday.

"Did I hear your name called for the promotion meeting yesterday, Claire?" Gene asked, as they were emptying new glassware into the cupboards. Promotion meetings were a time when teachers were on call to answer to the principal who spent a few days looking over every student's results to determine if the mark was a fair representation of the student's accomplishments. Usually the nod was given.

"Yup," Claire said as she wiped the back table. "You did."

"Okay, spill the beans. Who was it for?"

"Aisha Ames. She would have had a much better result if she hadn't been cyber-bullied. Twice."

"So you gave her a mark that better represented what she would have had otherwise?" Anne asked, looking up from cleaning the fish tank.

"We all did. It was like an auction—it was heartening how her teachers from both semesters stepped up to give her a mark that shows what she usually does," Claire answered as she arranged a tray of new Florence flasks on a shelf.

"Speaking of marks, did you hear that Mark Compren got his scholarship, even after that abominable scene he made at the dance?" Gene was boxing the plants from the windowsill. Natalie was going to put them in her garden until September.

"Unfortunately, I did," Claire said. "Shirley told me that Martin Parker and Bandhura Abbasi both had students they thought should have won that scholarship, but they were nice kids who didn't browbeat their teachers for extra marks or have a father working for the board," she said, as she placed the microscopes Anne had cleaned the other day into a cupboard.

She turned around and looked at her friends. "Martin was fuming. Bandhura just scowled." She went over to the drawer where the slides were kept and started to help Gene pick out the damaged ones. "At the other end of the scale, nobody—and I mean nobody—wanted to give Dwayne Dufresne anything so he could pass English, especially after he was caught with that bagful of marijuana. Bertha and Jack had to work hard to get the odd mark for him."

"Did he get any?"

"Not enough to pass, even with credit recovery. The English essay he handed in," Anne said, "...was a piece of crap."

"Well, I can't disagree, based on what I've heard about Dwayne... and... er... speaking of useless pieces of shit, how did Ricky fare?" Gene asked.

"Well, talk about a conflict of interest," Claire rolled her eyes to emphasize her absolute

disgust, "Bertha didn't ask Jack to step out, so nobody had the balls to say 'no' to Ricky. The fifty percent Muriel got him for credit recovery has been raised to fifty-six and he still hasn't done a lick of work himself."

"Where the hell was Kristen?" Gene turned to ask her.

"Come on, Gene. She can't outvote those two," Shirley, who had just arrived with lemonade for everybody, said shaking her head. "I suspect she's secretly trying to get at least one of

398

them transferred to another school but it's difficult, it can take years and it can be dangerous for her career too."

"So Ricky will pass and he'll suffer again." Gene sounded sad.

"He will...but we won't," Claire said with a wide grin on her face.

"Oh?"

"Fortunately for him and for Amberton, Jack and Muriel have decided to send him to Elgin Falls High School for a fresh start. I hope it will be good for him, but I have my doubts. He isn't changing his parents."

"That's where Bertha is sending Tommy and Logan," Gene said, his chin hanging in disbelief and his eyes a pair of saucers.

"Oh my God..." They all looked at each other, shaking their heads. They were speechless.

***

The light at the end of the tunnel arrived. The weather was warm and the sun was bright. The caretakers were happy, knowing that whatever they cleaned and polished would stay that way for a while.

The only thing left was the final staff meeting, always a pleasant affair held at a posh local venue. It started with a good breakfast. They all stood up and applauded as Paul Fraser arrived with Deirdre and his daughters.

The room was abuzz with year-end gossip. The staff laughed about incidents that, in retrospect, were hilarious. Breakfast over, Bertha, the chairperson for the occasion, smiled as she stood up to make her remarks. "I have a major announcement to make today," she started, as Kristen gave her the thumbs up. Everyone stopped talking. "The police have charged the driver who injured Paul Fraser." Every eye popped, every jaw dropped and every head turned to Paul. "The boy will spend the summer in youth detention—if not longer."

"Who was it?" an eager voice asked.

"As you all know, at the Graduation Ball Mark Compren was drunk and disorderly. He was fulminating. The police took him to the hospital and later to the police station for drunk and disorderly conduct and assaulting Ethan Boyd. At the station he continued his rants. They were about getting even, so the constables decided to record what he was saying. Last week, Mark was brought in. They played the tape and he confessed. He said his parents wanted him to get a certain scholarship. His math result was dragging down his average and the morning of January 24th he tried to coerce Paul into fixing his mark. Paul refused. Mark was afraid to tell his parents he'd missed the scholarship. I have a copy of the police report." She read from the report: "The afternoon of January 24th Mark Compren was upset and got into his mother's new silver Corolla and drove around and around the school.

"By four o'clock the weather worsened, visibility was bad and he decided to turn around in the school parking lot. The tires hit a large patch of black ice and Mr. Compren lost control of the car. He hit Mr. Fraser, then Mr. Mason's car. Mr. Compren panicked, put the car in reverse and backed over Mr. Fraser's foot as he left.

"He drove home and put the car in the garage. Mr. Compren told his parents he'd slid into a fire hydrant hidden in a snowdrift."

Bertha put the report down and sighed. "The police have matched the paint on the Compren car to that on Jethro's. It all matches and they have Mark's confession. Damian Stoker really did hit a tree, but Mark set him up because Damian had tripped him during the Amberton/Elgin Falls basketball game. To get back, Mark, having heard about Damian's accident, dropped hints around the school that Damian had hit Mr. Fraser. Ethan Boyd knew the truth and defended Damian, which is why Mark attacked him in the washroom."

There was a collective sigh of relief as everyone looked at Paul, who was looking at the floor in embarrassment. Deirdre and his daughters hugged him.

Then Bertha called attention to the teachers who were retiring. "First, there is Shirley Alquist," she said with politically correct feeling, "who has reached this milestone after twenty-nine years of excellence in the teaching profession, most of them here at Amberton District High. Eleanor? Pierce?"

Eleanor Davidson and Pierce Legault, who taught in the French department, walked to the lectern. "Shirley, please join us," Eleanor said with a welcoming wave. Shirley walked up to thunderous applause.

"Well, Shirley, you can finally stop counting the days! Here it is!" Eleanor said, leading to even more raucous applause. "Yup, no more alarm clocks!" Pierce added, as he took Gene's hammer from the shelf under the lectern and smashed a cheap alarm clock to smithereens. The room erupted in hoots of laughter. "We're here to honour Shirley's years of dedicated service to our students at Amberton District High and previous schools," Eleanor said. "Shirley is living proof that students appreciate teachers who teach lessons with substance."

"In 1983," Pierce said, "Shirley was teaching grade eight at the old Riverside Middle School. She always maintained first-rate discipline.

"Her classroom was on the third floor of the old school. One day, she heard ominous creaks from above and it wasn't the principal." He looked at Bertha, who grunted. "She told her pupils to get up, leave everything on their desks, and go stand against the wall in the hall. All except one girl obeyed. Shirley stood over her in a corner as the entire ceiling crashed down.

Not one child in her class had a scratch. Two neighbouring classes were not so lucky." The crowd clapped in admiration.

"Shirley is the embodiment of dedication to her students. For years—especially since she got a computer—if there wasn't an exercise or a book to teach something, Shirley wrote one. She has shared her work with many colleagues and never asked for a cent." Shirley stood beside them, blushing. "To her, the kids were the goal and their education was the only thing that counted. Several of her graduates from Amberton have become diplomats, translators and French teachers. We will all miss Shirley in the years to come. Pierce?"

"Yes. Shirley, the staff association would like to present you with a token of our appreciation and a souvenir of your years at Amberton. We won't forget you and we hope your years at Amberton will be a pleasant memory."

Eleanor, Pierce and Bertha all hugged Shirley before she turned and thanked her colleagues with trembling voice and proudly showed them the plaque with the school crest on it and her name engraved underneath.

"Thank you, Shirley, Eleanor and Pierce," Bertha said.

She waited as the three went back to their seats. "We're sorry to lose Dr. Chin Ho too," she continued, looking at Claire. There were murmurings of surprise. "He has been offered a position at Bellington University in the Ecology department. Angus, would you please say a few words about Dr. Ho?"

Claire was blindsided. She had no idea she was about to lose her best support at the school. She had assumed he would be there forever. Who would replace him? Who could possibly replace Chin?

Angus made his way to the podium. He focused on Chin Ho. "Thank you, Bertha. As you know, Chin has led the Amberton Science Department for eight years. He holds a doctorate in chemistry and has been a wonderful department head. He has helped save my sanity many times and he has a great sense of humour. He always saw the big picture, and zoomed in on the essence of a problem.

"I know I speak for everyone in the Science department when I say he has made our work much easier." Claire was in shock and barely heard the applause.

"Chin initiated the Amberton Science Fair and our students have done well in Bellington and at the provincials. He loves robots and rockets. Two years ago, his twins won scholarships at the Science Fair with a model robot. Now thanks to them, our Amberton students are into R & R too.

"At the same time, Dr. Ho was particular about the state of his department and every once in a while we got a tongue-lashing about equipment being missing, broken, out of place, or dirty. He runs a tight ship and we respect and love him for that. He has helped keep our stress manageable and moulded us into a team.

"Chin, we wish you well in your new endeavour. You will be sadly missed by every one of us in the Science department, the staff, and the whole student body. Please accept this engraved Amberton plaque in memory of eight wonderful years leading the science department at Amberton District Secondary."

"Chin! chin!" someone yelled. The crowd echoed the sentiment and they all raised their coffee mugs. Chin Ho looked at Claire as he thanked Angus and everyone for their gift and vowed that he too had enjoyed his eight years at Amberton and that he would never forget his colleagues.

Claire was dumbstruck. Why hadn't he told her? She felt betrayed. She wanted to flee the meeting, but something held her back— Shirley's hand was patting her arm.

In the fog, Claire saw Bertha stand up. What else could she come up with to ruin next year? Claire had her resignation letter ready to print. Then Bertha announced, "Gene Putnam will be the new Science Department head." Shirley looked at Claire and smiled. There was more applause with many nods of congratulations to Gene. Claire felt her senses return. Shirley gave her a look, which said, "We weren't allowed to tell you."

The meeting droned on. Bertha announced the names of other departing staff members. Bertha said she was sorry to lose them. Most of them were teachers who had given their best without support. They were looking for a better school, a stronger principal, or a less frustrating career.

"…and Naomi Harper," Bertha said. "We're very, very, sorry to see you go. You've done an excellent job."

Claire leaned across the table and rolled her eyes at Anne, who nearly choked on her coffee as she stifled a laugh. Heads turned, looking for Naomi. The transparent applause waned. She was nowhere to be seen. Neither was Chester.

"Finally, we are ecstatic to welcome back Paul Fraser." Bertha had to wait for the standing ovation from his friends and colleagues. And now, thank you everyone," Bertha gushed into the microphone. "It's been another excellent year! Have a safe and happy summer."

***

A half hour later, as an exhausted but relieved Claire pulled into her driveway, she spotted Matt on her front step with Boomer. Matt was in his favourite jeans and a new crisp casual shirt. His face lit up like a lighthouse as soon as he saw her.

Why wasn't he at work? What could be up?

Matt and Boomer bounded down the two steps to meet her. He leaned into her open driver's window. "I'm so excited. I've got some news."

"Oh?" Claire dragged herself out of the car and robotically reached for her briefcase on the back seat. "What's your news?" she asked passively as she gave him a peck hello.

"That's not enough," Matt said. He grabbed her briefcase, plunked it on the porch, took her hand and pulled her into a shady spot beside an overgrown climbing rose at the side of the house. He gave her a long deep, loving kiss. His excitement was contagious. "You know how interested Chin Ho is in the environment?" The name brought her close to tears. Matt didn't wait for an answer. "Well, we talked at the Science Fair and before one or two of the Eco club meetings. He was very interested in my work and told me he was negotiating for a new job in the Ecology Department at Bellington University. I wasn't to mention it to anyone."

Claire pushed him away. "You mean you *knew*?"

Matt pulled her back. "I'm sorry. I wanted to tell you but Chin wanted it kept totally confidential." He put his arms around her and looked into her eyes. "He knew my travels were causing problems for you … er …us. He didn't want the department to lose you. He told me about a friend of his in Colorado. He told him about my work at Ecohydrelco."

Matt's exhilaration was growing. Trembling with excitement, he grabbed her arms. "They sent me for a meeting with Chin's friend at Denver University. I showed him some of my stuff, Claire, my work with polluted water and my own designs for a more efficient system to clean it. He recommended me." Matt was grinning from ear to ear. "They need someone who knows the machines and I've been a nervous wreck, Claire… They've interviewed me three times since April."

Claire's eyes opened wide in fear. She stepped away from him.

Matt grabbed her shoulders. "I've been going *crazy*… waiting and wondering since April if I'd be considered for a job at the university. That's what I was doing in Denver that time, Clarikins, talking to his colleagues there for the third time."

Claire's eyes dug into his. "So you're moving to Colorado?"

"No, Clarikins. You're not getting it. Last week Bellington University offered me a position and I've accepted. I'll be working less than thirty kilometres from here. It starts in September. What do you think?"

It took a few seconds for Claire's head to stop spinning and register the news. "Oh, Matt! It's perfect," she finally sighed. Claire was now so happy she could only stutter. Her eyes were riveted to his. Matt pulled her back in for another hug and she relaxed into his arms.

"And now," Matt said, pulling away slightly, "Chin fixed it so that we've got a whole summer together. Ecohydrelco is giving me two months off. Starting in the Fall they're going to keep me on a contract basis. The jobs will complement each other. But I'm becoming a researcher and teacher at the university, so there won't be any trips during the school year. Most of my work will be done locally at Bellington University or in the Ecohydrelco lab."

"That's wonderful, Matt, I'm thrilled for you."

He looked at her, his eyes brimming. "For *us*, Claire, for *us*."

"So you don't think I should quit my job?" Claire gave him a suspicious look.

"No, Claire." Matt's face became serious. "Absolutely not. I saw you at the Science Fair, I saw you in Algonquin, I saw you at the Music Night, and I saw you at the Grad Dance. You are exceptionally capable with the students. No other job will give you such a chance to be an influence for good with youth. Even with all the stress and the frustrations, you have to teach. From now on I'm one hundred percent in your corner."

Claire melted into his arms again as they hugged and kissed. When their lips finally parted, Matt pulled a gorgeous bouquet of pink lilies out from behind a low hanging branch of the rose.

He gave her the flowers, got down on one knee and looked at the face he loved so much. Boomer, thinking Matt could only be on his knees to play with him, was licking his face. He gently brushed the dog away. Then, his emotions brimming over, he said, "Claire, love of my life, would you please do me the honour of becoming my wife? If you do, I promise to be a good and faithful husband, to do my share of the housework, pick up my dirty laundry and help take care of our child, the dog." He had to push Boomer away three times and was starting to laugh.

Claire got on her knees too, gently nudging the intrigued dog out from between them as she looked into his hazel eyes. "I've been longing to say this, Matt, yes…yes…yes!"

They both jumped to their feet and kissed and hugged and twirled through giddy laughter and tears of relief. When they stopped, Matt looked deep into her eyes. "You're glowing, Clarikins." He stepped back to look at her. "There's more than the usual sparkle in your eyes, Claire. Are you up to something? Is that all for me?"

Claire waited for a moment or two: "I'm so happy, Matt. I love you to pieces. I'm thrilled about your job and I'll be ecstatic to be your wife." Then stepping back, and giving him a coy look, slowly she said, "We have another reason to be happy though, Matt. I've kept a secret too. One I can now tell you. I hope you'll like it."

"Oh?" Matt said, his eyes searching hers.

"Boomer won't be the only child we'll have to care for."

Matt blinked and his jaw dropped. "You mean… you mean…?

"We're in the family way, Matt. You and I are going to be parents."

"When, Claire, when?"

"Late January…" Her eyes were riveted to his.

For a minute, Matt just stood there, mouth gaping, taking it all in, saying nothing. Then gently, he took Claire in his arms and carried her over her threshold. Boomer followed them into the little house.

For once Bertha had been right. It *had* been an excellent year.

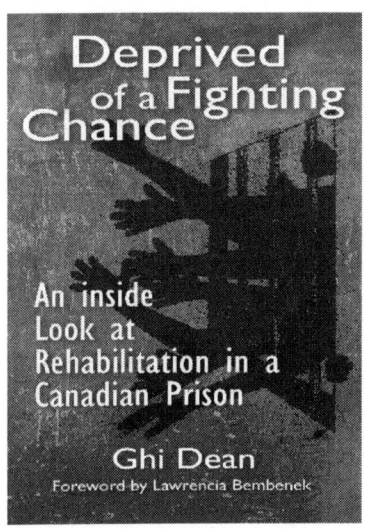

Nelson Mandela once said that a nation should not be judged by how it treats its highest citizens, but its lowest ones. Ghi Dean's novel shows us how one of the "advanced" countries in the world deals with its prisoners -and it's not a pretty sight. Rehabilitation clashes with punishment and inmates are given intermittent rays of hope while being stuck in an endless cycle of hopelessness and desolation. Ghi Dean's experiences were written with such emotional frankness that I found myself commiserating with her frustrations and celebrating with her whenever she encounters tiny triumphs.
Eduardo Aduna for Reader's Favorite Reviews.

Notes

Made in the USA
Columbia, SC
27 August 2017